Pressure Cookers

FOR

DUMMIES®

2ND EDITION

by Tom Lacalamita

WILEY

John Wiley & Sons, Inc.

Pressure Cookers For Dummies,® 2nd Edition

Published by
John Wiley & Sons, Inc.
111 River St.
Hoboken, NJ 07030-5774
www.wiley.com

Copyright © 2012 by John Wiley & Sons, Inc., Hoboken, New Jersey

Published by John Wiley & Sons, Inc., Hoboken, New Jersey

Published simultaneously in Canada

For general information on our other products and services, please contact our Customer Care Department within the U.S. at 877-762-2974, outside the U.S. at 317-572-3993, or fax 317-572-4002.

For technical support, please visit www.wiley.com/techsupport.

Wiley publishes in a variety of print and electronic formats and by print-on-demand. Some material included with standard print versions of this book may not be included in e-books or in print-on-demand. If this book refers to media such as a CD or DVD that is not included in the version you purchased, you may download this material at http://booksupport.wiley.com. For more information about Wiley products, visit www.wiley.com.

Library of Congress Control Number: 2012946053

ISBN 978-1-118-35645-6 (pbk); ISBN 978-1-118-41223-7 (ebk); ISBN 978-1-118-41222-0 (ebk); ISBN 978-1-118-41224-4 (ebk)

Manufactured in the United States of America

10 9 8 7 6 5 4 3 2 1

WILEY

About the Author

Tom Lacalamita is a bestselling author of eight appliance-related cookbooks. Nominated for a James Beard cookbook award, Lacalamita is considered to be a national authority on housewares and has appeared on hundreds of television and radio shows across the country, including *Good Morning America,* CNBC, and NPR. With a passion for food, cooking, and all sorts of kitchen gadgets, Tom is also a spokesperson for various food and housewares manufacturers.

Author's Acknowledgments

A book is an ongoing process that starts with an idea that continues to develop with the inspiration and the guidance of many individuals. I want to thank my family and friends for always providing me with the inspiration to cook and nurture them with my food. I thank Gary for so many years of support and encouragement and Cristina for always wanting me to cook for her. I sincerely thank the *Dummies* editorial and production team, especially acquisitions editor David Lutton and my project editor Jen Tebbe, two of the best editors I have had the pleasure of working with. Their calming demeanor and wisdom proved invaluable during this endeavor. The final product that this book became would not have been possible without the invaluable contributions made by the following people: copy editors Christy Pingleton and Danielle Voirol; Liz Bray, the technical editor who made sure that I conveyed clearly and precisely every nuance involved in pressure-cooking; Emily Nolan for her honest opinions and excellent input on the new recipes added to this revised edition, as well as Patty Santelli for the accompanying nutrition analysis.

Publisher's Acknowledgments

We're proud of this book; please send us your comments at http://dummies.custhelp.com. For other comments, please contact our Customer Care Department within the U.S. at 877-762-2974, outside the U.S. at 317-572-3993, or fax 317-572-4002.

Some of the people who helped bring this book to market include the following:

Acquisitions, Editorial, and Vertical Websites

Project Editor: Jennifer Tebbe

    (Previous Edition: Suzanne Snyder)

Executive Editor: Lindsay Sandman Lefevere

Copy Editors: Christine Pingleton, Danielle Voirol

    (Previous Edition: Tina Sims)

Assistant Editor: David Lutton

Editorial Program Coordinator: Joe Niesen

Technical Editor: Liz Bray

Recipe Tester: Emily Nolan

Nutritional Analyst: Patty Santelli

Editorial Manager: Christine Meloy Beck

Editorial Assistants: Rachelle S. Amick, Alexa Koschier

Art Coordinator: Alicia B. South

Cover Photo: © Agefotostock / Pixtal

Cartoons: Rich Tennant (www.the5thwave.com)

Composition Services

Project Coordinator: Sheree Montgomery

Layout and Graphics: Carl Byers, Erin Zeltner

Proofreaders: Melissa D. Buddendeck, Melissa Cossell

Indexer: Ty Koontz

Illustrator: Elizabeth Kurtzman

Publishing and Editorial for Consumer Dummies

    Kathleen Nebenhaus, Vice President and Executive Publisher

    Kristin Ferguson-Wagstaffe, Product Development Director

    Ensley Eikenburg, Associate Publisher, Travel

    Kelly Regan, Editorial Director, Travel

Publishing for Technology Dummies

    Andy Cummings, Vice President and Publisher

Composition Services

    Debbie Stailey, Director of Composition Services

Contents at a Glance

Recipes at a Glance

Desserts

Gluten-Free

Grains and Pasta

Poultry

Soups, Chili, and Chowder

Stews

Stocks

Vegan and/or Dairy-Free

**Recipes with ☾ are both*

Table of Contents

Introduction

· ·

The pressure cooker is one kitchen appliance that's long been misunderstood and underappreciated. Maligned for decades and the brunt of endless jokes and unwarranted stories, this kitchen wonder survived for years, once truly appreciated only by people in the know. Today's sleek, fast-cooking pressure cookers, however, have safety valves and other features that make them totally safe and easy to use — a far cry from the pressure cookers in use decades ago.

Wouldn't you like to have savory, delicious, homemade beef stew cooked in less than 45 minutes, compared to 90 minutes of simmering and stirring the old-fashioned way? What about nutritious dried beans or legumes that normally need to simmer up to 2 hours but can be yours in less than 20 minutes? Have I whetted your appetite yet? By cooking with a pressure cooker, you can have these fast-and-tasty foods and more.

About This Book

Chances are, you've never used a pressure cooker, or if you have, you may still have some questions or a few misconceptions about this gadget. So join me as I demystify pressure cookers and explain how they really work and what to expect as far as delicious, home-cooked foods are concerned. In fact, I share with you some of the all-time-best pressure-cooker recipes I know.

Conventions Used in This Book

A 6-quart pressure cooker can easily handle all the recipes in this book, even the two pressure-canning recipes in Chapter 5 (all the recipes in this book were developed and tested in 6-quart, stainless-steel pressure cookers). Just be sure to check with your pressure cooker's manufacturer before canning to make sure your unit can and will reach 15 pounds per square inch (psi) under high pressure.

With that out of the way, it's time to highlight some specific recipe-related conventions that apply throughout the book:

- ✓ Vegetarian recipes are marked with a tomato in the Recipes in This Chapter list, with the exception of Chapters 12 and 13, in which all the recipes are vegetarian. The fact that a given recipe is vegetarian is also included as a Note at the end of a vegetarian recipe (except in the aforementioned chapters). Sometimes a recipe can be made vegetarian with a simple tweak or two. For example, some otherwise meatless recipes may call for chicken stock; by replacing it with vegetable stock, the recipe becomes vegetarian. These types of alterations are included in the Vary It! comments that you'll see at the end of these recipes.

- ✓ If you're following a vegan, gluten-free, or dairy-free diet, these recipes have you covered too. Notes following the recipes indicate when recipes are vegan, gluten-free, and/or dairy-free when prepared as directed. If a recipe can be made vegan, gluten-free, and/or dairy-free by altering the recipe (for example, by replacing butter and cheeses with vegan equivalents), you'll find this information in the form of a Vary It! at the end of the recipe.

- ✓ Temperatures are all in Fahrenheit. (If you prefer working in the metric system, turn to Appendix B for help converting temperatures to Celsius.)

- ✓ All eggs are large.

- ✓ All dry ingredient measurements should be level. Spoon the ingredient into the appropriate-sized measuring cup and level off with the blunt edge of a knife. You don't need to pat down the ingredient (more is not necessarily better than less).

- ✓ Pepper should always be in the form of freshly ground black peppercorns for maximum flavor.

- ✓ I recommend using kosher salt because it doesn't contain additives and therefore has a "cleaner" taste. Unless you're on a sodium-free diet, judiciously salt your food to taste as it cooks rather than at the end, except for beans and dried legumes, which should be salted only after they have cooked.

I've also employed the following general conventions to help make reading *Pressure Cookers For Dummies,* 2nd Edition, even easier:

- ✓ **Boldface** denotes key words and phrases in bulleted lists. It also indicates specific action steps for you to take.

- ✓ *Italics* are my way of pointing out words I'm defining or emphasizing.

- ✓ `Monofont` lets you know that you're looking at a web address.

What You're Not to Read

Of course, I think all the material in this book is valuable, but if you're pressed for time, you're welcome to skip over the sidebars. *Sidebars* are gray-shaded boxes filled with interesting yet nonessential information.

Foolish Assumptions

Naturally, I made some assumptions about you, my dear reader, as I was writing. And now I confess them to you:

- ✔ **You don't necessarily already own a pressure cooker.** Perhaps you're planning to use this book as a guide to find out more about pressure cookers before taking the plunge and purchasing one. If that's the case, you're certain to find everything you need to know about the many different kinds of pressure cookers out there so you can make an informed purchase.

- ✔ **You do own a pressure cooker and you want to get more comfortable using it.** Rest assured, this book will get you started with pressure cooking. Who knows? You may never want to cook anything that's *not* under pressure again!

- ✔ **You enjoy cooking quickly.** Yes, everyone has to eat in order to survive, but some folks — like you and me — actually get a kick out of the cooking process, especially when it doesn't take all day to prepare a delicious meal.

How This Book Is Organized

This book is divided into five parts, and each part consists of two or more chapters chock-full of information that will get you pressure cooking quickly and successfully, each and every time. Here's a breakdown of what you can expect to find in each part.

Part 1: Stress-Free Cooking under Pressure

After giving you an overview of the wonderful world of pressure cooking, this part dispels all the many misconceptions surrounding the pressure cooker.

It also provides you with some insight into the different types of pressure cookers available (stovetop and electric) so you can pick the right one if you don't already own a pressure cooker — or if you're looking to upgrade to a more modern unit, like an electric pressure cooker that boasts slow cooking and rice cooking under pressure. As a bonus, I even give you some recipes designed to take advantage of an electric pressure cooker's slow cooker and rice cooker programs.

Part II: Making the Best and Safest Use of Your Pressure Cooker

In this part, I fill you in on exactly how pressure cookers work, what to expect as far as features and benefits when cooking under pressure, and why today's new models and styles (including electric pressure cookers) are safer and easier to use than ever before. I share with you some of the tricks I've learned along the way for getting the best results with the least amount of effort, as well as how to adapt your favorite conventional recipes for the pressure cooker.

Part III: Preparing Delicious Recipes in Your Pressure Cooker

Quick, delicious, homemade food is what pressure cooking is all about, and those are the results (not to mention the compliments) you're bound to get when you make any of the 97 recipes found in this part. As I compiled recipes for this book, I envisioned how I use my pressure cooker for maximum benefit, as far as convenience as well as from a healthy diet perspective.

Then I organized the recipes as you would expect them to be arranged in any well-organized cookbook. Chapter 7 presents dishes that you would eat with a spoon (think soups and grain dishes such as rice and quinoa). In Chapters 8 and 9 you find the meat dishes, specifically stew recipes and roast and poultry recipes. Then comes Chapter 10, with its recipes that highlight those other great sources of protein — beans and dried legumes. Chapter 11 is home to vegetable dishes, including some yummy sides, and Chapter 12 rounds out your meal with some truly delectable desserts. Last but not least, Chapter 13 explores a wide range of vegetarian, vegan, gluten-free, and dairy-free recipes because, hey, who isn't following a special diet these days (or at least trying to eat less meat)?

Part IV: The Part of Tens

Years ago, it was common practice for people to pick up the phone and call Mom with their cooking questions. You can still call Mom today, but you'll probably get her voicemail while she's out playing tennis, taking a class, or hitting the outlet stores. Instead, check out my Part of Tens, where I give you invaluable tips and troubleshooting hints.

Part V: Appendixes

Today, everyone is in a rush and no one has time to spare, so when in doubt and cooking under pressure, refer to Appendix A for recommended pressure-cooker cooking times. Also be sure to check out Appendix B for handy metric and other conversion information.

Icons Used in This Book

Icons are symbols or pictures that represent or convey an idea. I use four of them throughout this book wherever I think an idea or concept should be stressed for your benefit.

If you own (or plan to buy) an electric pressure cooker and want to be sure to review the information that's specific to this type of pressure cooker, keep your eyes peeled for this icon.

If you recall nothing else from this book but the information flagged with this icon, you're in good shape.

Simply stated, this icon points out tips or shortcuts I've picked up over the years that I share with you to make your pressure cooking more fun and less of a hassle.

When you see this icon, I'm warning you about a potential problem or pitfall. Rest assured, I wouldn't warn you without also telling you how to avoid or overcome the problem.

Where to Go from Here

Although the beginning is usually a good place to start, feel free to start reading whichever chapter (or section) is of the most interest to you. For example, if you're looking for a great pot roast recipe, turn to Chapter 9, which contains information about making roasts and other large cuts of meat in your pressure cooker. Wondering how to make quick-and-easy jams and chutney for holiday gift-giving? Then be sure to check out my recipes in Chapter 12.

Because I hope that you'll soon rely upon your pressure cooker for quick and easily prepared foods, I suggest you become well acquainted with your pressure cooker and your pressure-cooker manufacturer's documentation to better understand how it works. Naturally, I'm proud of all the information I've compiled in this book and hope that you'll take the time to read most of it. If you don't initially, that's okay, too, because I know that you'll like the recipes so much that, before you even realize it, you'll have ultimately read almost everything, from cover to cover! Or, if you'd like, you can start anywhere and read as little or as much as you want at a time. After all, it's your book.

Part I

Stress-Free Cooking under Pressure

"Now, it not only cooks fast, it looks fast."

In this part . . .

Chapter 1 is your crash course in how to maneuver through the world of pressure cooking. In Chapters 2 and 3, I tell you exactly what a pressure cooker is, how it works, and why you should use one every day when you cook! I also fill you in on how the pressure cooker has changed in the past 70 years, making it one of the fastest and safest methods of cooking. You find out what to expect in terms of new sizes and features, too.

Chapter 1

Cooking with Pressure 101

· ·

· ·

*A*lthough much maligned, in reality the pressure cooker is the harried cook's most valuable friend in the kitchen. Besides the fact that it cooks up to 70 percent faster, it can also save you money and cut down on kitchen cleanup because you do all your cooking in a totally closed and sealed pot. In this chapter, I present you with some very convincing arguments for why everyone needs to be cooking under pressure — more so today than ever before.

Not Your Parents' Pressure Cooker

I'm sure you've heard the story of a friend of a friend who experienced an exploding pressure cooker and wound up cleaning split-pea soup off the ceiling for a month. But come on, that was back in the 1940s! The modern pressure cooker is a far cry from what your parents and grandparents used in the past. Sleek and sophisticated, from stovetop to electric models, more pressure cookers are available for today's cook to choose from than ever before.

Better yet, all of these options are also safer. Manufacturers are always striving to make improvements on just about everything. The pressure cooker is no exception. As I mention in Chapter 2, there's no denying that earlier models weren't always as safe as they should have been and didn't have all the safety features that today's pots do. Since then, however, some of the best housewares engineers in the world, working in ultra-modern, state-of-the-art factories, have designed and added many features to traditional stovetop pressure cookers as well as the newer digital electric models. The result is pressure cookers that are nearly impossible to tamper with and super-easy to use (as you discover in Chapter 4).

What Makes a Pot a Pressure Cooker?

For a pot to work as a pressure cooker, it must create an airtight seal so that when hot cooking liquid comes to a boil, the steam it creates becomes trapped, ultimately creating pressure. When that pressure is applied to the food in the sealed pot, the food winds up cooking up to 70 percent faster than via conventional cooking.

All pressure cookers are made up of the same three basic parts: a metal cooker vessel or pot, a metal lid, and a rubber gasket within the lid that creates an airtight seal when the lid is locked in place. The pots and lids are made of aluminum or stainless steel, or, in the case of electric pressure cookers, nonstick-coated aluminum.

To make them safe, all pressure cookers have at least three safety valves in the lid as well as a valve that controls and releases pressure during and after cooking. A valve may be as simple as a small rectangular cutout in the lid to release excess pressure or as sophisticated as a spring-regulated valve that controls the amount of pressure needed to cook specific types of foods.

Surveying What's Out There

Go online any day of the week and you'll see that at least 75 different pressure-cooker models are available at retail, starting as low as $30 for a traditional jiggler-valve model and going up as high as $275 for a Swiss-made, stainless-steel version. Although they all have the same function of cooking under pressure, the aluminum, jiggler-valve pressure cooker is the most basic and therefore the least expensive. Size and country of origin are also determining factors when it comes to the price of stainless-steel models. The decision is yours as far as what to purchase and cook with.

If you're in the market for a new pressure cooker, you need to know about the different options available to you. Check out the following list for the basic details and turn to Chapter 3 for even more information:

✔ **Jiggler-valve pressure cooker:** If you like simplicity, this may be the pressure cooker for you. Aside from being the least-sophisticated option, this tried-and-true model is noisy, yet practical. It's also the least-expensive type of pressure cooker.

✔ **Developed-weight pressure cooker:** Consider this model a more updated version of its cousin, the jiggler-valve pressure cooker. But this model has no moving parts and requires no guesswork as to whether the level of pressure you want has been reached.

- **Spring-valve pressure cooker:** With the turn of a dial, this very modern pressure cooker eliminates most of the guesswork. It's the easiest to use of the stovetop models, a characteristic that comes at a price because the spring-valve pressure cooker is more expensive than the other stovetop units.

- **Electric pressure cooker:** Rapidly growing in popularity, the very-simple-to-use, multifunctional electric pressure cooker almost cooks by itself. Just choose high or low pressure, set the timer, and press Start. At the end of the cooking cycle, the pot will buzz to tell you it's done. You can either let the pressure cooker release the pressure naturally, or you can opt for a manual quick-release. And if that weren't enough, some models even have slow cooker, rice maker, and traditional cooking programs to choose from as well.

My advice for purchasing a pressure cooker is to go somewhere in the middle of the road pricewise, unless you can splurge — then, most definitely, go Swiss.

My electric love affair

Recently, for a variety of reasons, I've become a big fan of the electric pressure cooker, also known as a multicooker. First and foremost: I like not having to use my stove. Let me explain. I'm a clean freak and I hate a dirty stove as much as I hate having to clean one. I don't care how neat you are; cooking, browning, and sautéing are messy and leave the entire cooktop dirty, even when you use only one burner. Now, when you cook in an electric pressure cooker on your counter, everything stays in the removable, nonstick cooking pot. No mess, no muss. It's all self-contained.

Another reason why I'm such a big fan of this appliance, besides the obvious one of convenience, is the additional features it offers. While I haven't used every electric pressure cooker or multicooker on the market, I've cooked with some of the best, and they all do other cooking tasks besides pressure cooking. Following are two of my favorite appliances that some electric pressure cookers can double as:

- **Slow cooker:** Besides obviously cooking fast under pressure, my favorite electric multicookers also have a slow-cooker program that lets you cook as you would in your crock pot. With this in mind, I strongly suggest you try my delicious slow-cooker recipes found in Chapter 3, as well as those found in one of my other *For Dummies* cookbooks, *Slow Cookers For Dummies*, coauthored by Glenna Vance and published by Wiley.

- **Rice cooker:** I've been making fluffy, perfectly cooked rice in rice cookers for years. They make, by far, the world's best rice. Some multicookers have a rice-cooker program that (believe it or not) also makes fabulous fluffy rice under pressure.

Three great appliance functions in one neat package with digital controls and a timer make this slightly higher-priced gadget worth it!

Get Cookin'!

After you have your pressure cooker, the cooking fun can begin. You can prepare recipes specifically designed for the pressure cooker, like those found in Part III, or you can adapt conventional recipes you know and love so you can prepare them in less than half the time it normally takes.

Regardless of your recipe choices, cooking under pressure requires some know-how as far as how much liquid to use and how long to cook a particular type of food. Naturally, that's why you're reading this book. Understanding the particulars of cooking in a pressure cooker also makes sense. To that end, the following sections give you a quick overview of the basic steps for using your pressure cooker and adapting your favorite recipes.

Presenting six steps to cooking in your pressure cooker

I provide more detailed information on using your pressure cooker in Chapter 5, but if all you need are the basics, here's a six-step breakdown of the entire process:

1. **Choose the right recipe.**

   Whether you make a pressure-cooker-specific recipe or you adapt a conventional recipe, make sure the recipe contains at least 2 cups of water or cooking liquid. (The exception is when you're preparing a dish that cooks or steams in 10 minutes or less. Then you can use as little as 1 cup of liquid.)

   Never fill your pressure cooker more than two-thirds full, even when you're making soup.

2. **Do any browning or sautéing necessary.**

   For stovetop pressure cookers, you can brown and sauté in the pot over medium-high heat.

   For electric pressure cookers, simply use the Brown setting.

   Deglaze either pot as necessary with liquid.

3. **Set the pressure specified in your recipe.**

   With stovetop cookers, you need to start cooking over high heat to reach pressure. Once you do, you have to lower the burner enough to maintain, but not exceed, pressure. Over the course of cooking, you may need to raise the burner heat a bit to maintain pressure as needed.

With electric cookers, all you have to do is hit the high or low pressure settings; the appliance makes all the necessary adjustments.

4. **When the stovetop pressure cooker reaches the right pressure level, set a timer for the length of time your recipe requires. Your electric pressure cooker does this for you automatically.**

Get to know your stovetop cooker's pressure-regulator valve and find out how to determine when it reaches the level of pressure called for in your recipe.

5. **At the end of the specified cooking time, carefully release the pressure inside the pot using the release method specified in the recipe.**

I cover different release methods in Chapter 4.

6. **Check to see whether your food is done.**

Undercooking food is preferable to overcooking it; you can always cook food a bit more, but you can't unburn it! If the food tastes tough or hard when you test it, re-cover the pressure cooker, bring it back up to pressure, and cook for 3- to 5-minute intervals or until the food is cooked to your satisfaction.

When going from one function to another in your electric pressure cooker, always push Stop, choose another function, and then push Start.

Adapting your favorite recipes

Because, as a novice pressure-cooker user, you should always walk before you run, I strongly suggest that you start off following and cooking the pressure-cooker-specific recipes found in this book. After you get a better feel for pressure cooking, you can start experimenting and begin adapting your own recipes.

The first thing you should do when adapting a recipe is to consult the recommended cooking times that I provide in Appendix A. Compare the traditional cooking times with the shortened pressure-cooker times you find there. The next step is to rewrite the recipe. I discuss how to do this in Chapter 6. There you'll find four example recipes, with two parallel versions of each: the traditional version and the pressure-cooker one. Using the recommended cooking times in Appendix A and the recipe conversion information in Chapter 6, rewrite your recipes like I did and then try them out.

One thing to remember when cooking in a pressure cooker, and specifically when adapting recipes, is that not all foods cook at the same speed. For example, when making beef stew with vegetables, the meat naturally needs to cook longer. To avoid having mushy veggies, you can use the stop-and-go cooking method I describe in Chapter 5. Here's how it works in a nutshell: You start off by browning the meat in the pot as you normally would and then begin cooking the meat with some cooking liquid under pressure. You then stop the cooking process, open the lid, add some of the harder and longer-cooking veggies, like the potatoes and carrots, and partially cook them under pressure. You finish up by adding the faster-cooking ingredients, like mushrooms and perhaps fresh herbs. Simple enough, right?

So what are you waiting for? Join millions of others worldwide and get cooking under pressure!

Chapter 2

The Pressure Cooker: Fact versus Fiction

In This Chapter

▶ Tracing the evolution of pressure cookers, from bum rap to unbeatable value

▶ Appreciating the many advantages pressure cookers have to offer

A late Baby Boomer, I had heard about pressure cookers but had never really seen one in operation until, as an undergraduate, I went to study in Spain. I shared a furnished apartment with three native Spanish students where, because I was the only one who knew my way around a kitchen, I became the appointed cook. In the kitchen was an 8-liter, jiggler-valve pressure cooker. Not sure what to do with it — and in all honesty somewhat apprehensive about using it — I at first put it away in the back of the cupboard.

A few weeks later, I went home with one of my roommates. The first thing I noticed as we walked into his family's apartment was a terrible racket coming from the kitchen. There on the stove sat a very noisy pot with a valve that hissed and spit as it slowly spun around. After eating the delicious stew that had been made in the pressure cooker, my curiosity got the better of me and I asked tons of questions about pressure cooking. Before I knew it, I was using the pressure cooker three to four times a week and whipping up meals in about half the time!

Upon returning to New York, I bought an inexpensive aluminum pressure cooker. This was in 1979, and no one I knew owned a pressure cooker or had ever used one. Nevertheless, I cooked with mine as often as possible, amazing (and perhaps scaring) family and friends — back then, only health-food diehards and hippies were using pressure cookers, mostly to cook beans and grains. Now, a little more than 30 years later, more than 2 million pressure cookers are sold each year in this country alone!

I couldn't live without my collection of pressure cookers. In fact, I have at least seven or eight in my pantry on any given day, depending on whether or not my "loaners" have made it back home from friends who frequently borrow them. My pressure cookers get me out of many a mealtime dilemma when 6:00 rolls around and I have yet to begin cooking. Depending on how many people I have to cook for, I may have up to four pressure cookers cooking away on my stove! The pressure cooker enables me to get dinner on the table, on average, up to 70 percent faster than other cooking methods.

Time savings are just one of the many benefits pressure cookers have to offer. I tell you about the others later in this chapter. But first, I dispel some myths that have repressed the pressure cooker's popularity over the years.

Dispelling Fears about Pressure Cookers

No housewares product has ever been as misunderstood and underutilized in American kitchens as the pressure cooker. Even though pressure cookers are enjoyed by tens of millions of home cooks worldwide without fear and crimination, the United States appears to be the last place on earth where they're so underused, yet ironically, so much needed.

Why is it, then, that while everyone else around the world relies on pressure cookers, many Americans think pressure cookers are dangerous and terrifying? To understand why so many Americans are leery of using a pressure cooker, you need to understand something about the history of the pressure cooker and go back in time to the period just before and right after World War II.

A pre–WW II timesaver

Based on the success and popularity of 10-gallon home pressure canners, introduced in 1915, inventors began playing around with the idea of a smaller, more user-friendly pot for cooking food on the stovetop in less time. One of the inventors was Alfred Vischer Jr., who, after much trial and error, introduced his Flex-Seal Speed Cooker in 1938 at a New York City trade show. It was the first time a safe, easy-to-use, saucepan-sized pressure cooker was made available for consumer use. Department-store buyers clamored to be the first in town to offer their customers this cookware wonder that afforded home cooks convenience and speed never before seen in the kitchen. Success led to competition, with other American and European manufacturers introducing their own brands and models of saucepan-sized pressure cookers.

Today's pressure cookers are safe

Even though some poorly designed and post-war-manufactured American-made pressure cookers did indeed explode and rupture, many food-spewing incidents can be attributed to people not reading the instructions or not knowing how to use their pressure cookers properly.

Whereas today's new and improved pressure cookers can't be opened while cooking under pressure, this was not the case with the earlier units. Way too many times, an unsuspecting family member would want to get a peek at what was cooking for dinner and would remove the cover from a pressure cooker under pressure, causing an eruption of hot food. As Chapter 4 explains, this is impossible today unless you're using a vintage model, because the new pressure cookers have safety features that make it impossible to remove the lid as long as an iota of pressure is still inside.

Timing was critical, however, because just as pressure cookers were riding the wave of popularity, manufacturing came to a grinding halt as the United States entered World War II, bringing an end to all civilian production of cookware. This stoppage didn't hamper pressure-cooker use, however. Faced with limited food supplies and rationing during the war, pressure-cooker owners were encouraged by cookware manufacturers to be patriotic and share their pressure cookers with friends and family so that they, too, could enjoy the benefit of cooking cheap cuts of meat to tender perfection!

The untimely demise of the pressure cooker

At the end of the war, the success of the Vischer pressure-cooker saucepan (as pressure cookers were then called) and postwar consumer demand inspired 85 competitive brands of U.S. pressure-cooker saucepans to flood the market. Although that may seem like a good thing, it was actually the beginning of the end of the pressure-cooker boom — no pun intended!

With so many models to choose from, steep competition caused prices to drop, ultimately affecting the integrity and quality of the products. The all-too-familiar pressure-cooker horror stories that we hear over and over again date from this period — the late 1940s through the early 1950s. Some U.S. manufacturers began to produce inferior-quality pressure-cooker saucepans, and cooks were unhappy with the results. What once was the relatively safe pressure cooker, the home cook's friend, was now exploding and rupturing, spewing hot food all over clean kitchens. One by one, companies began to drop out of the business, with only those dedicated to the pressure cooker's development remaining in operation. The damage was done, however, and the pressure cooker's fate seemingly sealed. It took close to 50 years for American consumers to even consider cooking with a pressure cooker again.

Design changes: A safer, more convenient product

While America was getting on with life after the war, Europe was rebuilding, literally from the ground up. Civil production of most housewares didn't commence until the 1950s. Fortunately for us, though, our European counter-parts continued using their old, prewar pressure cookers after the war. With rapidly growing postwar families and lifestyle changes due to advances in technology, European housewives were concerned with providing their families with traditional home-cooked meals in a relatively short time. Because of this demand and an ongoing interest in pressure cooking, major European manufacturers didn't delay in improving the basic concept by developing new designs and incorporating improved safety features. (I talk about these features in Chapter 4.) Americans ultimately benefitted from these improvements and advances when major European housewares manufacturers began to ship pressure cookers to the U.S. in the late 1980s and early 1990s.

Looking at the Benefits of Using a Pressure Cooker

If asked to give a one-word reason why I own and use a pressure cooker, my answer would be "fast." Or perhaps "convenient." No, most definitely "fast" and, well, also "delicious" and "healthy," because so many nutrients and vita-mins are saved when food is cooked in a pressure cooker. Using a pressure cooker helps me produce fast, convenient, delicious, and nutritious food! I guess I'd be hard-pressed to use only a single adjective. For such a simple product, pressure cookers provide an awful lot of bang for the buck! In the following sections, I address these benefits in more detail.

Fixing food fast

Pressure cookers use a combination of pressure and intense high heat from built-up, trapped steam in order to cook food 38 degrees hotter than a conventional saucepan or skillet. By doing so, they cut down on cooking time by up to 70 percent on average. If given the option of spending, say, 30 minutes or an hour and a half cooking, which would you choose? Easy answer, huh? Then why aren't you using your pressure cooker each and every day?

Check out how much time you can save with just a few of the popular foods I list in Table 2-1.

Table 2-1	Comparing Cooking Times		
Food	*Pressure-Cooker Cook Time*	*Traditional Cook Time*	*Time Savings*
Mashed potatoes	17 min.	35 min.	18 min./ 51% faster
Minestrone soup	10 min.	55 min.	45 min./ 82% faster
Italian meat sauce	50 min.	110 min.	60 min./ 54% faster
Risotto	7 min.	28 min.	21 min./ 75% faster
Sauerbraten (a type of mari- nated, German pot roast)	60 min.	120 min.	60 min./ 50% faster

The best way to begin using your pressure cooker is to leave it out on the stovetop. This way, you'll be sure to see it when it comes time to cook. I can assure you that the more you use it and see how much time you save, the more cooking you'll do with it.

Making cooking convenient and clean

Unlike microwaves and other new fast-cooking gadgets, pressure cookers don't take up any counter space, nor do they require any special or expensive equipment. All you need is your gas or electric stove (halogen and glass cooktops work too) and a kitchen timer.

You can use your pressure cooker to make almost any conceivable type of food, as long as you prepare it with some liquid to create steam and pressure.

Cooking in a pressure cooker is also cleaner than using a conventional sauce-pan or skillet. First, because the pressure-cooker lid is locked in place, you eliminate the possibility of splattering cooking liquids all over the stove and surrounding areas. Second, when steam is emitted from a bubbling pot, it eventually settles on your stove and counters, leaving behind starch and mineral deposits. Because the steam is trapped in the pressure cooker, so are the starch and minerals.

Saving energy

Pressure cookers are energy efficient. Because they cook up to 70 percent faster on average and are on the stove for a much shorter period, by using them you ultimately reap the rewards of lower energy costs. Moreover, because all the steam stays in the pot while the food cooks, using your pressure cooker keeps your kitchen cooler in the summer than using conventional saucepans and skillets to simmer your food, thus reducing your need for fans or air conditioning. Just be sure to release the steam under a ventilator hood so the steam is vented to the outside.

Offering multifunctionality

When it was first introduced in the late 1990s, the electric pressure cooker had limited distribution and a high price tag. In the years that followed, technology improved, digital controls were added, and prices became more reasonable. Today, electric pressure cookers are the fastest-growing segment of the pressure-cooker category. Besides allowing you to brown food before cooking it under pressure, many of the newer models can also be used as an electric pot for conventional cooking by using the Brown and Keep Warm settings. But the most exciting aspect of electric pressure cookers is the capability some models have to be used as a slow cooker or a rice cooker. These features make this appliance essentially four products in one, eliminating the need to buy more than one gadget.

Doing food deliciously

Even though a pressure cooker cooks up to 70 percent faster on average than conventional cooking methods, you're basically cooking the food in the same way, building on flavor and appearance as you go along by sautéing, browning, and finishing the dish under pressure so that it cooks thoroughly. The resulting food is cooked to perfection, and it's tasty, too! And why shouldn't it be? This is scratch cooking, after all, just sped up by about 70 percent!

Keeping nutrients in and contaminants out

At the risk of showing my age, I'll ask this question: Do you remember a television commercial from years back for grape jelly that was cooked in a device that looked like a copper still? The gist of the commercial was that all the natural goodness was trapped in the copper tubes to keep in all the good flavor. Guess what? They were right, plus, the jelly probably had more nutrients in it, too!

Studies performed at the Analytic Chemical Laboratory at the Agronomic National Institute in Paris, France, show that valuable minerals and vitamins normally wash out and are poured down the drain when foods are cooked in conventional saucepans of water. These vitamins and minerals are retained to a much higher degree when steamed or cooked in a pressure cooker.

Because steam replaces the air space in the pot that isn't occupied by food, the food doesn't oxidize and change color as quickly. Furthermore, the longer food is cooked, the more color and flavor it loses. That's why green veggies come out greener and carrots stay brighter when cooked in a pressure cooker, not to mention their more intense flavor!

Using your pressure cooker may also help you avoid food poisoning. All too often, you hear about outbreaks of illness related to food contamination. Food poisoning is avoidable, however, especially when you're in control of your kitchen. I go over some of the safe cooking practices you should follow every day in Chapter 14. Nevertheless, you should know that because your pressure cooker cooks under pressure between 220 and 250 degrees (8 to 38 degrees hotter than boiling water), most harmful bacteria are killed off when meat is cooked until done (see Table 2-2).

Table 2-2	Cooking Temperatures of Commonly Prepared Meats
Food	*Safe Internal Cooking Temperature*
Ground meat	
Turkey or chicken	165°
Beef, veal, lamb, or pork	160°
Fresh beef	
Medium	160°
Well done	170°
Fresh lamb	
Medium	160°
Well done	170°

(continued)

Table 2-2 *(continued)*

Food	Safe Internal Cooking Temperature
Fresh pork	
Medium	160°
Well done	170°
Poultry	
Chicken	180°
Turkey	180°

Chapter 3

Exploring Modern Pressure-Cooker Options to Find What You Like Best

*F*or the most part, today's pressure cookers are sleek and shiny, bearing little resemblance to the industrial-looking, earlier models of the 1940s and '50s with their off-putting gauges and valves. Available in a variety of sizes and styles, ranging from 3 to 10 quarts, there's a pressure cooker for every personal preference and budget.

From a 6-quart aluminum pot with a time-tested jiggler-valve priced at $30 to the Cadillac of the category, a $350, Swiss-made, 5-quart stainless-steel model with a spring-loaded pressure-release valve, you have more options available to you than ever before if you're in the market for a pressure cooker. You can even choose from electric models that cost about $100 a pop and do everything automatically but serve the food!

How do I navigate all these amazing options, you ask? Start by determining what you want to base your decision on. Do you want to set a budget and stick to it? Or do you want to pick between a traditional pressure cooker and an electric model? Pick your path and then use this chapter as your guide.

If you choose a model that has the capability to double as a slow cooker and/or rice cooker, be sure to check out the recipes later in this chapter that take advantage of these programs.

Putting Price First

So, you've decided you're going to pick out your pressure cooker based on a set budget, and you know exactly how much you're willing to spend. Here are the options available, based on average price point:

- ✔ Aluminum pressure cookers with jiggler valves are the least-expensive option, ranging from a bargain-basement price of $20 to around $50 for a 6- to 8-quart model.

- ✔ Sturdier and easier to maintain, stainless-steel 6- and 8-quart pressure cookers range from approximately $90 to $130, depending on the features they include.

- ✔ Electric pressure cookers range in price from $100 to $150 and typically come in 5- to 7-quart sizes. They look like tall, round, digital slow cookers capped by a lockable lid with a spring valve.

Although it's the least attractive of all the models, the old-fashioned-looking and noisy jiggler-valve pressure cooker is extremely economical and practical. If you want good results without having to break the bank, this model is a good bet.

Naturally, price matters. Nevertheless, a sturdy, well-made pressure cooker that is well taken care of is an investment that will pay for itself, year after year, for many years to come. As a point of reference, my Spanish mother-in-law used the same heavy-duty Hispano-Suizo-manufactured, 8-liter pressure cooker almost daily for well over 50 years. Even though it had its dings and dangs, it withstood the test of time and provided the family with thousands of home-cooked meals.

Picking the Stove or the Plug

Stovetop pressure cookers were the sole pressure-cooking game in town from World War II on — until electric pressure cookers arrived on the market in the late 1990s. Over the past few years, electric pressure cookers have become not only more affordable but also readily available, manufactured and marketed by leading cookware manufacturers such as Cuisinart, Fagor, and T-fal. The following sections go into more detail about stovetop and electric pressure cookers to help you make the right purchase for your household.

To get a better idea of available retail options, I suggest you do a little homework. The easiest thing to do is go online and perform an Internet search. Type in "pressure cookers" and see what pops up. A good place to start is a site called "Top 50 Pressure Cookers" at www.compare99.com/p/Pressure-Cookers. See what your money can get for the features that you want.

On the stove

Stovetop pressure cookers come in two different finishes: aluminum and stainless steel. The majority of pressure cookers sold worldwide, primarily in developing nations, are the aluminum kind that rock and roll and spew and hiss as the pressure in the sealed pot builds, causing the valve sitting on the vent pipe to spin. If you're a novice cook, you may want to start with an aluminum model, although I still suggest you explore your options.

Stainless-steel models all come with triple-clad metal bottoms, sandwiching an aluminum or copper heat-conducting core of metal between two sheets of stainless steel, which provides a nice heat barrier from the burner. This barrier, in turn, reduces the risk of foods burning and sticking.

Besides the finish, another factor to take into consideration is the pressure regulator. All pressure cookers have a series of built-in safety valves to help regulate pressure as well as make the pressure cooker safe to use. In addition to the jiggler-valve-type aluminum pressure cookers, there are easier-to-use pressure cookers with different types of valves. These include two basic types that are referred to as *developed-weight-valve-regulated* and *spring-valve-regulated* pressure cookers. These valves are usually found on models with stainless-steel pots and lids and, naturally, cost more. (For the full scoop on pressure-regulator valves, see Chapter 4.)

With a cord

One of the fastest-growing segments of the pressure-cooker category is the electric pressure cooker. In addition to cooking food in a fraction of the normal time with just the push of a few buttons, electric pressure cookers offer a lot more for the money. Completely self-contained, most models offer digital countdown timers and perform multiple functions that allow you to brown meat and poultry, as well as cook vegetables before pressure cooking. They also have "warm" settings that simmer foods as well as keep them warm after they're done cooking.

What makes an electric pressure cooker unique is that it's completely automatic. Plug it in, add the food, press a few buttons, and it's ready to go. It automatically rises to and maintains the pressure level you choose. The built-in digital timer regulates the cooking time, and when the dish is done cooking, the pressure is automatically released. The appliance then switches itself off, beeping to tell you that it's done cooking and keeping the food warm until needed.

Beyond Pressure: Exploring Other Features of Electric Cookers

Besides cooking under pressure, some electric models have unique features not normally associated with pressure cookers. Some models have special programs that let you use the appliance as a rice cooker, a steamer, and even as a slow cooker. Who could ask for more? Three of the most popular, 21st-century kitchen must-haves in one appliance! Got your interest? Read on to find out more about my two favorite electric pressure-cooker features, as well as recipes that make the most of each one.

Slowing it down: The slow-cooker program

Slow cooking is the total opposite of pressure cooking. Whereas pressure cooking involves cooking about 70 percent faster under pressure, slow cooking involves heating food over very low heat for hours, no supervision required. Slow cookers, also known as crock pots, are among the most popular small electric appliances sold today.

The slow-cooker program on an electric pressure cooker gives you the option of cooking immediately under pressure or using the program so the food is ready at the exact moment that you want to serve it, later in the day. Just be sure to choose a brand and model of electric pressure cooker that offers high and low slow-cooking settings with a timer, as found today on all conventional slow cookers.

As coauthor of *Slow Cookers For Dummies* with Glenna Vance (also published by Wiley), I'm naturally an advocate of slowing things down when appropriate. Whereas I used to pull out my old tried-and-true crock pot, I now typically use my Fagor electric pressure cooker and select the slow-cooker program to prepare my favorite recipes. And because I want you to enjoy using the slow-cooker program as much as I do, I'm sharing six recipes that I'm certain you'll enjoy.

The top five reasons to consider purchasing an electric pressure cooker

Following are the top five advantages of using an electric pressure cooker as opposed to a stovetop pressure cooker:

1. They're multifunctional. Electric pressure cookers are great for home cooks short on space and everyone else who thinks less is more! The leading brand and model browns food, cooks under pressure, slow-cooks, makes rice, and keeps food warm.

2. They're totally automatic, thereby eliminating all the guesswork.

3. They're programmable. Put everything in the pot and push a few buttons. Now, go put your feet up and wait until you hear it beep!

4. They're cleaner to cook with. Because electric pressure cookers are self-contained and used on the countertop, you don't have to worry about getting grease and oil all over your stove when browning or sautéing.

5. They keep the kitchen cool when you're cooking during the dog days of summer. You'll generate less heat in the kitchen without your stovetop burner on.

Chicken Stroganoff

Prep time: 15 min • **Cook time:** High 3–4 hr; Low 6–7 hr • **Yield:** 6 servings

Ingredients	*Directions*
2 pounds boneless skinless chicken breast halves	*1* Cut chicken into bite-sized pieces and toss in a bowl with the poultry seasoning, salt, and black pepper.
2 tablespoons poultry seasoning	
1½ teaspoons salt	*2* Select the Brown setting and heat the olive oil in the electric pressure cooker. Add the seasoned chicken pieces and brown on all sides. Add the onion and garlic and cook 2 minutes longer.
½ teaspoon black pepper	
1 tablespoon olive oil	
1 large onion, chopped	
1 tablespoon minced garlic	*3* In a mixing bowl, combine the mushroom soup and water. Pour over the chicken.
Two 10¾-ounce cans condensed cream of mushroom soup	*4* Cover; select the Slow Cooker setting. Cook on high for 3 to 4 hours or on low for 6 to 7 hours, or until the chicken is fork-tender.
⅓ cup water	
One 8-ounce container sour cream	*5* Remove the cover and stir in the sour cream and parsley. Taste and adjust for salt and pepper before serving. Serve over the cooked noodles.
¼ cup chopped parsley	
12 ounces wide egg noodles, cooked according to package directions	

Per serving: Calories 570 (From Fat 212); Fat 24g (Saturated 9g); Cholesterol 147mg; Sodium 1,196mg; Carbohydrate 48g (Dietary Fiber 3g); Protein 41g.

Beer-Braised Sausages and Sauerkraut

Prep time: 15 min • **Cook time:** High 3 hr • **Yield:** 8 servings

Ingredients	*Directions*
2 pounds sauerkraut **2 tablespoons vegetable oil**	*1* Place the sauerkraut in a colander to drain the brine. Press to release most of the excess liquid and set aside.
2 pounds garlic sausage, kielbasa, knockwurst, bratwurst, or any combination **2 onions, peeled and sliced** **2 cloves garlic, minced**	*2* Select the Brown setting and heat the vegetable oil in the electric pressure cooker. Add the sausage and brown on all sides. If necessary, cut the sausage into smaller pieces to fit in the pot. Remove and set aside.
2 bay leaves **1½ teaspoons black peppercorns** **1 teaspoon mustard seed** **1½ cups chicken stock**	*3* Add the onion and garlic. Cook until the onion is soft. Add the drained sauerkraut and stir to combine. Add the bay leaves, peppercorns, mustard seed, chicken stock, and beer. Stir to combine. Place the browned sausage on top of the sauerkraut mixture.
1½ cups beer **Spicy mustard to taste**	*4* Cover; select the Slow Cooker setting. Cook on high for 3 hours. Serve immediately with spicy mustard or leave covered on the Warm setting until ready to serve.

Per serving: *Calories 426 (From Fat 322); Fat 36g (Saturated 12g); Cholesterol 73mg; Sodium 2,136mg; Carbohydrate 11g (Dietary Fiber 4g); Protein 15g.*

Note: This recipe is dairy-free.

Vary It! For a gluten-free recipe, use sausage made without fillers that contain gluten and use gluten-free beer made with sorghum.

Tip: If your kielbasa comes in a coil, it will fit in your pressure cooker as-is. If it comes in a horseshoe shape, you'll likely need to cut it into smaller pieces.

Pulled-Chicken Soft Tacos

Prep time: 15 min • **Cook time:** High 4–5 hr; Low 8–9 hr • **Yield:** 6 servings

Ingredients	*Directions*
2 pounds boneless skinless chicken breast halves	*1* Add the chicken, onion, garlic, cilantro, southwest seasoning, chili powder, paprika, cayenne pepper, salt, oregano, chicken stock, and lime juice to the electric pressure-cooker pot. Stir to combine. Cover.
1 small onion, cut in half and sliced	
2 cloves garlic, minced	*2* Select the Slow Cooker setting. Cook on high for 4 to 5 hours or on low for 8 to 9 hours until the chicken is falling-apart-tender, stirring occasionally.
2 tablespoons chopped fresh cilantro	
1 tablespoon southwest seasoning powder	*3* Carefully remove the chicken from the pot and transfer it to a bowl. Shred the chicken by moving two forks in opposite directions.
1 tablespoon chili powder	
1 teaspoon smoked paprika	
½ teaspoon cayenne pepper	*4* Pour the cooking liquid from the pot into a bowl and set aside. Add some of the liquid to the meat to moisten. Adjust the seasoning if necessary.
1 teaspoon salt	
1 teaspoon dried oregano	
¾ cup chicken stock	*5* Use the pulled chicken to fill the warmed tortillas. Garnish with a squeeze of fresh lime juice.
Juice of one lime	
Soft flour tortillas, warmed	

Per serving: Calories 387 (From Fat 80); Fat 9g (Saturated 2g); Cholesterol 84mg; Sodium 1,065mg; Carbohydrate 38g (Dietary Fiber 3g); Protein 37g.

Tip: Serve with your choice of lime wedges, guacamole, salsa, black beans, diced avocadoes, sour cream, and/or shredded cheddar cheese.

Slow-Cooked Ziti

Prep time: 15 min • **Cook time:** Low 4–5 hr • **Yield:** 8 servings

Ingredients	*Directions*
1 tablespoon olive oil **2 pounds Italian sausage, casings removed** **Two 24-ounce jars your favorite pasta sauce** **2 cups water** **1 pound ziti pasta, uncooked** **1 pound ricotta cheese** **5 cups shredded mozzarella** **⅓ cup grated pecorino Romano or Parmesan cheese** **2 tablespoons chopped basil**	*1* Heat the olive oil in a large saucepan over medium-high heat. Add the sausage and cook, breaking up pieces with a spoon, until no longer pink. Add the pasta sauce and water. Bring to a simmer. Remove from the heat. *2* Spread a thin layer of sauce on the bottom of the electric pressure-cooker pot. Cover with a single layer of ziti. Dot with ⅓ cup of ricotta. Cover with 2 cups of sauce. Sprinkle with 1 cup of mozzarella and 1 tablespoon of grated Romano or Parmesan cheese. *3* Repeat the layering four more times, starting with the pasta and ending with the grated cheese. *4* Cover; select the Slow Cooker setting. Cook on low for 4 to 5 hours, or until the pasta is tender. *5* Sprinkle the basil on top of the pasta before serving.

Per serving: Calories 816 (From Fat 399); Fat 44g (Saturated 21g); Cholesterol 131mg; Sodium 1,607mg; Carbohydrate 61g (Dietary Fiber 5g); Protein 43g.

Jambalaya

Prep time: 25 min • **Cook time:** Low 3½ hr • **Yield:** 4 servings

Ingredients	*Directions*
2 tablespoons olive oil	**1** Select the Brown setting and heat the olive oil in the electric pressure cooker. Add the onion, garlic, celery, and bell pepper. Cook until the onion is soft.
1 large onion, chopped	
3 cloves garlic, minced	
2 stalks celery, chopped	**2** Add the ham, tomatoes, parsley, thyme, salt, black pepper, hot sauce, and rice. Stir to combine.
1 green bell pepper, cored, seeded, and chopped	
2 cups diced smoked ham	**3** Cover; select the Slow Cooker setting. Cook on low for 3 hours.
One 28-ounce can crushed tomatoes	
1 tablespoon flat-leaf parsley	**4** Stir in the shrimp. Continue cooking 30 minutes longer on low or until the shrimp are pink. Taste and adjust for salt.
1 teaspoon dried thyme	
2 teaspoons salt	
¼ teaspoon black pepper	
Hot pepper sauce to taste	
1 cup uncooked, long-grain rice	
1 pound large shrimp, shelled and deveined	

Per serving: Calories 475 (From Fat 93); Fat 10g (Saturated 2g); Cholesterol 195mg; Sodium 2,370mg; Carbohydrate 59g (Dietary Fiber 5g); Protein 36g.

Note: This recipe is dairy-free.

Vary It! For a gluten-free recipe, use sausage made without fillers that contain gluten.

Vegetable Curry

Prep time: 15 min • **Cook time:** High 4–4½ hr; Low 5–5½ hr • **Yield:** 4 servings

Ingredients	*Directions*
2 tablespoons olive oil	*1* Select the Brown setting and heat the olive oil in the electric pressure cooker. Add the onion, garlic, and bell peppers. Cook until the onion is soft. Add the curry powder, minced ginger, and salt. Cook for 2 minutes, stirring the mixture as it cooks.
1 medium onion, chopped	
2 cloves garlic, minced	
1 each red and green bell pepper, cored, seeded, and chopped	
2 tablespoons curry powder	*2* Add the cauliflower, potatoes, carrots, celery, tomatoes, stock, coconut milk, salt, and pepper. Stir well to combine.
1 tablespoon minced ginger	
2 teaspoons salt	
1 medium head cauliflower, cut into florets	*3* Cover; select the Slow Cooker setting. Cook on high for 4 to 4½ hours or on low for 5 to 5½ hours. Cook the vegetables until fork-tender, stirring occasionally.
2 large Yukon gold potatoes, peeled and diced	
3 carrots, sliced	
2 stalks celery, sliced	*4* Taste and adjust for salt and pepper. Stir in the yogurt and green peas just before serving. Let warm through, about 10 to 15 minutes. Serve the curry over the jasmine rice.
One 14.5-ounce can petit diced tomatoes, undrained	
2½ cups vegetable stock	
½ cup coconut milk	
1 teaspoon salt	
½ teaspoon black pepper	
1 cup plain yogurt	
2 cups frozen green peas, defrosted	
2 cups cooked jasmine rice	

Per serving: Calories 561 (From Fat 139); Fat 16g (Saturated 7g); Cholesterol 4mg; Sodium 2,725mg; Carbohydrate 92g (Dietary Fiber 17g); Protein 20g.

Note: This recipe is vegetarian and gluten-free.

Vary It! To make this recipe vegan or dairy-free, substitute soy yogurt for the dairy version.

Fluffing it up: The rice program

In a prior life, as the marketing and product manager for a leading housewares manufacturer, I traveled to Japan frequently for business and discovered that everyone in Japan has at least one automatic electric rice maker. Not having grown up eating a lot of rice, I could never grasp the significance of automatic rice makers. Why purchase another gadget when you can simply use a saucepan, right? Wrong! Rice makers make the most amazing, fluffy rice.

Electronic rice makers use a lot less water than stovetop saucepans. Additionally, the rice kernels steam rather than boil, keeping them firm and fluffy, not at all mushy or sticky. The rice is truly delicious, and using a rice maker became the only way I made rice — until I got my Fagor electric pressure cooker with its unique rice program that makes rice under pressure. With a push of a button, I can now prepare rice — or any rice-based dish — in just 6 minutes. Talk about being truly outstanding, much like the following recipes, which I prepare on a regular basis.

If you have or purchase an electric pressure cooker, check to see whether it has a special rice setting. If it doesn't, program it as you normally would for high pressure, setting the digital timer for 6 minutes of cooking time.

Browsing manufacturers' websites

The manufacturer is the best place to get started when checking out the features and functions of various pressure cookers. Your personal computer makes it as easy as surfing the web. The following is a list of companies that make pressure cookers, along with their websites and notes on whether they manufacture stovetop cookers, electric cookers, or both:

- ✔ **Cuisinart:** www.cuisinart.com; electric
- ✔ **Fagor:** www.fagoramerica.com; stovetop and electric
- ✔ **Kuhn Rikon:** www.kuhnrikon.com; stovetop
- ✔ **Manttra:** www.manttra.com; stovetop and electric
- ✔ **Magefesa:** www.magefesausa.com; stovetop
- ✔ **Mirro:** www.mirro.com; stovetop
- ✔ **Presto:** www.gopresto.com; stovetop
- ✔ **Tefal:** www.t-falusa.com/; stovetop and electric
- ✔ **WMF:** www.wmfamericas.com; stovetop
- ✔ **Wolfgang Puck:** www.wolfgangpuck.com; electric

Greek Lemon Rice

Prep time: 15 min • **Cook time:** 6 min • **Yield:** 4 servings

Ingredients	Directions
2 tablespoons olive oil **1 medium onion, chopped**	*1* Select the Brown setting and heat the olive oil in the electric pressure cooker. Add the onion. Cook until the onion is soft.
1½ cups uncooked rice (long-grain white, basmati, or jasmine) **2 cups chicken or vegetable stock**	*2* Add the rice and cook 2 minutes, stirring constantly. Add the stock and stir well.
Salt to taste	*3* Cover; select the Rice setting. Press Start.
Black pepper to taste **¼ cup freshly squeezed lemon juice**	*4* At the end of the rice-cooker program, release the pressure using the quick-release method. Unlock and remove the cover.
1 tablespoon snipped fresh dill **1 cup crumbled feta cheese**	*5* Fluff the rice. Season with salt and pepper to taste. Add the lemon juice and dill.
¼ cup toasted pine nuts **1 lemon, cut into wedges**	*6* Put the cover on the pot and select the Warm setting. Let the rice rest 10 minutes.
	7 Remove the cover. Transfer to a serving plate. Top with the feta and toasted nuts. Serve with the lemon wedges.

Per serving: Calories 517 (From Fat 195); Fat 22g (Saturated 8g); Cholesterol 36mg; Sodium 1,067mg; Carbohydrate 66g (Dietary Fiber 2g); Protein 14g.

Note: This recipe is gluten-free. For a vegetarian version, choose vegetable rather than chicken stock.

Vary It! For a vegan recipe, use vegetable stock and a vegan substitute for the feta cheese. For a dairy-free version, use a vegan substitute for the feta cheese.

Cajun Dirty Rice

Prep time: 10 min • **Cook time:** 6 min • **Yield:** 4 servings

Ingredients	*Directions*
1 tablespoon olive oil	*1* Select the Brown setting and heat the olive oil in the electric pressure cooker. Add the garlic, onion, celery, and green bell pepper. Cook until the vegetables are crisp-tender.
2 cloves garlic, minced	
1 large onion, chopped	
1 stalk celery, chopped	
1 green bell pepper, cored, seeded, and chopped	*2* Add the sausage and cook, breaking up the meat with a spoon, until no longer pink. Add the rice, stock, and Worcestershire sauce. Stir well.
1 pound sweet or hot Italian sausage, casing removed	
½ cup uncooked white long-grain rice	*3* Cover; select the Rice setting. Press Start.
1⅓ cups chicken or vegetable stock	*4* At the end of the rice-cooker program, release the pressure using the quick-release method. Unlock and remove the cover.
1 teaspoon Worcestershire sauce	
Salt to taste	*5* Fluff the rice. Taste and add salt and pepper as desired.
Black pepper to taste	

Per serving: *Calories 352 (From Fat 179); Fat 20g (Saturated 6g); Cholesterol 47mg; Sodium 1,040mg; Carbohydrate 28g (Dietary Fiber 2g); Protein 15g.*

Note: This recipe is gluten-free and dairy-free.

Tip: Serve with hot sauce on the side for those who prefer a spicier dish.

Mac 'n' Cheese

Prep time: 5 min • **Cook time:** 6 min • **Yield:** 4 servings

Ingredients	*Directions*
2 cups uncooked small pasta like elbows, shells, rotini, or farfalle	*1* Place the pasta and stock in the electric pressure-cooker pot. Stir well to combine.
1¾ cup chicken or vegetable stock	*2* Cover; select the Rice setting. Press Start.
¾ cup whole milk	*3* At the end of the rice-cooker program, release the pressure using the quick-release method. Unlock and remove the cover.
2 cups shredded sharp cheddar cheese	
1 tablespoon butter	*4* Add the milk, cheese, butter, black pepper, and cayenne pepper. Stir well.
Black pepper to taste	
1 pinch cayenne pepper	*5* Reposition the cover on the pot. Select the Warm setting and let the pasta rest for 10 minutes before serving.

Per serving: Calories 402 (From Fat 227); Fat 25g (Saturated 15g); Cholesterol 75mg; Sodium 812mg; Carbohydrate 24g (Dietary Fiber 1g); Protein 20g.

Note: This recipe is vegetarian when made with vegetable rather than chicken stock.

Tip: Double this recipe for leftovers or whenever you have visitors.

Almond Rice Pudding

Prep time: 15 min • **Cook time:** 6 min • **Yield:** 4 servings

Ingredients	*Directions*
1 cup long-grain or jasmine rice	*1* Place the rice, almond milk, sugar, raisins, and vanilla extract in the electric pressure-cooker pot. Stir well to combine.
2½ cups sweetened almond milk	
¼ cup sugar	*2* Cover; select the Rice setting. Press Start.
½ cup golden raisins	*3* At the end of the rice-cooker program, release the pressure using the quick-release method. Unlock and remove the cover. Stir well.
1 teaspoon vanilla extract	
½ cup slivered almonds	
	4 Add the slivered almonds. Serve warm or cold.

Per serving: Calories 437 (From Fat 82); Fat 9g (Saturated 1g); Cholesterol 0mg; Sodium 103mg; Carbohydrate 81g (Dietary Fiber 4g); Protein 8g.

Note: This recipe is vegetarian, vegan, gluten-free, and dairy-free.

Part II
Making the Best and Safest Use of Your Pressure Cooker

The 5th Wave
By Rich Tennant

"Here's the basics of pressure cooking. You have 9 people coming to dinner in 2 hours. Rather than divorcing your husband for not defrosting the roast and slitting your wrists for forgetting to soak the beans, you use the pressure cooker."

In this part . . .

Here is where I reveal some of the finer points concerning the use and care of pressure cookers and share some of the tricks I've learned along the way for getting the best results with the least amount of effort. You also discover how to use your pressure cooker for canning and how to convert your favorite recipes designed for use with traditional cooking methods into recipes for the pressure cooker.

Chapter 4

Understanding How Pressure Cookers Work

• •

In This Chapter

▶ Becoming acquainted with your pressure cooker

▶ Getting some operational guidelines

▶ Releasing the steam

▶ Testing your pressure cooker

• •

*T*he pressure cooker has come a long way from its early days when it resembled a cast-iron cannonball that was heated in the hot cinders of the hearth until the cook "guessed" that the food was done (back in the days of our great-great grandparents!). It's different even from what it looked like a short 85 years ago when it was made from die-cast metal. Aside from being cosmetically different, today's stamped-aluminum or stainless-steel pressure cooker has at least three safety valves, making it the safest pressure cooker invented yet.

If you've never used a pressure cooker before, or if you have but plan to start using one of the new-and-improved versions, carefully read through this chapter. In it, I tell you everything you ever wanted to know about how this kitchen wonder works and what to expect along the way as it does its thing.

The Science of the Pressure Cooker

With the exception of oil and fat, all liquids that contain water boil at 212 degrees. When water boils, steam, which is hotter than boiling water, is produced.

For a moment, imagine a pot of boiling water that's producing steam. You cover the pot and close the cover in such a way that the pot is sealed and the steam can't escape. As long as the liquid boils, the trapped steam continues to increase, eventually condensing with nowhere to go and building up inside the pot. The pressure of this trapped steam can be measured in pounds per square inch, or psi.

Now pretend that the pot contains a 1-x-1-inch cube, and you're applying approximately 10 to 13 pounds of force, or pressure, on all six sides of the cube. With the combined heat and pressure, the temperature increases by about 38 degrees and the cube starts to break down, which is exactly what happens to food when you prepare it in a pressure cooker. See Figure 4-1 for an illustration of cooking under pressure.

Figure 4-1:
Trapped steam creates high pressure and a high cooking temperature.

Illustration by Elizabeth Kurtzman

The Nuts and Bolts of Stovetop Models

Stovetop pressure cookers are deceptively simple-looking. When you consider that they consist of only four main components, it's pretty amazing that you can cook such delicious food, so quickly, in such a simple product. But don't be fooled. Each part plays an important role in getting the job done! I tell you about the most important parts — the pot and its cover, the rubber gasket, and the pressure-regulator valve — in the sections that follow. (***Note:*** The electric pressure cooker, which I describe in the later section "Examining the Cord, Plug, and Buttons of Electric Models" has all these same parts.)

Looking at the pot and its cover

The two main components of the pressure cooker are the pot and cover. Originally made from die-cast metal, pressure cookers have been made of stamped metal ever since this process was introduced in France in the 1950s. Today's stamped-aluminum or stainless-steel (usually high-quality, 18/10 stainless) pressure cookers are usually sold in a variety of sizes ranging from 4 to 8 quarts. The most commonly offered size is 6 quarts, which can easily accommodate 4 to 8 servings.

Whether you purchase and use an aluminum or stainless-steel pressure cooker is up to you. Aluminum is usually less expensive. However, because I use my pressure cooker almost each and every day, I prefer a heavier, stainless-steel model.

Most stainless-steel pressure cookers have a thick, three-ply plate attached to the bottom of the pot that comes in direct contact with the burner. Comprised of a sheet of aluminum or copper sandwiched between two sheets of stainless steel, this plate evenly distributes heat, eliminating hot or cold spots. Because I like to sauté and brown in the same pressure-cooker pot before cooking under pressure, I prefer a heavy-bottomed pot for even cooking.

Also, the heavier the bottom, the less likely the food is to stick and burn when cooking under pressure. Some less-expensive aluminum pressure cookers have thin metal bottoms, which increase the risk of food sticking and burning over high heat as the pressure cooker is brought up to pressure.

Both aluminum and stainless-steel pressure-cooker pots tend to have two heat-resistant plastic handles. The pot cover has two matching handles. These handles are important for two reasons:

✔ **They make it easier to move the pressure cooker from the countertop to the burner.** Pressure-cooker pots are heavy. A 6-quart stainless-steel pot can weigh about 7 to 8 pounds empty; add some cooking liquid and food, and that pot gets awfully heavy mighty fast.

✔ **They help ensure you close the pressure cooker properly.** If you look at the underside of a pressure-cooker cover and the top of the pot, you'll see a jarlike locking mechanism for closing and sealing the pressure cooker. When the pressure cooker is closed properly, the top handles on the cover line up with the bottom handles on the pot. Some pressure-cooker cover handles also have a locking mechanism incorporated in the handle that has to be activated in order to lock the cover in place. Others self-lock when the cover is turned and locked in position.

Regardless of the design, modern pressure cookers can't be opened until the pressure has dropped to 0 psi. This is an important safety feature. Early model pressure cookers, for the most part, didn't explode. People opened them under pressure, causing food to fly all over the kitchen! Fortunately, this scenario is no longer a possibility. If you happen to have one of those older models, say from the '40s or '50s, save it as a conversation piece — they're no longer meant for cooking!

Relying on the ever-important rubber gasket

An important feature invented by Alfred Vischer, Jr., and incorporated in his 1938 Flex-Seal Speed Cooker (which I tell you about in Chapter 2) was the rubber seal or gasket. The gasket creates an air- and steam-tight seal when the cover is locked in place. All pressure cookers must have this feature because they don't work without it.

Here's why. Because metal expands when heated, the rubber gasket allows for a constant tight seal between the cover and the pot. By having this constant seal, air can't get into the pressure cooker. The steam that's created by the boiling cooking liquid is trapped inside the sealed pot and builds into pressure, which ultimately cooks the food up to 70 percent faster than using a regular pot and cover.

In order to perform as required, the gasket must be clean and flexible. Over the course of time, it can dry out and harden, losing its elasticity. If that happens, replace the gasket immediately. Make a habit of checking the gasket each time you use your pressure cooker (for more info, see Chapter 5). Most manufacturers suggest that the gasket be replaced at least once a year. Never use your pressure cooker without the rubber gasket properly positioned. Don't use a damaged gasket because the cover won't lock into place properly and/or steam won't build up and may even escape.

Regulating pressure (and safety) with valves

In much the same way that electric appliances have on/off switches and temperature controls or settings, pressure cookers have pressure-regulator valves that allow you to control the amount of pressure inside the closed pot. Some of these valves have been around for decades; others are new and quite innovative. The kind of valve determines the type of pressure cooker you have. Basically, stovetop pressure cookers come in three varieties (as you can see in Figure 4-2): jiggler-valve cookers, developed-weight-valve cookers, and spring-valve cookers.

It's rock 'n' roll regulator time!: The jiggler valve

The jiggler valve is one of the oldest pressure-regulator methods around. People who recall that old, noisy pressure cooker sitting on top of their stove are thinking about the jiggler-valve type of pressure cooker.

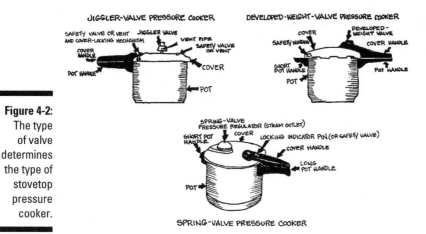

Illustration by Elizabeth Kurtzman

Figure 4-2:
The type of valve determines the type of stovetop pressure cooker.

The jiggler valve is a round, metal weight that sits on top of a thin metal tube, or vent pipe, in the center of the cover of some pressure-cooker models. As pressure builds inside the pressure cooker, steam comes out through the vent pipe, causing that metal weight to rock back and forth and slowly turn. As pressure increases, so does the movement of the jiggler valve. In fact, the only method you have for figuring out the approximate level of pressure you're cooking with is one of trial and error. Exceed pressure, and the infamous jiggler valve hisses and spits steam and condensation at you with no mercy.

Today's jiggler-valve pressure cooker really hasn't changed too much since its introduction. It has some additional safety features, like preventing removal of the cover while under pressure. Unlike the earlier ones made from die-cast metal, today's versions are made from stamped aluminum or, in some cases, stainless steel.

The heavyweight: The developed-weight valve

A takeoff of the jiggler valve is the developed-weight valve. This pressure-regulator valve is positioned on the vent pipe (most are located on the cover handle) and locked in place by the user. When pressure is achieved, the weight rises up ever so slightly and steam is emitted, indicating to the user that maximum pressure has been reached and that the moment has arrived to adjust the burner heat to a level that's low enough to maintain pressure.

It's all in the turn of the dial: Spring-valve pressure regulators

Over the course of time, manufacturers have devised easier ways to regulate pressure, the best of which is the spring-valve pressure regulator.

The design of the spring-valve pressure regulator is different from brand to brand, although two common types exist:

✔ **A plastic dial that's located on top of the cover (refer to Figure 4-2):** Inside or under the removable dial is a spring mechanism. If you gently press down on the dial, you can feel the spring action. The dial usually has numerical settings and a burst-of-steam symbol that allow you to choose the level of pressure you want and release pressure after cooking. The following list gives a detailed description:

• **Setting 0:** Releases the dial, allowing you to remove the cover for cleaning.

• **Setting 1:** Used for low pressure (10 psi). Perfect for cooking soft foods, such as berries or fish, so they retain their shape.

• **Setting 2:** Works for high pressure (13 to 15 psi, depending on brand and model). I use this setting most frequently when cooking under pressure.

• **Steam:** Used to release pressure immediately after cooking.

✔ **A plastic or metal rod that's built into the cover:** This valve rises as pressure builds in the cooker. The spring-regulated rods indicate the level of pressure reached by color and/or height. Some models also have a pressure selector switch built into the handle that allows you to select a level of pressure, such as low (10 psi), medium (13 psi), or high (15 psi).

Hearing lots of hissing? It's the safety valves!

After the cover is positioned on the pressure cooker and locked in place, the pressure cooker can be heated and brought up to maximum pressure over high heat. Steam pressure gradually builds up. Excess steam begins to come out of the pressure-regulator valve, and an audible hissing sound is heard. These things happen with all pressure cookers, regardless of the type of pressure-regulator valve.

If the burner heat isn't adjusted and lowered, steam continues to come out as a safety feature. As pressure continues to build, the other safety valves also activate. All pressure cookers have at least three safety valves. Their function is to permit excess pressure to escape if too much pressure builds up due to one or more of the following reasons:

✔ The heat is too high, creating too much steam.

✔ A pressure-regulator valve is malfunctioning or obstructed.

✔ The pressure cooker is overfilled.

Although every manufacturer refers to these valves by different names, for the most part they're very similar in operation. Basically, by making so much racket, the pressure cooker reminds you to lower the burner heat to a simmer.

So where are these safety valves located? In addition to the pressure-regulator valve, another safety valve is usually located in the cover. This valve may be as simple as a rubber stopper or plug or as sophisticated as a metal lug-nut-type valve. In addition, depending on the design of the pressure cooker, some type of safety valve is usually located in the cover handle. A cutout in the cover rim allows for expansion of the rubber gasket under extreme excess pressure. Together, all these safety valves provide the user with a pressure cooker that's safer to use than ever before. Nevertheless, all the valves must be kept unobstructed and clear of any food buildup to work properly.

Examining the Cord, Plug, and Buttons of Electric Models

Electric pressure cookers provide the gadget-savvy consumer with a totally new and innovative way to cook under pressure, as well as slow cook and even make rice, all in one appliance (see Chapter 3).

This appliance works on the same premise as a stovetop pressure cooker with a spring-valve pressure regulator (refer to Figure 4-2 to see what this stovetop model looks like). The electric pressure cooker (pictured in Figure 4-3) is made up of a metal electric base that houses the heating element, a cord and plug, and a control panel. The nonstick pot is easy to remove for washing. Depending on the brand and model, electric cookers come with a 5-, 6-, or 7-quart cooking pot made of nonstick aluminum. The base usually has two side handles, making it easier to move and carry the appliance.

Figure 4-3:
Electric pressure cookers look nothing like their stovetop counterparts.

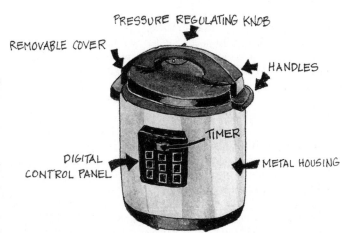

PRESSURE REGULATING KNOB

REMOVABLE COVER

HANDLES

TIMER

DIGITAL CONTROL PANEL

METAL HOUSING

Illustration by Elizabeth Kurtzman

The removable lid, which locks into place when turned clockwise, is very similar to that found on a stovetop pressure cooker. At least three safety valves are built into the lid, including the spring-valve pressure regulator. The underside of the lid also has a removable rubber gasket.

Besides the cord and plug, the one feature that really differentiates the electric pressure cooker from the stovetop version is the electronic control panel on the front of the base (see Figure 4-4). Made up of a push pad and a digital clock, the control panel is the brain of the appliance. By pushing a button, you program the pressure cooker to do the things that you would otherwise have to do manually. The electric pressure cooker can brown and sauté, simmer, cook under high or low pressure, *and* keep the cooked food warm when done. The countdown clock/timer allows you to set the pressure cooker for the cooking time specified in the recipe. After the desired pressure is reached, the timer kicks in, and the pressure cooker beeps at the end of the selected cooking time. Easy, no?

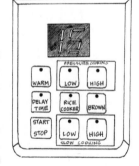

Figure 4-4:
The control pad of an electric pressure cooker.

Illustration by Elizabeth Kurtzman

Say you want to make my Sunday Pot Roast recipe in Chapter 9. After adding the oil to the pot, you simply press the Brown and Start buttons. After 60 seconds of preheating, the oil is hot enough to begin cooking. After browning the meat and onions, you add the broth and press the Stop button. After positioning the lid on the pressure cooker and locking it in place, you press the High pressure button and, according to the recipe directions, set the programmable timer for 60 minutes. After that, you simply press Start and let the pressure cooker do its thing. The electric pressure cooker heats up, creates steam, and reaches high pressure, after which it stabilizes on its own and cooks the meat to perfection. At the precise moment that the pressure cooker reaches the chosen level of pressure, the countdown timer kicks in, and at the end of the cooking cycle, the appliance "beeeeeeps," telling you that it's done cooking. On most models, the pressure cooker automatically switches over to Keep Warm. At this moment, you're ready to release the pressure by using either the natural-release method or the automatic-release method, both of which I tell you about in the later "Letting Off Some Steam" section.

Guidelines for Easy Pressure Cooking

As with any appliance or gadget, you have some basic, fundamental rules to follow to get the best results before and while you use your pressure cooker. Here's what to keep in mind:

- **Never fill the pressure cooker more than half full with food or two-thirds full with liquid when making soups or sauces.** Food, especially liquid, boils harder and faster under pressure, which means it has a tendency to increase in volume. Fortunately, most pressure cookers have a two-thirds mark stamped on the inside of the pot, eliminating any guesswork.

  Never pack food down into the pressure cooker because that defeats the purpose of fast cooking by inhibiting the very hot steam from circulating around the food.

- **Maximize flavor by browning meat and poultry directly in the pressure cooker.** When food is cooked quickly over high heat in a small amount of fat, such as canola or olive oil, it browns. The natural sugar found in food caramelizes in the hot fat, giving the food great color and intense flavor. I therefore always brown or sauté meat, poultry, chopped onions, carrots, celery, and (at times) hearty herbs such as thyme or sage, to give the food I'm preparing better flavor and, ultimately, texture.

- **When browning, you want the temperature to be hot enough to sear in the juices and flavor, but not burn the food.** When you think the oil is hot enough, add a piece or two of food. If it sizzles without sputtering, the oil is at the ideal temperature. Add about half of the food to be browned and cook it evenly on all sides. If you add too much at once, the oil and pot drop in temperature and the food simmers rather than browns. Cooking food in small quantities at a time rather than all at once is called cooking in batches. Deglaze the pan before proceeding to cook under pressure to remove cooked-on particles of food as well as any cooked-on juices. Deglazing also makes the finished product superflavorful.

  Always brown with the cover off and usually over high or medium-high heat in order to sear the outer surface of the meat. Marinated foods should be well drained, and all meat and poultry should be patted dry before being placed in the hot oil.

  When using an electric pressure cooker, select the Brown setting and proceed as previously described.

- **Never force the cover when closing it.** If the cover won't easily close and lock, remove it from the pressure cooker and make sure the rubber gasket is properly positioned. The cover should sit squarely on the center of the pressure cooker before you try to close it.

Remember, a pressure cooker lid is like a jar top: Put it on the wrong way and you may not be able to open the jar easily or at all. The same is true with your pressure cooker. If you have to force the cover closed, either the lid isn't sitting correctly on the pot or the rubber gasket may be twisted or improperly aligned. You'll probably have a hard time getting the lid off the pressure cooker, if you can even get it off.

Some covers lock in place by being positioned on the pressure cooker and turned clockwise. These units usually have an arrow or some type of indicator mark that you need to line up with the long pot handle. Making sure that the cover is sitting flush to the pot, carefully turn clockwise. Because of the tight fit of the rubber seal gasket, some covers may offer more resistance than others when you're closing the pressure cooker. Regardless, never force the cover shut.

Some pressure cookers have a self-locking cover mechanism. You simply position the cover on the pressure cooker in accordance with the manufacturer's instructions and lock it in place.

✔ **Start the countdown time for cooking when the pressure cooker reaches the chosen level of pressure, not before.** Pressure is rated in psi. As Table 4-1 indicates, the higher the pressure, the hotter the food is cooking.

The electric pressure cooker makes it even easier for you. Choose the level of pressure you want (high or low), set the timer, and press Start. When the pressure cooker reaches pressure, the countdown timer kicks in and beeps when done.

✔ **Follow cooking times carefully.** Because pressure cookers cook up to three times faster than conventional cooking methods, food can overcook quickly! Either refer to the cooking times indicated in pressure-cooker recipes or use a suggested cooking times chart. If you're uncertain about the exact time to cook something, undercook it. Undercooked food can easily be cooked under pressure an additional minute or two, whereas overcooked food usually becomes puree!

Table 4-1	Temperature-Pressure Ratios	
Pressure Setting	*Cooking Temperature*	*Pressure Level*
High pressure	250 degrees	13–15 psi
Medium pressure	235 degrees	10 psi
Low pressure	220 degrees	3 psi

Letting Off Some Steam

Unless otherwise indicated in a recipe, pressure should always be released immediately after the required length of cooking time to prevent overcooking. There are three methods to release the steam: the natural-release method and two quick-release methods.

When releasing pressure, always choose the appropriate method for your model of pressure cooker or in accordance with the recipe's instructions.

Natural-release method

The natural-release method can be used with all types of pressure cookers, including electric versions. Here's how it works:

1. **After cooking for the prescribed length of time, remove the pressure cooker from the burner and let it cool to room temperature.**

   As it cools, the pressure diminishes and eventually drops completely. The exact amount of time it takes depends on how full the pressure cooker is.

   When cooking with an electric pressure cooker, the appliance automatically goes into the Keep Warm cycle. Press Stop when done cooking and the pressure will diminish automatically.

2. **Open the pressure cooker when all the pressure has been released.**

   If using a jiggler-valve or weighted-valve pressure cooker, you can tell that the pressure has been released when you can touch or remove the valve and it no longer makes any noise. Pressure has been released in a spring-valve or electric pressure cooker when the pressure indicator pin drops all the way.

Save the natural-release method for when you're cooking large, tough cuts of meat that won't break down and get mushy, or when you're making stock or broth and the solids (vegetables, poultry, meat, and so on) will be discarded. These foods benefit from the additional cooking time in a closed pot. For example, pot roast becomes more tender, and stock becomes more flavorful.

Quick-release methods

The two quick-release methods — the cold-water-release method and the automatic-release method — are the two most commonly used ways of releasing pressure. The method you use is determined by the model and type of pressure cooker you have, so check your manufacturer's instructions.

Cold-water-release method

The cold-water release is the method to use if you have a jiggler valve, developed-weight valve, or spring-regulated valve pressure cooker *without* a pressure selector.

1. **When finished cooking, remove the pressure cooker from the stove using potholders to grab the two handles, and place it in the sink.**

2. **Run cold water over the top side of the pressure cooker until all the pressure has been released.**

   If using a jiggler-valve or developed-weight-valve pressure cooker, you can tell that the pressure has been released when you can touch or remove the valve and it no longer makes any noise. Pressure has been released in a spring-valve pressure cooker when the pressure indicator pin drops all the way.

3. **Open the pressure cooker when all the pressure has been released.**

When cooking in an electric pressure cooker, never use the cold-water-release method, or you run the risk of electrocution!

Automatic-release method

Use the automatic-release method to release pressure after cooking if your pressure cooker has a pressure selector with steam release, usually indicated by a burst-of-steam symbol. The same holds true with electric pressure cookers.

1. **Carefully turn or push the pressure selector to the steam setting.**

   The pressure cooker automatically and safely releases all the built-up steam through the spring-regulator valve.

2. **Open the pressure cooker when all the pressure has been released.**

   You can tell the pressure has been released when the pressure indicator pin drops all the way.

In the event that you're unable to open the cover of your stovetop pressure cooker, try the cold-water-release method because some pressure may still remain.

If you experience difficulties opening your electric pressure cooker, unplug it and contact the manufacturer's customer service department.

Doing a Trial Run

The easiest way to get a feel for how to use a pressure cooker is by putting it through a test run and heating some water under pressure before you begin cooking any food.

Follow these steps for heating water:

1. **Fill the pressure-cooker pot with 2 cups of water.**

2. **Cover the pot.**

   Look for the two arrows or triangles that are engraved in the top of the cover. Place the cover on the pot, matching the arrows with the long pot handle. Turn clockwise until the cover and long pot handles line up and you hear a click. If your pressure cooker isn't shown in Figure 4-2, or if you're using an electric pressure cooker, check the owner's manual for instructions.

    Before positioning and locking the cover in place, always check the rubber gasket to make sure it's in good condition. Position it properly on the underside of the cover. Always check the owner's manual to see whether the gasket has to be positioned in a specific fashion or location because some gaskets have small cutouts or openings that must be lined up in order for the pressure cooker to work properly.

    Never force the cover when turning it to close. It should sit level on top of the pressure cooker and turn without much resistance. If you encounter difficulties, refer to Chapter 14.

    If you don't hear a click when closing the pressure cooker, the cover isn't locked and the cooker won't operate properly. In that case, inspect the gasket, cover, and pressure-cooker pot for possible damage.

3. **For a jiggler-valve or developed-weight-valve pressure cooker, place the weighted valve on the vent pipe. If you have a spring-valve pressure cooker and it has a pressure selector, set the regulator for the level of pressure desired, in this case, high.**

4. **Place the pressure cooker on the stove and bring the water to a boil over high heat.**

    For electric pressure cookers, select high pressure, set the timer for 5 minutes, and press Start.

   As the water boils, steam is produced.

   If your pressure cooker is the jiggler-valve type, the jiggler valve will slowly begin to turn and rock as steam pressure builds up. With the developed-weight-valve type, the valve will rise slightly.

   The mode of operation with spring-valve pressure regulators is even more diverse: Some have a pressure indicator pin that rises up until it's level with the top of the cover. Others have a pressure-regulator valve that rises higher than the cover itself. Regardless, once the valve is up, your pressure cooker has reached the level of pressure you chose to cook with.

5. **If using a stovetop pressure cooker, lower the burner heat to simmer to maintain pressure.**

   The pressure cooker is now cooking under pressure, which is when you start to clock the cook-down time.

If you're using an electric pressure cooker, the appliance's built-in timer will automatically kick in.

If you don't own a digital kitchen timer, now is the time to purchase one. Available in the gadget section of most housewares stores and supermarkets, digital timers allow you to control the exact cooking time without any guesswork. If your stove has a digital timer, you can use that instead.

Make sure to watch for the following things when using a stovetop pressure cooker:

✔ After you raise the heat to high, the pressure cooker will eventually start to hiss at you as it releases excess steam and pressure through the pressure selector. The pressure cooker is signaling you that it has reached the level of pressure you selected and it's time for you to immediately lower the burner heat to a low setting, which on my gas range is a simmer.

✔ If the pressure cooker is still pretty noisy after lowering the heat (with the exception of the jiggler- and weighted-valve versions, which normally operate with a certain amount of noise), turn the spring-valve pressure regulator to the steam release setting for a couple seconds to release some of the excess pressure. Things should now be stabilized, the pressure cooker almost quiet, and hardly any steam coming out of the pressure regulator.

✔ If the jiggler valve slows down or stops spinning or if the weighted valve or indicator pin begins to lower while you're cooking, raise the burner heat slightly so the valves remain operational.

To remove the cover after cooking, follow these steps:

1. **Turn off the burner heat and remove the pressure cooker from the stove.**

2. **Release the pressure.**

   If using a jiggler- or weighted-valve pressure cooker or a spring-valve pressure cooker without a pressure selector switch, remove the pressure cooker from the stove and place it in the sink. Run cold water over the top side of the pressure cooker until all the pressure has been released.

   For a spring-valve pressure cooker with a pressure selector, turn the selector to the steam setting to release the pressure.

   When using an electric pressure cooker, press Stop when the pressure cooker beeps and release the pressure using the automatic-release method.

3. **Unlock the cover.**

   You can't remove the cover until after all the steam has been released. As long as any pressure remains in the pot, a safety-locking valve kicks in and makes removing the cover impossible, whether you have a stovetop unit or an electric one.

Chapter 5

Pressure Cooking Basics from Start to Finish

Recipes in This Chapter

◔ Garlic Dill Pickles

◔ Strawberry Jam

*Y*our pressure cooker will last you quite a while if you take good care of it, which is why this chapter gives you some pointers on how to maintain it in perfect working shape for optimum use day after day, year after year. It also offers tips on what to look for every time you use your pressure cooker and introduces you to the concept of pressure canning for those times when you want to preserve the season's best produce.

If you haven't looked at Chapter 4 yet, you may find it helpful to read that information first so you're more familiar with the basic pressure-cooker parts and techniques that I refer to in this chapter.

First Things First To Get Cooking Under Pressure

The following five sections explain in detail the steps involved in using a pressure cooker successfully. Much easier than you probably imagine, it's all a matter of finding out what to do and following a basic routine, as you would with any style of cooking. Observing each of the steps that follow will ensure many happy and successful hours of pressure cooking.

Keep it clean

Always wash the pressure cooker well after every use and when you haven't used it for an extended period of time. Never leave any food or residue in or on the pot or cover. If you see something that doesn't look like it belongs there, wash it off. For more pointers on cleaning your pressure cooker, flip to the later "Keeping Your Pressure Cooker Squeaky Clean and Shiny" section.

Remove the gasket from the cover and check to see that the gasket, the inner part of the cover, and the outer rim of the pot are clean. (See the next section for how to inspect and replace the gasket.) Making sure these areas are clean reduces the risk of the cover sticking when you go to open it after the pressure has been released.

Inspect the gasket

The rubber sealing gasket or ring is what makes the pressure cooker airtight so that it can maintain pressure. Every time you use the pressure cooker, whether you have a stovetop model or an electric one, make sure that the rubber gasket is still flexible and hasn't dried out.

I always remove the gasket and check it visually for any tears or cracks *before* I start cooking. Here's the method that works best: Take the gasket in two hands, twist it into a figure eight, and stretch it. There should be some give. If not, or if you notice any signs that the gasket is dry or damaged, replace it immediately with a new gasket, obtainable from the manufacturer.

After checking the gasket, put it back in the rim on the underside of the cover. The gasket must slide flatly under the rim. Some pressure-cooker gaskets have markings or cutouts that indicate where to position them.

Check the valves

Just as you would never drive a car with a leaking gas tank, you should never use a pressure cooker that leaks. Routinely check your pressure cooker for leaks as well as blockages in the safety valves.

Each manufacturer's design varies, so check the owner's manual for the exact requirements for maintaining the safety valves in working order. The following are some of the things I look for:

 ✔ If your pressure cooker has a jiggler valve or developed weight with a vent pipe, stick a pipe cleaner or toothpick through the opening to make sure that the vent pipe is clean and not blocked. Also check the underside of the jiggler valve or weight and remove any caked-on food residue. Some of these pressure cookers have a rubber, stopperlike valve on the top of the cover. Be sure that it's securely positioned and hasn't dried out. Others have a brass or steel nutlike valve on the underside of the cover. Make sure that no food or residue has collected in the center of the nut.

✔ If your pressure cooker has a spring valve, press or pull gently on the valve (depending on the design) to make sure that it moves without any resistance. Visually check any remaining valves on the underside of the cover. For the most part, these valves resemble brass or steel nutlike valves.

✔ Another place to look for valves is in the handle assemblies. Here, too, remove any caked-on food or food residue.

Fill the pressure cooker properly

Filling your pressure cooker with the right amount of ingredients is critical. If you use too little cooking liquid, the pressure cooker may never reach the desired pressure. On the other hand, if you fill the pressure cooker with too much food or liquid, the steam and pressure will force the food or liquid up toward the cover and safety valves. As the pressure builds, food and liquid will be forced out through the valves, which is dangerous because food particles can become lodged in the valves and clog them, causing the safety system of valves to kick in, stop the cooking process, and continuously release pressure.

If you can remember the following points, you'll always have a properly filled pressure cooker:

✔ Never fill the pressure cooker more than two-thirds full.

✔ Always use at least 2 cups of cooking liquid to obtain maximum pressure output.

Look, listen, and smell

As the pressure cooker begins to do its job, keep your senses alert.

✔ **Look** to see that the pressure regulator valve is operating properly and that the pressure cooker isn't taking longer than the anticipated amount of time to reach pressure. A good ballpark amount of time is about 5 to 10 minutes.

If you happen to see condensation leaking from the cover onto the stove as the pressure cooker reaches or is cooking under pressure, you don't have an airtight seal or the pressure cooker was overfilled. Stop everything and do the following: Release any pressure in the pot, remove the cover, and check to make sure that the gasket is indeed there and that it's properly positioned and not damaged. Remove any excess food if the pot is more than two-thirds full.

Electric pressure cookers operate a bit differently. Because they're electronically controlled, steam hardly ever comes out of the pressure-regulator valve. The only thing that may come out is a bit of condensation that collects in the small, clear plastic reservoir located on the base handle.

✔ **Listen** to the pressure regulator valve as it talks to you. Jiggler-valve pressure cookers are the noisiest kind there are. In order to cook under pressure, some steam and pressure have to come out of the vent pipe that the jiggler valve sits on; as it does, it makes a hissing sound. No sound, no pressure! The more sound the jiggler valve makes, the higher the level of pressure you're cooking at.

Weighted-valve and spring-valve pressure cookers should make noise only when the pressure cooker exceeds the level of pressure chosen for the recipe or food being cooked. For example, suppose that you choose to cook at low pressure and set the pressure cooker accordingly, either with a low-pressure valve (a weighted-valve model) or by setting the spring valve on low. Once the pressure exceeds low, the excess pressure has to go somewhere. Slowly but surely, it's released through the pressure-regulator valve and starts to make a racket. This is an essential safety feature on stovetop cookers. Basically, the pressure cooker is telling you, "Hey, you set me on low pressure; I got there, so why don't you lower the burner to a simmer instead of making me sweat it out!"

✔ **Smell** (from a safe distance!) and you will notice that the steam coming out of the pressure release valve is odorless; rarely will you smell anything while cooking under pressure. Rest assured, however, that if you cook at temperatures that are way too high, the food will stick and eventually burn. The food will also stick and burn, scorching the pot, if you don't use enough liquid and it evaporates.

Surveying the Three Ways to Cook in a Pressure Cooker

There's more one than one way to cook food in a pressure cooker. You can do any of the following:

✔ **Steam under pressure by using water and some sort of a steaming basket or tray.** This technique is perfect for cooking farm-fresh vegetables and fresh lobster. You can also steam desserts such as cheesecake, puddings, and custards, which you would normally bake in the oven in a hot water bath — otherwise known as a *bain-marie.*

If your pressure cooker has a metal steaming basket, you'll no longer end up with waterlogged veggies, and you'll be able to create pressure-cooker-baked goodies like my cheesecake recipes in Chapter 12. Fill the pressure cooker with 2 to 3 cups of water. Put the trivet in the pot and the steaming basket on top. Fill with vegetables or whatever food you want to steam. Then cover and cook under pressure for the recommended cooking time.

✔ **Prepare foods that contain a lot of liquid, like soups, under pressure.** You can prepare some of my favorite soup recipes (see Chapter 7) in a fraction of the time it would take using conventional methods, simply by using your pressure cooker.

✔ **Make an endless variety of entree and side dishes.** Start off as you normally would by browning or sautéing in the open pressure cooker first (see Chapters 4 and 8 for more information) and then finish up the dish with a quick braise under pressure (see Chapter 9 for information on braising). This two-step cooking process is probably my favorite way to use the pressure cooker, especially when time is short and I need to get dinner on the table in less than an hour. See Chapters 8 and 9 for some top-notch main-dish recipes and Chapter 11 for some tasty side dishes.

Whatever you do, *never* deep-fry in a pressure cooker. Oil is a flammable liquid that's rated by *smoke point* (the temperature at which the oil bursts into flames). Because you have no way to gauge the internal temperature of the hot oil as it heats in a closed pressure cooker, you have no idea how hot it is. Oil that reaches or exceeds its smoke point combusts and bursts into flames. You don't want to remove the pressure-cooker cover to find flames shooting out of the pot. If you want to deep-fry foods, invest in an electric deep-fryer or use a frying pan.

Introducing Stop-and-Go Cooking

Not all food needs to cook for the same length of time (see Appendix A for recommended pressure-cooking times categorized by type of food). So what happens when you're preparing a dish such as stew, which contains meat that needs to cook at least 20 minutes and vegetables that cook in less than half that time? If the vegetables are added at the beginning with the meat, they'll cook too much and become mushy. The only way to avoid this is by cooking under pressure in steps, or — as I like to call it — *stop-and-go cooking.* To give you a better idea of what I mean, refer to the following two scenarios.

Scenario 1: The long and the short of it

Pretend you're cooking My Favorite Beef Stew recipe in Chapter 8. To be fork-tender, stew meat needs to cook at least 20 minutes under pressure. The green beans, carrots, celery, and potatoes, collectively, need less than 10 minutes;

the mushrooms need only 60 seconds. What's a cook to do? You have to group and cook the ingredients in stages, starting with the longest-cooking ingredients and finishing up with the shortest. Think of it in terms of steps:

1. **Cook the meat under pressure for 15 minutes. Then release the pressure using a quick-release method.**

   I explain how to release the pressure in your cooker in Chapter 4.

2. **Add all the veggies except the mushrooms and cook them with the meat for 8 minutes. Release the pressure using a quick-release method.**

   As the vegetables cook with the meat, a wonderful gravy is made with all the juices and the red wine.

3. **Add the mushrooms and cook them with the meat and other vegetables for 1 minute under pressure.**

All together, the meat cooked for 15 minutes, plus 8 minutes, plus another 1 minute, for a total of 24 minutes under pressure. The meat is fork-tender, having been cooked to perfection for the right amount of time; the faster-cooking vegetables have also been cooked for the right amount of time, so they retain their shape and flavor. And because all the ingredients were cooked together, the stew gravy is amazingly flavorful.

Scenario 11: Soup versus stock

Another good example of how different cooking times affect the results of a dish is the comparison of chicken soup to chicken stock (see Chapter 7). Both recipes have similar ingredients. How they're handled, however, determines the end result.

When making chicken soup, you want to extract enough flavor from the chicken and the vegetables so that you have a good broth. The chicken pieces need only about 15 minutes to cook, whereas small-cut veggies are done in under 5 minutes. Because dry, tasteless chicken and mushy vegetables aren't on the menu, you have to cook them for different lengths of time by following these steps:

1. **To make the broth, first cook the chicken in salted water, under pressure, to completion in 15 minutes.**

   So that the chicken doesn't overcook, release the pressure using a quick-release method.

2. **After removing the cooked chicken, add the vegetables to the chicken broth and cook them for only 4 minutes under pressure.**

   So that the veggies don't get mushy, release the pressure using a quick-release method.

3. **Add some cooked noodles and the cooked chicken that you cut into chunks while the vegetables were cooking.**

   The soup is now ready to serve.

The broth has the rich taste of the chicken and vegetables that were cooked in it. The chicken is tender and juicy; the vegetables are cooked to perfection!

Although chicken stock is basically made from the same ingredients as chicken soup, the process and end result are different. The objective in making chicken stock is to extract as much flavor from the chicken and vegetables as possible. To do so, forget about stop-and-go cooking. Instead, cook all the ingredients together for the same amount of time until they're so soft that they're virtually tasteless. To make sure this happens, remove the pressure cooker from the stove and let the pressure release on its own by using the natural-release method. As long as any pressure is left in the closed pot, whatever is inside continues cooking.

Looking at the High and Low of Pressure

When you cook with conventional cookware and bakeware, either on the stovetop or in the oven, you can always take a look at the food to see how it's coming along or whether it's done cooking. Because a pressure cooker is a sealed pot, you can't peek in without releasing the pressure and stopping the whole cooking process. Timing is therefore of the utmost importance.

The whole idea of using a pressure cooker is to save time. In fact, food cooks up to 70 percent faster, on average, in a pressure cooker than by most conventional methods. To get things going quickly, you always want to begin cooking over high heat. If you're using a stovetop pressure cooker, after it reaches the desired pressure, you need to lower the burner to a near simmer, or whatever it takes to maintain pressure without exceeding it, as I explain in detail later.

As mentioned earlier, the process is easier with electric pressure cookers because they electronically control the cooking temperature and steam output; there's no human intervention.

But if the cover is locked in place, how do you know when to lower the heat to start the countdown for cooking? That's easy — you set the timer once the pressure cooker reaches and maintains the level of pressure you've chosen. When you bake a cake in the oven, you always preheat the oven before baking, right? The same holds true when a pressure cooker is coming up to pressure. You bring it up to pressure over high heat. It's like preheating before you're ready to start cooking under pressure.

The following sections fill you in on how to determine and maintain pressure.

Determining whether your cooker has reached high pressure

If you use a jiggler-valve-type pressure cooker (see Chapter 4), you know that the pressure cooker is up to pressure when the jiggler valve is rockin' 'n' rollin' at an even pace and some hissing is going on. Now's the time to lower the burner to a simmer or thereabouts and start the cooking countdown time.

With a developed-weight-valve or a spring-valve model (see Chapter 4), you know that the pressure cooker has reached pressure when the weighted valve rises up or when the pressure regulator indicator is in the upright position. Wait until the pressure cooker begins to make just a bit of noise, and then lower the burner heat. Set the kitchen timer for the recommended cooking time, and you're on your way.

If you're using an electric pressure cooker, all you have to do is select high or low pressure and set the timer. The appliance self-adjusts when the level of pressure is reached and then cooks for the length of time selected.

Maintaining pressure

You know that you've exceeded pressure when the pressure release valve and safety valves start to make a hissing noise. Basically, the pressure cooker is telling you to lower the burner heat. How you do it depends on whether you're using an electric or stovetop pressure cooker and, if the latter, the type of stove you have.

Electric pressure cookers

An electric pressure cooker makes maintaining pressure very easy for you because the appliance is self-regulating. After it reaches the level of pressure you choose on the control panel, it stabilizes the heat to maintain the heat and pressure for the cooking time chosen.

Gas stoves

If you cook on a gas stove, you already know that a simple turn of the burner knob one way causes the heat to go up immediately; turn it in the opposite direction, and it drops almost instantaneously.

So what are you waiting for? Turn down the heat, almost to a simmer or until you're able to maintain pressure without exceeding it. Within a minute or so, the pressure cooker will get quiet again.

Element hopscotch

If you have an electric range, you know that, unlike gas stoves, turning the dial does not elicit an instant response from the element. Electric elements take longer than gas burners to react when you raise or lower the heat. This delayed reaction can be a problem when you cook with a pressure cooker. To overcome this problem, I suggest that you play "element hopscotch."

In simple terms, element hopscotch means that you cook on two elements: one set on high heat and one set on a lower setting, whatever keeps water boiling at a simmer on your range. Use the element set on high heat to heat the pressure cooker for browning or sautéing the food and to bring the pressure cooker up to pressure once the cover is in place and locked into position.

After the pressure cooker reaches pressure, transfer it to the element that's preheated to the lower setting. (**Note:** Don't forget to turn off the high-heat element after the transfer!) This element must be set low enough so that the pressure cooker doesn't exceed pressure. On the other hand, it has to be hot enough so that the pressure cooker can maintain the level of pressure it has reached without dropping. Otherwise, the food may take longer to cook.

Now You're Cooking

After the stovetop pressure cooker reaches the desired pressure, the burner heat is lowered, and the kitchen timer is set, the pressure cooker should be fine doing its own thing. For the most part, you can take a breather, but don't go too far from the kitchen. You need to be around in case the pressure cooker gets too hot and begins to exceed pressure. There's really no need to be alarmed if it does, however. If you happen to hear it making a racket, just lower the burner heat until it stops.

Is it done yet?

Remember to remove the pressure cooker from the burner heat and release the pressure when the kitchen timer rings. Use one of the quick-release methods discussed in Chapter 4 or use the natural-release method.

Always choose the appropriate release method for the type of food you're making. Use the natural-release method when preparing foods like large cuts of meat or stocks that benefit from the additional cooking time as the pressure drops on its own. For all other foods, use a quick-release method.

After releasing the pressure and removing the cover (see the following section for safety tips), check to see that the food is cooked. If it's not to your liking, replace the cover and cook for an additional couple minutes under pressure.

Opening the pressure cooker safely

The food in the pressure cooker is extremely hot, so be careful opening and removing the cover. Hold the griplike handle on the pot with one hand and turn the cover counterclockwise by grasping and turning the cover handle. If you have a pressure cooker with a self-locking cover, check the owner's manual for information on how to open and close the cover.

Regardless of the method you use to release the pressure, always remember the following when opening and removing the cover:

- **Always place the pressure cooker on a heatproof, stable surface.** You don't want to burn a table or countertop, and you certainly don't want the pot to topple over.

- **Steam is hotter than boiling water and can cause serious burns.** Even though there's no further pressure in the pressure cooker, the cooked food will be very hot, and some steam will rise up out of the pressure cooker. Avoid contact with this hot steam when releasing pressure and removing the cover.

  To avoid getting burned, never hold your face over the pressure cooker as you remove the cover. Also, if you use an automatic quick-release method (see Chapter 4), watch where your hands are in relation to where the steam comes out when the pressure is released.

A Primer on Pressure Canning

Canning involves packing hot food into special, sterilized canning jars; capping them; and then submerging them in a hot water bath and heating them over a prescribed period of time to kill dangerous bacteria that can spoil food. At the end of the process, the special canning jar lid forms a vacuum seal and the cooled jar of canned food can be stored without refrigeration. This process, called water-bath canning, is labor-intensive and time-consuming.

Pressure canning is an easier canning method and is the only method that's safe for some foods. To pressure-can, you simply place the covered canning jar filled with hot food in a 6-quart or larger stainless-steel pressure cooker that has a high pressure setting of 15 pounds per square inch (psi). At 15 psi, the internal temperature of the pressure cooker reaches and may even exceed 240 degrees — the necessary temperature for destroying the hard-to-kill bacteria found in low-acid foods, including all fresh vegetables and some fruits. These foods require a higher temperature for processing than the water-bath method, which heats foods only to 212 degrees, provides.

Because electric pressure cookers don't reach 15 psi, you can't use them to pressure-can.

Pressure canning, which is simple and quick, requires only a few special tools that are readily available at your local hardware store, supermarket, or online. I tell you all about these tools and walk you through the basic pressure-canning process in the next sections. I also provide you with a list of recommended pressure-canning times and share with you a couple fun pressure-canning recipes to try.

Having the right equipment on hand

Making sure you have the proper equipment for pressure canning means first checking to see that you have the right pressure cooker for the job. Because most small pressure cookers don't reach 15 psi, only 6-quart or larger, stainless-steel models are recommended for pressure canning, preferably one with a developed-weight or spring valve because jiggler valves can be tricky. Check your owner's manual to verify that your pressure cooker reaches 15 psi at high pressure. If you're still not sure after checking the documentation, contact the manufacturer.

The basic equipment for canning is the same whether using the traditional hot water bath method or a pressure cooker for pressure canning. The following is a list of the must haves:

- ✔ **Canning jars** in 4-, 8-, 12-, or 16-ounce sizes, which are the sizes that fit best in a pressure cooker
- ✔ **Two-part lids** (complete with lid bands and caps)
- ✔ **A canning or metal rack** that fits on the bottom of the pressure cooker to place the jars on
- ✔ **A wide-mouth funnel** to make it easy to fill the jars
- ✔ **A plastic bubble releaser** to make sure that there are no air pockets in the jar of food you plan to can

Special pressure-canning kits, like the one in Figure 5-1, are available online. These kits make it easier to can under pressure and usually come with a rack to set the jars on, as well as a jar lifter. Some kits also include wide-mouth funnels and a bubble releaser, as well as a magnetic lid lifter and a jar wrench to tighten the lids. Amazon (www.amazon.com) is a good source to check for availability.

Here are some important equipment recommendations to follow:

✔ When using a developed-weight model, be sure to use the 15 psi weight. With a spring-valve model, set the dial on high pressure *only*.

✔ Only use well-cleaned and sterilized ½- or 1-pint canning jars and lid bands that are in excellent condition.

✔ Only use new lids, never used or damaged ones.

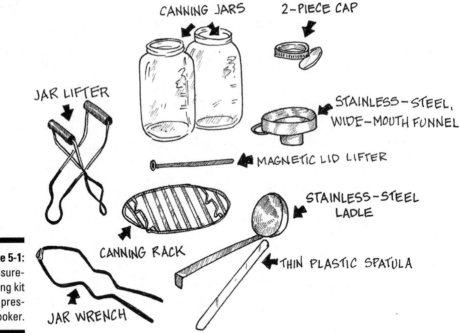

Figure 5-1:
A pressure-
canning kit
for a pres-
sure cooker.

Illustration by Elizabeth Kurtzman

Knowing how long to cook

With the pressure-canning method, jars of hot food are placed in 2 to 3 inches of boiling water in a pressure cooker and heated under pressure at a temperature of at least 240 degrees or 15 psi for a length of time specified by either a recipe or a cooking chart, like the one in Table 5-1.

The pressure-canning times listed in Table 5-1 begin when the pressure cooker reaches and stabilizes at high pressure or 15 psi. Don't reduce the recommended times, and be sure to allow the pressure to drop naturally. Also, when filling the jars with food, remember to leave the appropriate amount of *headspace* (the space between the inside of the lid and the top of the food or liquid in your jar), as specified either in the recipe or in Table 5-1. Headspace is necessary so that the jar doesn't explode or crack when being heated during the canning process.

Table 5-1	Recommended Pressure-Canning Times and Headspace		
Food	*Pressure Canning Time in Minutes*	*Headspace*	*Your Notes*
Fruits, all	10	½ inch	
Asparagus	25	1 inch	
Beans, lima	40	1 inch	
Beans, snap	25	1 inch	
Beets, whole/sliced	25	1 inch	
Carrots	25	1 inch	
Corn, whole kernel	60	1 inch	
Cucumbers (brined)	10	½ inch	
Greens, all kinds	45	1 inch	
Mushrooms	30	1 inch	
Okra	25	1 inch	
Okra and Tomatoes	25	1 inch	
Peas, green	40	1 inch	
Peas, black-eyed	40	1 inch	
Potatoes, new (whole)	30	1 inch	
Squash, cubed	30	1 inch	
Sweet potatoes	60	1 inch	
Tomatoes	10	½ inch	

Walking through the steps

After you've gathered your equipment and checked how long it will take to pressure-can the desired food, you're ready to get started. Follow these steps to pressure-canning success:

1. **Prepare the food you want to can as directed by your recipe.**

   Regardless of what you're making, all foods must be carefully washed in order to kill all bacteria. The food and/or canning liquid must be at least 212 degrees (the boiling point) when filling jars.

2. **Wash all canning equipment, jars, and lids and sterilize them in boiling water.**

3. **Using a food funnel, carefully ladle the hot food and/or canning liquid into the clean, sterilized jars, leaving ample headspace to form a tight vacuum seal.**

   Consult your recipe or Table 5-1 to determine how much headspace to leave.

4. **Release any air bubbles with a nonreactive utensil, preferably plastic, adding additional food or liquid to maintain the proper headspace.**

5. **With a clean, damp cloth, wipe the rims of the jars; then seal the jars with two-piece caps, hand-tightening the bands.**

6. **Set the processed jars on a wire rack in the pressure cooker without allowing them to touch, so steam can flow around each jar.**

7. **Pour boiling water between the jars in the pressure cooker until the jars are sitting in 2 to 3 inches of water.**

8. **Cover and bring the pressure cooker to high pressure, over high heat.**

9. **Lower the heat to stabilize the pressure and process for the time indicated in your recipe or Table 5-1.**

   Check frequently to make sure the pressure is constant and doesn't drop below 15 psi.

10. **When the processing is complete, turn off the gas or remove the pressure cooker from the electric burner.**

11. **Release the pressure using the natural-release method.**

     Never use one of the quick-release methods because you run the risk of the jars of hot food exploding inside the pressure cooker when the pressure is released quickly.

12. **After the pressure releases naturally, wait 10 minutes longer before opening so that the pressure in the jars stabilizes.**

13. **Carefully open the pressure cooker.**

14. **Use a jar lifter to carefully remove the jars from the cooker.**

15. **Place the hot jars on a cooling rack or dry kitchen towels.**

     Leave at least 1 inch of space between the jars. Do not tighten the lids.

16. **Allow the jars to cool, untouched, for 12 to 24 hours, and then tighten the lid bands.**

     Most two-piece canning lids will seal with a popping sound as they cool on the counter. When the jars are completely cooled, test each lid by pressing it gently in the center. It should curve down with no give. If a jar isn't sealed properly (there's give in the lid), refrigerate it and use the contents within a couple days.

Always examine jars of home-canned food before serving. If the contents smell foul or appear spoiled, don't taste them; discard them immediately. Other telltale signs of spoilage are bulging lids and leaking jars.

For more information on pressure canning and other great canning tips and suggestions, I suggest you consult the latest edition of *Canning and Preserving For Dummies* by Amelia Jeanroy and Karen Ward (Wiley).

Diving into pressure canning

What good is a bunch of pressure canning advice without the chance for some practical application? Following are two recipes, including one of my favorite recipes for garlic dill pickles.

Garlic Dill Pickles

Prep time: 15 min • **Cook time:** 10 min under pressure • **Yield:** 4 pints

Ingredients	*Directions*
Twelve 4-inch gherkin cucumbers	*1* Wash the cucumbers and quarter each one lengthwise. Place in a large bowl. Cover with a layer of ice cubes; refrigerate 4 hours. Drain completely.
1½ cups white vinegar	
2¼ cups water	*2* In a medium saucepan, combine the vinegar, water, and salt and bring to a boil over high heat.
¼ cup noniodized salt	
4 tablespoons fresh chopped dill weed	*3* Pack the cucumbers into 4 clean, sterilized pint jars. Leave 1 inch of headspace. Place 1 tablespoon of the dill, 4 garlic cloves, 1 teaspoon of the mustard seed, and 4 peppercorns into each jar.
16 garlic cloves, unpeeled	
4 teaspoons mustard seed	*4* Pour the hot vinegar brine over the cucumbers and spices in each jar, leaving ½ inch of headspace. Cap and seal. Place the jars in the pressure cooker with 2 to 3 inches of boiling water.
16 black peppercorns	
	5 Cover and bring to high pressure over high heat. Lower the heat to stabilize the pressure. Process for 10 minutes.
	6 Remove from the heat. Use the natural-release method to release the pressure.
	7 Wait 10 minutes longer so that the pressure in the jars stabilizes.
	8 Carefully open the pressure cooker.
	9 Use a jar lifter to carefully remove the jars from the canner. Place the hot jars on a cooling rack or dry kitchen towels. Leave at least 1 inch of space between the jars. Allow the jars to cool, untouched, for 12 to 24 hours; then tighten the lid bands.

Per serving (1 pickle spear, or ¼ of a pickle): Calories 5 (From Fat 0); Fat 0g (Saturated 0g); Cholesterol 0mg; Sodium 292mg; Carbohydrate 1g (Dietary Fiber 0g); Protein 0g.

Note: This recipe is vegetarian, vegan, gluten-free, and dairy-free.

Strawberry Jam

Prep time: 60 min • **Cook time:** 10 min under pressure • **Yield:** 4 pints

Ingredients	Directions
5 cups strawberries 7 cups sugar, divided Small pinch salt One 1¾-ounce package powdered pectin	**1** Wash the strawberries. Remove the stems and cut off any white parts. Cut the berries into quarters and place in a large saucepan. Add 2 cups of the sugar, stir well, and let sit at room temperature for 30 minutes.
	2 With a potato masher or fork, mash the strawberries. Cook over medium-high heat, stirring constantly. Bring to a boil. Add the remaining sugar and, stirring constantly, bring to a second boil. Remove from the heat. Skim off any foam.
	3 Ladle the jam into 4 clean, sterilized pint jars. Leave ½ inch of headspace. Cap and seal the jars. Place in the pressure cooker with 2 to 3 inches of boiling water.
	4 Cover and bring to high pressure over high heat. Lower the heat to stabilize the pressure. Process for 10 minutes.
	5 Remove from the heat. Use the natural-release method to release the pressure.
	6 Wait 10 minutes longer so that the pressure in the jars stabilizes.
	7 Carefully open the pressure cooker.
	8 Use a jar lifter to carefully remove the jars from the canner. Place the hot jars on a cooling rack or dry kitchen towels. Leave at least 1 inch of space between the jars. Allow the jars to cool, untouched, for 12 to 24 hours; then tighten the lid bands.

Per serving (1 tablespoon): Calories 46 (From Fat 0); Fat 0g (Saturated 0g); Cholesterol 0mg; Sodium 3mg; Carbohydrate 12g (Dietary Fiber 0g); Protein 0g.

Note: This recipe is vegetarian, vegan, gluten-free, and dairy-free.

Keeping Your Pressure Cooker Squeaky Clean and Shiny

Clean and maintain your pressure cooker like any other piece of quality cookware. By doing so, you'll get many years of quick and easy-to-prepare meals out of it.

Before putting your stovetop pressure cooker away, perform this cleaning process:

1. **Remove the gasket from the cover and wash it separately by hand.**

2. **Wash the pressure cooker cover, pot, and gasket with a mild, liquid dishwashing soap and a nonabrasive sponge after each use. Rinse well under clean water.**

   Consult Chapter 14 if you have any problems getting your pressure cooker clean.

   Never immerse the cover in water because it may affect and damage the safety valves. Also, never wash the pressure cooker in the dishwasher. Food particles in the recycling wash water or even dishwasher detergent can collect in and clog the pressure-regulator and/or safety valves.

3. **Towel-dry all parts and properly reposition the rubber gasket under the cover.**

   Some gaskets have to be lined up a specific way. Make sure that you replace the gasket correctly.

Some manufacturers suggest that you disassemble and clean the pressure regulator valve after each use. Check the manufacturer's instructional materials for further information.

Always wash your electric pressure cooker thoroughly after every use. Unplug and let it cool before cleaning (do not wash any parts in the dishwasher except for the removable cooking pot). Remove the removable cooking pot and wash it with warm, soapy water or in the dishwasher. Rinse and dry thoroughly. Wipe the outer housing and the lid with a clean, damp cloth. The temperature sensor and heating element, located on the inside of the outer housing, must be cleaned after each use. Wipe with a soft, damp cloth and be sure to dry thoroughly; do not submerge the housing in water. Remove the condensation reservoir from the outer housing handle by pulling it down. Wash it with warm, soapy water. Rinse and dry thoroughly. Replace by pushing it into place. Remove the gasket from the underside of the lid and wash it in warm, soapy water. Rinse and dry thoroughly. Replace the gasket by positioning it inside the edge of the lid. Never use abrasive cleaners or scouring pads to clean any of the parts. Only use clean, soft cloths and mild, liquid dishwashing soap.

Storing Your Pressure Cooker

Storing your pressure cooker properly is essential to maintaining its long and useful life. Here are some pointers on what *not* to do:

- ✔ **Never store the pot with food inside.** Doing so is inefficient because the pressure cooker would take up too much room in the refrigerator. Furthermore, the food may stain the interior surface or pick up odd flavors. Always clean and dry your pressure cooker thoroughly before putting it away.

- ✔ **Never lock the cover in place because doing so can damage the rubber gasket seal or ring.** Over an extended period of time, the rubber gasket can dry out and form a permanent bond between the pot and cover, making it nearly impossible to open the pressure cooker. Moisture can also prevent you from opening the cover because it can create an almost permanent seal.

The best way to store the cover is to place it upside down on top of the cooker.

Help Is But a Phone Call Away

Although I've tried to anticipate and answer any questions or concerns that I think you may have, you may need to contact your pressure cooker's manufacturer if you have specific questions about your particular cooker. All the manufacturers have fully staffed customer service departments with trained representatives who are happy to answer your questions. Either check your owner's manual for the manufacturer's customer service number or look it up online.

Chapter 6

From the Pot to the Pressure Cooker

Many people are reluctant to cook because they think they don't have the time to do it. If you use a pressure cooker, however, you don't need a lot of time. You can get a nutritious, home-cooked dinner ready after you come home from work instead of relying on take-out and processed foods. The great thing about this kitchen cooking wonder is that you can use it to cook just about anything. In fact, many great dishes cook up to 70 percent faster when prepared in a pressure cooker.

With a couple of minor tweaks here and there, most recipes can be easily adapted to a pressure cooker. It's all a matter of knowing what ingredients work, how much of these ingredients to use, and how long to cook them. I cover all these topics in this chapter, and then provide some examples of conventional recipes that I've converted for use in the pressure cooker.

Preparing the Best Ingredients for Pressure Cooking

Although you can cook almost anything in a pressure cooker, some foods are better suited than others for this appliance. Foods that normally cook quickly, such as seafood, shellfish, and soft fruits (berries, for example), are better suited for conventional cooking methods. Ideal candidates for the pressure cooker include soups, stocks, stews, and braised and slow-roasted meats, made with less-expensive cuts of meat; some poultry; steamed and braised vegetables; dried beans and grains; and slow-simmered recipes such as tomato sauce and fruit preserves. Following are some tips for preparing different types of foods.

Meat and poultry

Because many cuts of meat generally take so long to cook using conventional cooking methods, you'll be surprised and pleased by how quickly they cook up in the pressure cooker. Here are some tips for cooking meat and poultry:

- ✔ Always pat meat and poultry dry before seasoning with salt and freshly ground black pepper.
- ✔ Sear and brown meat in hot oil for the best flavor and texture, unless otherwise indicated in the recipe.
- ✔ Feel free to prepare poultry with or without the skin.
- ✔ Try tougher, less-expensive cuts of meat; cooking under pressure breaks down the fibers for fork-tender results.
- ✔ Make sure that meat and poultry are adequately cooked. When in doubt, check the cooking time chart for meat in Appendix A.
- ✔ Always let cooked roasts and whole poultry sit for 10 to 15 minutes before carving.
- ✔ Slice most roasts against the grain.

For more detailed information on cooking meat and poultry, consult Chapter 9.

Fruits and vegetables

Fruits and vegetables cook quickly in the pressure cooker, so always use an accurate kitchen timer. Here are some tips for cooking fruits and vegetables in the pressure cooker:

- ✔ Cook most fresh fruits on low pressure because fruit is soft and cooks quite fast.

  The only fruits I usually cook in a pressure cooker are apples for applesauce or dried fruits for a compote. These do well on high pressure.
- ✔ Cut thoroughly washed fruits and vegetables into equal-sized pieces.
- ✔ When making a stew or pot roast, add vegetables toward the end of the cooking time so they don't overcook.

✔ When cooking only fruits and vegetables, steam them in a steaming basket placed on a trivet in the cooking liquid. This way, they'll retain their flavor and bright color.

✔ Always release pressure with a quick-release method (see Chapter 4).

For more detailed information on cooking fruits and vegetables, consult Chapters 11 and 12, as well as Appendix A.

Dried beans, legumes, and grains

If I could use my pressure cooker for cooking only two types of food, they would, without a doubt, be beans and grains, which seem to take forever when cooked the conventional way. Here are some tips for cooking dried beans, legumes, and grains in the pressure cooker:

✔ Pick over dried beans, legumes, and grains to remove any pebbles, twigs, dirt, or foreign particles. Rinse under cold water.

✔ Soak dried beans and legumes — with the exception of lentils and split peas — overnight in room-temperature water or for one hour in boiling water before cooking.

✔ Always cook these foods in at least twice as much liquid. For example, for every 1 cup of dried beans, legumes, or grain, use 2 cups of water.

✔ Never add salt to the cooking liquid when cooking dried beans or legumes because it toughens the skin. Add salt after the food is cooked.

✔ Add a tablespoon of oil to the water to reduce the foaming that beans often cause.

For more detailed information on cooking dried beans, legumes, and grains, consult Chapters 7 and 10, as well as Appendix A.

Adjusting Liquids

Never lose sight of the fact that a pressure cooker can't work without liquid. Without liquid, you don't get steam, and without steam, there's no pressure.

But liquid can be much more than plain, old water. You can use all kinds of cooking liquids in the pressure cooker, including water, broth or stock, fruit juice, vegetable puree, wine, beer, and so on. The liquid doesn't even have to be part of the finished food — I've made custards, casseroles, puddings, and cheesecakes in my pressure cooker by putting the food on a rack and setting up a steam bath. (See Chapter 12 for tips on using your pressure cooker as a *bain-marie*.)

With the exception of soups, broth, stock, and sauces, the amount of liquid used in a pressure cooker recipe is usually less than that used in a traditional recipe. Because you're cooking in a sealed pot for a much shorter period of time, less liquid evaporates.

When converting a recipe, use approximately one-third to one-half of the liquid called for in the traditional recipe. However, most pressure cookers need at least 1 to 2 cups of liquid in order to build up and maintain pressure. Check the owner's manual for the exact amount needed.

Filling the Pressure Cooker

If you're adapting a traditional recipe that makes enough to serve a crowd, you may need to scale back the recipe so you don't overfill the pressure cooker. On the other hand, you may decide to double a small recipe to give the pressure cooker enough liquid to maintain pressure.

A 6-quart pressure cooker is the ideal size for preparing most recipes that yield 4 to 6 servings. Remember, however, that the pot must never be filled with 6 quarts of anything. In fact, pressure cookers should never be filled more than half full with food. Also, never fill the pressure cooker more than two-thirds full with cooking liquid.

The reasons not to overfill are quite simple. Because a pressure cooker cooks hotter than boiling water, the cooking liquid in the pot seems to expand and increase in volume with all the bubbling going on. Furthermore, the steam produced by this constant boiling needs room in which to be contained. If filled more than two-thirds full, the pressure cooker may not perform properly, and you may find cooking liquid coming out of the pressure indicator and release valves.

Determining Cooking Times

When you cook in an open pot, you can easily taste and test the food as it cooks to determine when it's done. But you can't do this with a pressure cooker. To cook under pressure, the cover must be locked in place, meaning that you can't sample the food quite as often during the cooking process. The only way to physically test something is to remove the pressure cooker from the heat, release the pressure, and remove the cover.

The easiest way to determine cooking times is to refer to the cooking time charts in Appendix A. You can find complete charts for grains, dried beans and legumes, meat, poultry, vegetables, and fruits. Table 6-1 is an abbreviated pressure-cooker cooking-time chart for the most commonly prepared foods. The cooking times in the table begin when the pressure cooker reaches high pressure. Always start with the shortest cooking time for an ingredient; you can always continue cooking under pressure for an additional minute or two until the desired texture is reached.

All cooking times are, at best, approximations and should be considered a general guideline. Not all types of potatoes cook for the same amount of time, for example. You may also find that your particular brand or model of pressure cooker cooks faster or even a bit slower. Therefore, feel free to note any cooking time differences in the right-hand column of the table.

If your recipe combines ingredients that don't cook for the same length of time — for example, stew meat and tender vegetables — you need to cook in stages, adding the long-cooking ingredients to the pressure cooker first. Partway through, you release the pressure, unlock the lid, add more ingredients, and then cook everything under pressure again. I cover this type of stop-and-go cooking in Chapter 5.

Table 6-1	Recommended Pressure-Cooker Cooking Times	
Food	*Cooking Time (in Minutes)*	*Your Notes*
Apples, chunks	2	
Artichokes, whole	8 to 10	
Asparagus, whole	1 to 2	
Barley, pearl	15 to 20	
Beans, fresh green or wax, whole or pieces	2 to 3	
Beans, lima, shelled	2 to 3	
Beets, ¼-inch slices	3 to 4	
Beets, whole, peeled	12 to 14	
Broccoli, florets or spears	2 to 3	
Brussels sprouts, whole	3 to 4	
Cabbage, red or green, quartered	3 to 4	
Carrots, ¼-inch slices	1 to 2	
Cauliflower, florets	2 to 3	
Chicken, pieces	8 to 10	
Chicken, whole	15 to 20	
Corn on the cob	3 to 4	
Meat (beef, pork, or lamb),1-inch cubes	15 to 20	

(continued)

Table 6-1 *(continued)*

Food	Cooking Time (in Minutes)	Your Notes
Meat (beef, pork, or lamb), roast	40 to 60	
Peas, shelled	1 to 1½	
Potatoes, pieces or sliced	5 to 7	
Potatoes, whole, medium	10 to 12	
Potatoes, whole, small or new	5 to 7	
Rice, brown	15 to 20	
Rice, white	5 to 7	
Spinach, fresh,	2 to 3	
Squash, fall, 1-inch chunks	4 to 6	
Squash, summer, sliced	1 to 2	
Stock	30	
Sweet potatoes, 1½-inch chunks	4 to 5	
Turnips, sliced	2 to 3	

Another way to figure out how long to cook something is by following a similar recipe in this book. Match up your traditional recipe to a pressure-cooker one and modify the cooking steps and times accordingly.

Converting Favorite Recipes for the Pressure Cooker

Although I know you'll enjoy the recipes that I developed especially for this book, I also know that at times you'll want to eat something of your own creation. One way to adapt a favorite recipe designed for conventional cooking is to find a similar pressure-cooker recipe and use it as your guide. For example, if you want to make your favorite beef stew recipe, you can look to My Favorite Beef Stew recipe (see Chapter 8) as a guide. Following that recipe, you brown the meat in batches in hot oil in the pressure cooker to sear in the juices and flavor. Next, you cook some onion in the same oil. When the onions are soft, you add some wine (or other cooking liquid) and then tomatoes to deglaze the bottom of the pot, dissolving the cooked-on juices and any cooked-on particles. Now you're ready to cook the meat under pressure. When the meat is almost done, you add the vegetables. (You don't add them at the beginning because if you do, they'll overcook and come out mushy.) By following these same steps and using my recipe cooking times as a guide, you can adapt your beef stew recipe for the pressure cooker.

For successful results when adapting recipes, never lose sight of the fact that pressure cookers cook differently than other conventional cooking methods in terms of timing, ingredients, and the amount of liquids.

Even though electric pressure cookers come with a cord and plug and are used on the counter and not the stove, they are functionally identical to their traditional counterparts. All the recipes in this book work equally as well in a stovetop pressure cooker as in an electric version. I've included instructions for both styles with each recipe. Just be sure to carefully read the manufacturer's use and care instructions so that you understand how your appliance works.

To further show you how to convert your own recipes for use in the pressure cooker, I chose four of my all-time favorite recipes and adapted them. In making my selection, I looked for recipes that, although perhaps not exactly difficult to prepare, had long cooking times or were somewhat labor intensive, requiring frequent stirring and pot-watching. The pressure-cooker versions of these original recipes, on the other hand, save you time and work. After the pressure-cooker cover is locked in position and the cooking pressure is reached and stabilized, you're no longer needed in the kitchen until the timer goes off announcing that dinner is ready!

I give you both versions of each recipe: the original version and the pressure-cooker adaptation. Here's some information on what I did to adapt each recipe. I hope that you, too, will be inspired to experiment and convert some of your favorite traditional recipes for use in the pressure cooker.

- ✔ **Meat sauce:** This is my mom's recipe for basic meat sauce. She used to make it specifically for preparing pasta dishes such as lasagne and stuffed shells. To save time, she made the sauce a day in advance. If only she had had a pressure cooker! This recipe was very easy to adapt. The only thing that needed changing was the cooking time. I was able to shave 60 minutes off my mom's recipe. Everything else stayed the same.

- ✔ **Minestrone soup:** Made with eight different vegetables and fragrant herbs and spices, this Italian classic is the quintessential vegetable soup. With my pressure-cooker adaptation, you'll have dinner on the table in half an hour! Because cabbage takes on a pungent taste and smell when cooked too long, it's added toward the end of the cooking time in the original recipe. I was able to shorten the entire cooking time from 50 to a very short 10 minutes for the pressure-cooker version, so you can now add the cabbage along with the other veggies.

✔ **Mushroom risotto:** You've probably enjoyed this classic dish at your favorite Italian restaurant, and now you can make it at home. This simple recipe requires a simmering flavorful broth and short-grain Italian rice. If you don't have the time or patience to spend 30 minutes standing at the stove stirring a *slowly* simmering saucepan of rice and broth, try the pressure-cooker version of the recipe. The rapid bubbling of the broth and rice in the pressure cooker under high pressure replaces having to stand over a hot stove stirring constantly. Because there is virtually no evaporation, I cut back on the chicken or vegetable stock by ¼ cup.

✔ **Sauerbraten:** With a delicious balance of sweet and tangy flavors, this German pot roast is an American favorite. Because the meat must marinate three days in the brine before cooking, you have to plan accordingly when using the traditional recipe. Besides cutting the cooking time in half, the pressure-cooker adaptation eliminates the need to first marinate the meat. The rich flavor of the marinade infuses through the roast as it cooks under high pressure.

Dishes that don't play nice with the pressure cooker

The following are a few cooking methods and foods that just don't lend themselves to a pressure cooker, along with the reasons why.

✔ **Deep-frying:** As I discuss in Chapter 5, never deep-fry foods such as chicken, potatoes, fish sticks, jalapeño poppers, and so on in your pressure cooker. The hot temperature of the oil can damage the rubber gasket and valves, not to mention, the oil can burst into flames over high heat in the closed pot.

✔ **Baking:** Certain desserts that don't necessarily need to brown while cooking, such as cheesecake, custards, and crisps, "bake up" nicely in a pressure cooker when prepared in a sealed pan resting on a rack over hot water. Cookies, cakes, pies, and pastries, which require steady dry heat, don't and should not be made in your pressure cooker.

✔ **Expanding or foaming foods:** Things that get all frothy when cooked or that expand considerably should be avoided or cooked in small quantities. These foods include oatmeal, split peas, cranberries, and rhubarb. When these foods expand or get frothy, they may block the pressure-regulator valve or vent tube, causing the pressure cooker to go into "melt-down" mode and the safety valves to activate (see Chapter 4 for more info on how pressure cookers work).

Traditional Meat Sauce

Prep time: 10 min • **Cook time:** 1 hr, 50 min • **Yield:** 8 servings

Ingredients	Directions
2 tablespoons olive oil	**1** Heat the olive oil in a 6-quart saucepan over medium-high heat. Add the onion, garlic, carrot, and celery. Cook until the onion is soft.
1 small onion, finely chopped	
2 cloves garlic, minced	
1 carrot, finely chopped	**2** Add the ground beef and cook until no longer pink, breaking up large chunks with a spoon. Add the parsley, tomato puree, sugar, salt, and pepper.
1 stalk celery, finely chopped	
1½ pounds lean ground beef	
¼ cup flat-leaf parsley, chopped	**3** Bring the sauce to a boil. Lower the heat. Cover and simmer for 90 minutes, stirring every 10 minutes.
Two 28-ounce cans or 7 cups tomato puree	
1 teaspoon sugar	**4** Remove from the heat. Season to taste with salt and pepper. Serve over pasta cooked al dente (tender but still firm).
4 teaspoons salt	
1 teaspoon pepper	

Per serving: Calories 291 (From Fat 132); Fat 15g (Saturated 5g); Cholesterol 56mg; Sodium 2,001mg; Carbohydrate 22g (Dietary Fiber 5g); Protein 20g.

Note: This recipe is dairy-free and gluten-free.

MINCING PARSLEY + OTHER FRESH HERBS

1. RINSE AND DRY WELL.

2. CHOP ROUGHLY

✳ NOTE: FOR HERBS LIKE ROSEMARY AND THYME, REMOVE AND CHOP LEAVES. DISCARD THICK STEM.

3. GATHER AND CHOP SOME MORE! USE A ROCKING MOTION MOVE KNIFE AROUND

Illustration by Elizabeth Kurtzman

Pressure-Cooker Meat Sauce

Prep time: 25 min • **Cook time:** 30 min under pressure • **Yield:** 8 servings

Ingredients	*Directions*
2 tablespoons olive oil	*1* Heat the olive oil in a pressure cooker over medium-high heat. Add the onion, garlic, carrot, and celery. Cook until the onion is soft. (*For Electric:* Select the Brown setting.)
1 small onion, finely chopped	
2 cloves garlic, minced	
1 carrot, finely chopped	*2* Add the ground beef and cook until no longer pink, breaking up large chunks with a spoon. Add the parsley, tomato puree, sugar, salt, and pepper.
1 stalk celery, finely chopped	
1½ pounds lean ground beef	
¼ cup flat-leaf parsley, chopped	*3* Cover and bring to high pressure over high heat. Lower the heat to stabilize the pressure. Cook for 30 minutes. (*For Electric:* Select high pressure and set the timer for 30 minutes.)
Two 28-ounce cans or 7 cups tomato puree	
1 teaspoon sugar	*4* Remove from the heat. Release the pressure with a quick-release method. Open and remove the cover.
4 teaspoons salt	
1 teaspoon pepper	*5* Season to taste. Serve over pasta cooked al dente.

Per serving: Calories 291 (From Fat 132); Fat 15g (Saturated 5g); Cholesterol 56mg; Sodium 2,001mg; Carbohydrate 22g (Dietary Fiber 5g); Protein 20g.

Note: This recipe is dairy-free and gluten-free.

Tip: If you have a food processor, use it to chop the onions, garlic, carrots, and celery. Begin by placing the onion and garlic in the food processor bowl. Press pulse a couple times until coarsely chopped. Add the carrot and celery (cut into 1-inch pieces) and pulse a couple times until finely chopped.

Traditional Minestrone Soup

Prep time: 15 min • **Cook time:** 50 min • **Yield:** 6 servings

Ingredients	Directions
3 tablespoons olive oil	*1* Heat the olive oil in a 6-quart saucepan over medium-high heat. Add the onion, garlic, and Italian seasoning. Cook until the onion is soft.
1 medium onion, chopped	
3 cloves garlic, minced	
1 tablespoon dried Italian seasoning	*2* Add the tomatoes, carrots, celery, zucchini, and potatoes and cook for 5 minutes. Add the string beans, salt, pepper, and water. Stir well.
One 14½-ounce can basil-, oregano-, and garlic-flavored diced tomatoes	
1 cup diced carrots	
1 cup diced celery	*3* Bring to a boil over high heat. Lower the heat. Cover and cook at a simmer for 45 minutes, stirring every 10 minutes.
1 cup diced zucchini	
1 cup peeled and diced potatoes	
1 cup bite-sized pieces of string beans	*4* Drain the kidney beans and rinse them under cold water. Add the beans and the cabbage to the saucepan. Cover and cook for 10 minutes longer.
1 tablespoon salt	
½ teaspoon pepper	
8 cups water	*5* Add the ditalini and the cheese. Season with salt and pepper to taste.
2 cups shredded cabbage	
One 19-ounce can red kidney beans	
1½ cups ditalini, cooked al dente	
½ cup freshly grated Parmesan or pecorino Romano cheese	

Per serving: Calories 358 (From Fat 85); Fat 9g (Saturated 2g); Cholesterol 5mg; Sodium 1,920mg; Carbohydrate 55g (Dietary Fiber 9g); Protein 16g.

Note: This recipe is vegetarian.

Vary It! For a vegan or dairy-free version of this recipe, omit the cheese or substitute a vegan variety. For a gluten-free version, substitute gluten-free pasta for the ditalini.

Tip: Ditalini is a small, tube-shaped pasta. You can substitute any similar type of pasta you may have on hand.

Pressure-Cooker Minestrone Soup

Prep time: 20 min • **Cook time:** 10 min under pressure • **Yield:** 6 servings

Ingredients

3 tablespoons olive oil

1 medium onion, chopped

3 cloves garlic, minced

1 tablespoon dried Italian seasoning

One 14½-ounce can basil-, oregano-, and garlic-flavored diced tomatoes

1 cup diced carrots

1 cup diced celery

1 cup diced zucchini

1 cup peeled and diced potatoes

1 cup bite-sized pieces of string beans

2 cups shredded cabbage

1 tablespoon salt

½ teaspoon pepper

8 cups water

One 19-ounce can red kidney beans

1½ cups ditalini, cooked al dente

½ cup freshly grated Parmesan or pecorino Romano cheese

Directions

1 Heat the olive oil in the pressure cooker over medium-high heat. Add the onion, garlic, and Italian seasoning. Cook until the onion is soft. (*For Electric:* Select the Brown setting.)

2 Add the tomatoes, carrots, celery, zucchini, and potatoes and cook for 5 minutes. Add the string beans, cabbage, salt, black pepper, and water. Stir well.

3 Cover and bring to high pressure over high heat. Lower the heat to stabilize the pressure. Cook for 10 minutes. (*For Electric:* Select high pressure and set the timer for 10 minutes.)

4 Remove from the heat. Release the pressure with a quick-release method. Open and remove the cover.

5 Drain the kidney beans and rinse them under cold water. Add the beans, ditalini, and cheese to the pot. Season with salt and pepper to taste.

Per serving: Calories 358 (From Fat 85); Fat 9g (Saturated 2g); Cholesterol 5mg; Sodium 1,920mg; Carbohydrate 55g (Dietary Fiber 9g); Protein 16g.

Note: This recipe is vegetarian.

Vary It! For a vegan or dairy-free version of this recipe, omit the cheese or substitute a vegan variety. For a gluten-free version, substitute gluten-free pasta for the ditalini.

Tip: Serve this soup with fruit and fresh, crusty bread for a quick-and-easy, complete meal.

Traditional Mushroom Risotto

Prep time: 10 min • **Cook time:** 28 min • **Yield:** 4 servings

Ingredients	Directions
2½ cups chicken or vegetable stock	*1* Bring the stock to a simmer in a small saucepan. Continue simmering.
3 tablespoons unsalted butter	
1 small onion, finely chopped	*2* Melt the butter in a 3-quart pot over medium heat. Add the onion and cook until soft. Do not brown. Add the mushrooms and cook for 2 minutes. Add the rice and cook for 1 minute to coat with butter.
8 ounces white button or crimini mushrooms, sliced	
1 cup Italian Arborio or other short-grain rice	*3* Stirring continuously, add about ½ cup of the hot stock. As the rice absorbs the stock, add another ½ cup. Repeat the process, stirring continuously, until there is no more stock and the risotto is cooked al dente.
⅓ cup grated Parmesan cheese	
Pepper to taste	
	4 Remove from the heat. Stir in the Parmesan cheese and season with pepper.

Per serving: Calories 363 (From Fat 124); Fat 14g (Saturated 8g); Cholesterol 33mg; Sodium 781mg; Carbohydrate 48g (Dietary Fiber 2g); Protein 9g.

Note: This recipe is vegetarian (if made with vegetable rather than chicken stock) and gluten-free.

How to Trim and Slice Mushrooms

1. wipe away dirt using a paper towel or a dish towel

2. Cut off stem

3. slice

Illustration by Elizabeth Kurtzman

Pressure-Cooker Mushroom Risotto

Prep time: 10 min • **Cook time:** 7 min under pressure • **Yield:** 4 servings

Ingredients	Directions
3 tablespoons unsalted butter	*1* Melt the butter in a pressure cooker over medium heat. Add the onion and cook until soft. Add the mushrooms and cook for 2 minutes. Add the rice and cook for another 2 minutes. Add the stock and stir to combine. (*For Electric:* Select the Brown setting.)
1 small onion, finely chopped	
8 ounces white button or crimini mushrooms, sliced	
1 cup Italian Arborio or other short-grain rice	*2* Cover and bring to high pressure. Lower the heat to stabilize the pressure, and cook for 7 minutes. Release the pressure with a quick-release method. Open and remove the cover. (*For Electric:* Select high pressure and set the timer for 7 minutes.)
2¼ cups chicken or vegetable stock	
⅓ cup grated Parmesan cheese	
Pepper to taste	*3* Stir in the Parmesan cheese. Season with pepper.

Per serving: Calories 361 (From Fat 122); Fat 14g (Saturated 8g); Cholesterol 33mg; Sodium 719mg; Carbohydrate 48g (Dietary Fiber 2g); Protein 9g.

Note: This recipe is vegetarian (if made with vegetable rather than chicken stock) and gluten-free.

Traditional Sauerbraten

Prep time: 20 min plus 3 days marinating time • **Cook time:** 2 hr, 30 min • **Yield:** 8 servings

Ingredients	*Directions*
4-pound beef chuck or rump roast	*1* Place the meat, carrots, celery, onions, garlic, and bay leaves in a large glass or stainless-steel bowl. In another bowl, combine the water, vinegar, wine, brown sugar, ground cloves, and 2 teaspoons salt.
2 large carrots, coarsely chopped	
2 stalks celery, coarsely chopped	*2* Pour the liquid mixture over the meat. The meat should be submerged in the marinade. If not, transfer to a smaller container. Cover and refrigerate for 3 days.
2 large onions, coarsely chopped	
1 clove garlic, crushed	*3* Remove the meat from the marinade. Pat dry with paper towels. Generously salt and pepper.
2 bay leaves	
1 cup water	
½ cup red wine vinegar	*4* Heat the oil in a Dutch oven over medium-high heat. Brown the meat evenly on all sides.
½ cup dry red wine	
¼ cup firmly packed brown sugar	*5* Pour in the reserved marinade and vegetables. Cover and bring to a boil. Lower the heat and simmer until the meat is fork-tender, about 2 hours.
1 teaspoon ground cloves	
2 teaspoons salt plus salt to taste	*6* Remove the meat to a serving platter and cover with foil. Discard the bay leaves. Add the gingersnaps to the cooking liquid to make a gravy. Stir until well blended. Pour the gravy into a food processor or food mill and process until smooth. Season to taste.
Pepper to taste	
2 tablespoons vegetable oil	
¾ cup finely crushed gingersnaps	*7* Slice the meat across the grain into thick slices and serve with the gravy on the side.

Per serving: Calories 654 (From Fat 386); Fat 43g (Saturated 18g); Cholesterol 146mg; Sodium 783mg; Carbohydrate 23g (Dietary Fiber 2g); Protein 41g.

Note: This recipe is dairy-free.

Pressure-Cooker Sauerbraten

Prep time: 20 min • **Cook time:** 60 min under pressure • **Yield:** 8 servings

Ingredients	*Directions*
1 cup water	*1* Combine the water, vinegar, wine, brown sugar, cloves, and 2 teaspoons salt. Set aside.
½ cup red wine vinegar	
½ cup dry red wine	*2* Generously salt and pepper the meat.
¼ cup firmly packed brown sugar	
1 teaspoon ground cloves	*3* Heat the oil in a pressure cooker over medium-high heat. Brown the meat evenly on all sides. (*For Electric:* Select the Brown setting.)
2 teaspoons salt plus salt to taste	
Pepper to taste	*4* Add the carrots, celery, onions, garlic, crushed ginger-snaps, and bay leaves. Pour the mixture from Step 1 over the meat. Stir to combine. Cover and bring to high pressure. Lower the heat to stabilize the pressure, and cook for 60 minutes. (*For Electric:* Select high pressure and set the timer for 60 minutes.)
2 tablespoons vegetable oil	
4-pound beef chuck or rump roast	
2 large carrots, coarsely chopped	
2 stalks celery, coarsely chopped	*5* Remove from the heat. Release the pressure using a quick-release method. Open and remove the cover.
2 large onions, coarsely chopped	*6* Remove the meat to a serving platter and cover with foil. Discard the bay leaves. To make the gravy, pour the cooking liquid into a food processor or food mill and process until smooth. Season to taste.
1 clove garlic, crushed	
¾ cup finely crushed gingersnaps	
2 bay leaves	*7* Slice the meat across the grain into thick slices and serve with the gravy on the side.

Per serving: Calories 654 (From Fat 386); Fat 43g (Saturated 18g); Cholesterol 146mg; Sodium 783mg; Carbohydrate 23g (Dietary Fiber 2g); Protein 41g.

Note: This recipe is dairy-free.

Tip: Serve this dish with broad egg noodles or Grandma's Mashed Potatoes in Chapter 11.

Part III

Preparing Delicious Recipes in Your Pressure Cooker

The 5th Wave   By Rich Tennant

I'm glad the 'Tin Man's head is a pressure cooker too. It just gives me the creeps having his body standing around like that during dinner.

In this part . . .

I share with you some of my favorite pressure-cooker recipes in the following pages. These recipes run the gamut from soups, pilafs, and an amazing variety of bean dishes to succulent roasts and stews and mouthwatering desserts. I also share a variety of recipes that are friendly to vegetarian, vegan, dairy-free, and gluten-free diets.

The absolute best part about all of these recipes is that they're quick and easy to prepare — and delicious to eat!

Chapter 7

Spoon Foods: Stocks, Soups, and Great Grain Dishes

In This Chapter

▶ Making and storing stocks

▶ Coaxing out the flavor in soups

▶ Getting the goods on grains

I always find it reassuring to eat almost anything from an oversized bowl with a big spoon. I guess I'm not alone, because many restaurants are serving diners all kinds of comfort foods in soup bowls nearly the size of serving pieces.

Soupy-type foods are among my favorites. They're warm and nourishing. Although some also contain meat or poultry, they almost always have lots of good vegetables in a flavorful stock or sauce. Some are smooth in consistency, and others are so chunky that you may want to eat them with a fork. Whatever your preference, these are dishes that taste good and make you feel warm and cozy all over.

In this chapter, I show you how to cook up four delicious varieties of stock that you can keep on hand for making homemade soups. I also reveal how you can use your pressure cooker to make tasty grain dishes in nearly no time at all. And of course, I share some of my favorite recipes along the way.

Stocking Up on Stocks

Stock is the rich, concentrated, liquid essence of the ingredients that are used to make it. For me, having small containers of frozen stock in the freezer is like having money in the bank. They can be taken out of the freezer, thawed, and then used as the base for endless soups, stews, and chilis. So easy and quick to make in the pressure cooker, yet so flavorful!

I fill you in on the basics of making, using, and storing stock in the next sections. I also share my tried-and-true pressure-cooker recipes for the four main types of stock — chicken, beef, vegetable, and fish — along with a few tidbits about each one.

Making stock

The first place to start in making great soup, or other dishes calling for stock or broth, is with full-flavored cooking liquid or stock. To make stock, you cook lots of vegetables, alone or with poultry, meat, or seafood, in less water than you'd normally use to make soup. Traditional, slow-simmered stock takes up to 2 to 3 hours to make; pressure-cooker stock takes about one-third of the time: 30 minutes of cooking under pressure and about another 30 minutes for the pressure to drop on its own.

Regardless of the method you use, once the stock is done, you need to remove the solid ingredients with a slotted spoon and filter the remaining liquid through a fine mesh strainer. Because most of the flavor from the solids has been extracted, the solids are, for the most part, now flavorless and should be discarded, except for perhaps meaty chicken pieces that you can remove from the bone and reserve for adding to soup or making chicken salad.

Using and storing stock

The rich, flavorful stock makes a great base for soups, or you can boil down some of it to concentrate the flavor even more to make sauces or gravies. After cutting the fat (which you can see how to do in Figure 7-1), I freeze any leftover stock to have on hand. Sometimes I even freeze reduced stock in ice cube trays. Once frozen, I store the concentrated stock cubes in small plastic bags to use when a recipe calls for a small amount of stock or broth.

Freezer space is always an issue for me. I never seem to have enough of it, and plastic containers take up a lot of valuable space. I like to freeze liquids such as sauces, soups, and stocks in 1-quart or 1-gallon resealable plastic freezer bags. Always write on the outside what's in the bag and the date it was frozen so you know exactly what's in it and how long it has been in there. After filling the bag, seal it, being careful to squeeze out as much air as possible. Wipe off any spilled liquid and lay the bag flat in the freezer, stacking the bags on top of each other.

Figure 7-1:
Defatting
your stock.

Illustration by Elizabeth Kurtzman

Acquiring the key ingredients

Here's how to stock up on the base ingredients for each of the main types of stock:

- ✔ **Chicken stock:** Whenever I buy a whole chicken to cut up, I always put aside the neck, wings, and back. I freeze these in a large plastic bag. When I've accumulated enough pieces, I take them out and make a big pot of stock; if I'm in a rush and come up short, I add some legs or thighs from the supermarket.

- ✔ **Beef stock:** There's more than one way to make beef stock, depending on your mood and the time available. If I'm feeling lazy, I throw the bones into the pot to make a very acceptable, good-flavored beef stock. Or, if I have time, I salt and pepper the bones and roast them until golden brown in a 400-degree oven for about 45 minutes to an hour. After roasting the bones, I then prepare the stock as detailed in this chapter, blotting the bones with paper towels to remove any melted fat. The ensuing stock is deeper in flavor and darker in color than the stock that you get by the quicker method.

- ✔ **Vegetable stock:** Cleaning out the veggie bin in the fridge is a good excuse to make vegetable stock, especially because it doesn't matter whether the vegetables are a bit limp or not exactly at their very best, as long as they aren't rotten. I even save clean vegetable peelings from carrots and other root vegetables, as well as end pieces from celery and leafy greens, and I freeze them in a large plastic bag. When I've accumulated enough pieces, I take them out and make a big pot of stock.

- ✔ **Fish stock:** Fish stock is extremely economical to make; just become friends with the fishmongers at your local seafood store or supermarket. Most will gladly set aside and give away the fish skeletons and heads from fish they've filleted.

Chicken Stock

Prep time: 10 min • **Cook time:** 30 min under pressure • **Yield:** About 2 quarts

Ingredients	*Directions*
3 to 4 pounds of chicken pieces (necks, wings, backs, legs, and thighs), with skin	*1* Rinse the chicken pieces under cold water. Place the chicken, onion, carrots, celery, parsnip, tomato, garlic, parsley, peppercorns, and water in a pressure cooker.
1 large onion, peeled and quartered	
3 carrots, cut into 1-inch pieces	*2* Cover and bring to high pressure over high heat. Lower the heat to stabilize the pressure. Cook for 30 minutes. (*For Electric:* Select high pressure and set the timer for 30 minutes.)
3 stalks celery, cut into 1-inch pieces	
1 parsnip, cut into 1-inch pieces	*3* Remove from the heat. Let the pressure drop using the natural-release method.
1 large tomato, quartered	*4* Unlock and remove the cover. Let the stock cool to room temperature.
3 cloves garlic	
2 sprigs parsley	*5* Remove the chicken and vegetables. Remove the chicken from the bone; dice and save for another use. Discard all the vegetables with a slotted spoon. Pour the stock through a fine strainer into a large storage container. Season with salt.
½ teaspoon whole black peppercorns	
8 cups (2 quarts) water	
Salt to taste	
	6 Refrigerate overnight. Remove and discard any congealed fat.

Per serving (2 cups): Calories 26 (From Fat 0); Fat 1g (Saturated 0g); Cholesterol 16mg; Sodium 336mg; Carbohydrate 3g (Dietary Fiber 0g); Protein 3g.

Note: This recipe is gluten- and dairy-free.

Vary It! Next time you roast a turkey, save the carcass after carving to make turkey stock. Simply rinse the carcass under water and place it in the pressure-cooker pot instead of the chicken pieces. If the carcass is too big, simply compact it by pressing down on it with the heel of your hand on a hard, clean work surface.

Beef Stock

Prep time: 10 min • **Cook time:** 30 min under pressure • **Yield:** About 2 quarts

Ingredients	*Directions*
3 pounds meaty beef bones	*1* Rinse the bones under cold water. Place the bones, onion, carrots, celery, tomatoes, garlic, parsley, bay leaf, peppercorns, and water in a pressure cooker.
1 large onion, peeled and quartered	
3 carrots, cut into 1-inch pieces	*2* Cover and bring to high pressure over high heat. Lower the heat to stabilize the pressure. Cook for 30 minutes. (*For Electric:* Select high pressure and set the timer for 30 minutes.)
3 stalks celery, cut into 1-inch pieces	
2 large tomatoes, quartered	*3* Remove from the heat. Let the pressure drop using the natural-release method.
3 cloves garlic	
3 sprigs parsley	*4* Unlock and remove the cover. Let the stock cool to room temperature.
1 bay leaf	
½ teaspoon whole black peppercorns	*5* Remove and discard the bones and all the vegetables with a slotted spoon. Pour through a fine strainer into a large storage container. Season with salt.
8 cups (2 quarts) water	
Salt to taste	*6* Refrigerate overnight. Remove and discard any congealed fat.

Per serving (2 cups): Calories 22 (From Fat 0); Fat 1g (Saturated 0g); Cholesterol 13mg; Sodium 317mg; Carbohydrate 1g (Dietary Fiber 0g); Protein 4g.

Note: This recipe is gluten- and dairy-free.

Vegetable Stock

Prep time: 10 min • **Cook time:** 15 min under pressure • **Yield:** About 2 quarts

Ingredients	*Directions*
1 large onion, peeled and quartered	*1* Place the onion, carrots, celery, parsnip, turnip, tomato, garlic, parsley, bay leaf, peppercorns, and water in a pressure cooker.
2 carrots, trimmed and cut into 1-inch pieces	
2 stalks celery, trimmed and cut into 1-inch pieces	*2* Cover and bring to high pressure over high heat. Lower the heat to stabilize the pressure. Cook for 15 minutes. (*For Electric:* Select high pressure and set the timer for 15 minutes.)
1 parsnip, cut into 1-inch pieces	
1 medium turnip. chopped	*3* Remove from the heat. Let the pressure drop using the natural-release method.
1 large tomato, cored and quartered	
4 cloves garlic	*4* Unlock and remove the cover. Let the stock cool to room temperature.
6 sprigs parsley	
1 bay leaf	*5* Pour the stock through a large, fine strainer into a large storage container, pressing gently on the vegetables to extract as much liquid from them as possible. Discard the veggie solids. Season with salt.
½ teaspoon whole black peppercorns	
8 cups (2 quarts) water	
Salt to taste	

Per serving (2 cups): Calories 9 (From Fat 0); Fat 0g (Saturated 0g); Cholesterol 0mg; Sodium 229mg; Carbohydrate 2g (Dietary Fiber 0g); Protein 0g.

Note: This recipe is vegetarian, vegan, gluten-free, and dairy-free.

Fish Stock

Prep time: 10 min • **Cook time:** 30 min under pressure • **Yield:** About 2 quarts

Ingredients	Directions
2 pounds white fish skeletons with heads	*1* Rinse the fish skeletons and heads under cool water. Place them along with the onion, carrots, celery, tomato, garlic, parsley, bay leaf, peppercorns, and water in a pressure cooker.
1 large onion, peeled and quartered	
2 carrots, trimmed and cut into 1-inch pieces	*2* Cover and bring to high pressure over high heat. Lower the heat to stabilize the pressure. Cook for 15 minutes. (*For Electric:* Select high pressure and set the timer for 15 minutes.)
2 stalks trimmed celery, cut into 1-inch pieces	
1 large tomato, cored and quartered	*3* Remove from the heat. Let the pressure drop using the natural-release method.
2 cloves garlic	
2 sprigs parsley	*4* Unlock and remove the cover. Let the stock cool to room temperature.
1 bay leaf	
½ teaspoon whole black peppercorns	*5* Remove and discard the skeletons and heads. Pour the stock through a large, fine strainer into a large storage container, pressing gently on the vegetables to extract as much liquid from them as possible. Discard the veggie solids. Season with salt.
8 cups (2 quarts) water	
Salt to taste	

Per serving (2 cups): Calories 9 (From Fat 0); Fat 0g (Saturated 0g); Cholesterol 0mg; Sodium 221mg; Carbohydrate 1g (Dietary Fiber 0g); Protein 1g.

Note: This recipe is gluten-free and dairy-free.

Vary It! Besides fish skeletons and heads, you can also use shrimp or lobster shells for a mild-tasting seafood stock. Figure on the shells from 1 pound of shrimp or about two lobster shells.

Soup under Pressure

Good soup normally simmers to allow the cooking liquid to slowly coax out all the different flavors from the ingredients as they blend together to create a delicious, flavorful broth. The pressure cooker is unique in that it allows this flavor mingling but at a much higher temperature in a fraction of the time.

This section is home to seven soup recipes for the pressure cooker that I turn to frequently when the craving for a piping-hot bowl of soup strikes me. The following list notes some delicious accompaniments for each dish:

- **Chunky Chicken Noodle Soup:** This soup screams "soup and sandwich night." Why not add another chicken breast or two to Step 1 of the soup recipe and use the cooked chicken meat to make your favorite chunky chicken salad served on toasted white bread with lettuce and sliced tomatoes?

- **Corn Chowder:** Try serving this chowder with homemade jalapeño cornbread and honey butter. The mellow sweetness of the butter contrasts wonderfully with the heat of the jalapeño peppers in the bread.

- **French Onion Soup:** Carry the French theme even further with some homemade quiche and a fresh green salad tossed with a Dijon vinaigrette.

- **Warm Louisiana Yam Soup with Snipped Chives:** For a taste of the bayou, serve this soup with steamed shrimp in their shell, made with Old Bay Seasoning (you'll find the recipe on the back of the can).

- **Potato and Leek Potage:** This is the perfect winter soup. I like serving it in mugs, along with grilled Polish kielbasa sausage and spicy, dark mustard.

Salt in soups and stocks

Salt is added to food to enhance its flavor. Stocks and soups have little taste if not salted adequately, even if they're made with many flavorful ingredients such as poultry, meat, and vegetables. Unless you're on a sodium-restricted diet, don't be alarmed by the amount of salt you need to use to get the desired flavor. Start off with a couple of teaspoons and gradually add more, little by little, until you achieve the desired flavor.

Tip: If you're on a sodium-restricted or reduced-sodium diet, try replacing the salt in soup and stock recipes with other flavorful ingredients, such as celery seed and garlic or onion powder.

The hand blender: My best kitchen buddy (after the pressure cooker, that is)

Did you know that you can puree hot food directly in the pressure cooker (or any pot or bowl, for that matter) if you have a hand blender (also known as an immersion blender or stick mixer)? This nifty, small electric appliance, approximately 16 to 18 inches long, makes pureeing hot soups and sauces a breeze. You simply hold the hand blender vertically, inserting the blade part into the food you want to puree. Push and hold down on the on/off button. With the blade always in the food, you puree away as the food is pulled in through the bottom and side cutouts or openings. Naturally, the food must be cooked until very soft and in a liquid base. Never lift the hand blender up and out of the hot food while it's operating, because you'll get splattered and possibly burned!

Hand blenders are also great for making malteds and smoothies. Many come with a mini-chopper attachment and, in some cases, even a whisk.

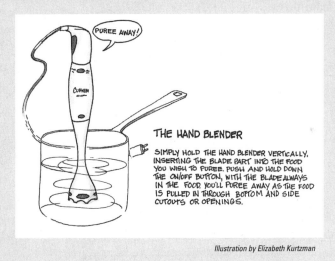

PUREE AWAY!

CUMIN

THE HAND BLENDER

SIMPLY HOLD THE HAND BLENDER VERTICALLY, INSERTING THE BLADE PART INTO THE FOOD YOU WISH TO PUREE. PUSH AND HOLD DOWN THE ON/OFF BUTTON, WITH THE BLADE ALWAYS IN THE FOOD YOU'LL PUREE AWAY AS THE FOOD IS PULLED IN THROUGH BOTTOM AND SIDE CUTOUTS OR OPENINGS.

Illustration by Elizabeth Kurtzman

✔ **Creamy Cauliflower Soup:** This soup is a family favorite on Thanksgiving, especially because locally grown Long Island cauliflower always appears at farm stands around the middle of November after the first frost of the season.

✔ **Split Pea Soup:** A throwback to the '60s when I was growing up, I never tire of having an old-fashioned grilled cheese sandwich alongside a steamy hot bowl of split pea soup.

Chunky Chicken Noodle Soup

Prep time: 10 min • **Cook time:** 19 min under pressure • **Yield:** 6 servings

Ingredients	*Directions*
2 split chicken breasts with bone and skin, about 1½ pounds	*1* Rinse the chicken under water. Place in a pressure cooker with the water and 1 tablespoon salt.
8 cups (2 quarts) water	*2* Cover and bring to high pressure over high heat. Lower the heat to stabilize the pressure. Cook for 15 minutes. (*For Electric:* Select high pressure and set the timer for 15 minutes.)
1 tablespoon salt	
2 large leeks (or 1 large onion) washed well, white and light green parts only, thinly sliced	
	3 Remove from the heat. Let the pressure drop using a quick-release method.
3 carrots, peeled and cut into ¼-inch rounds	
3 stalks celery, cut into ¼-inch slices	*4* Unlock and remove the cover. Remove the chicken with a slotted spoon. Skin and debone the chicken. Cut it into bite-sized chunks and set aside.
Salt and pepper to taste	
2 cups broad egg noodles, cooked al dente	*5* Strain the broth into a 3-quart container. Rinse out the pressure cooker and replace the broth. Add the leeks, carrots, and celery.
1 tablespoon chopped fresh parsley or snipped dill	
	6 Cover and bring to high pressure over high heat. Lower the heat to stabilize the pressure. Cook for 4 minutes. (*For Electric:* Select high pressure and set the timer for 4 minutes.)
	7 Remove from the heat. Let the pressure drop using a quick-release method.
	8 Unlock and remove the cover. Season with salt and pepper to taste. Add the cooked chicken, noodles, and parsley, and serve.

Per serving: Calories 149 (From Fat 16); Fat 2g (Saturated 0g); Cholesterol 40mg; Sodium 1,239mg; Carbohydrate 21g (Dietary Fiber 3g); Protein 12g.

Note: This recipe is dairy-free.

Vary It! To make this recipe gluten-free, replace the egg noodles with rice or gluten-free pasta.

Corn Chowder

Prep time: 10 min • **Cook time:** 8 min under pressure • **Yield:** 6 servings

Ingredients	*Directions*
2 tablespoons vegetable oil 1 small onion, chopped 1 red bell pepper, cored, seeded, and diced 2 carrots, peeled and cut into ¼-inch rounds 2 stalks celery, cut into ¼-inch slices 1 large all-purpose potato, peeled and diced 2 cups frozen corn kernels 1 cup frozen green peas 6 cups chicken or vegetable stock Salt and pepper to taste 2 cups broad egg noodles 1 tablespoon chopped fresh parsley or snipped dill 2 cups cooked diced chicken (optional)	*1* Heat the vegetable oil in a pressure cooker over medium-high heat. Add the onion and red pepper. Cook until the onion is soft. Add the carrots, celery, potato, corn, and peas. Cook for 2 minutes. Add the stock. (*For Electric:* Select the Brown setting.) *2* Cover and bring to high pressure over high heat. Lower the heat to stabilize the pressure. Cook for 8 minutes. (*For Electric:* Select high pressure and set the timer for 8 minutes.) *3* Remove from the heat. Let the pressure drop using a quick-release method. *4* Unlock and remove the cover. Season with salt and pepper. *5* Bring the chowder to a boil. Add the noodles and cook until al dente. Stir in the parsley and, if desired, the chicken. Serve immediately.

Per serving: *Calories 245 (From Fat 90); Fat 10g (Saturated 2g); Cholesterol 15mg; Sodium 1,162mg; Carbohydrate 35g (Dietary Fiber 5g); Protein 7g.*

Note: This recipe is dairy-free.

Vary It! To make this recipe gluten-free, replace the egg noodles with rice or gluten-free pasta. For a vegetarian or vegan recipe, use vegetable stock in place of chicken stock and don't add the optional chicken.

French Onion Soup

Prep time: 15 min • **Cook time:** 6 min under pressure • **Yield:** 6 servings

Ingredients	Directions
1½ cups of ¾-inch square French bread cubes	**1** Preheat the oven to 350 degrees. Toss the bread cubes in a large bowl with 2 tablespoons of the olive oil. Place on a baking sheet and toast in the oven for 15 minutes or until crisp, shaking periodically. Set aside to cool.
4 tablespoons olive oil, divided	
6 cups thinly sliced Spanish or Vidalia onions	**2** Heat the remaining 2 tablespoons olive oil in the pressure cooker over medium-high heat. Add the onions and garlic. Cook for 5 minutes. Add the thyme, dry sherry, and 2 cups of the stock. (*For Electric:* Select the Brown setting.)
4 cloves garlic, sliced thin	
1 tablespoon dried thyme	
⅔ cup dry sherry or white vermouth	**3** Cover and bring to high pressure over high heat. Lower the heat to stabilize the pressure. Cook for 6 minutes. (*For Electric:* Select high pressure and set the timer for 6 minutes.)
4 cups beef stock, divided	
Salt and pepper to taste	**4** Remove from the heat. Let the pressure drop using a quick-release method.
1 cup grated Gruyère or Swiss cheese	
	5 Unlock and remove the cover.
	6 Preheat the broiler. Add the remaining 2 cups of stock and bring to a simmer. Season with salt and pepper. (*For Electric:* Select the Warm setting.)
	7 Ladle the soup into heatproof bowls. Float some bread cubes on top and sprinkle with the Gruyère cheese. Place the soup bowls on a baking pan and set under the broiler until the cheese melts and is bubbly, about 1 to 3 minutes.

Per serving: Calories 247 (From Fat 139); Fat 15g (Saturated 5g); Cholesterol 20mg; Sodium 890mg; Carbohydrate 17g (Dietary Fiber 3g); Protein 11g.

Warm Louisiana Yam Soup with Snipped Chives

Prep time: 15 min • **Cook time:** 10 min under pressure • **Yield:** 6 servings

Ingredients	Directions
2 tablespoons olive oil **2 pounds yams or sweet potatoes, peeled and cut into 1-inch cubes** **1 large onion, chopped** **2 cloves garlic, crushed**	**1** Heat the olive oil in a pressure cooker over medium-high heat. Add the yams, onion, garlic, and gingerroot. Cook for 5 minutes. Add the stock. (*For Electric:* Select the Brown setting.)
	2 Cover and bring to high pressure over high heat. Lower the heat to stabilize the pressure. Cook for 10 minutes. (*For Electric:* Select high pressure and set the timer for 10 minutes.)
1½-inch slice fresh gingerroot, peeled and thinly sliced **4 cups vegetable or chicken stock**	**3** Remove from the heat. Let the pressure drop using a quick-release method.
	4 Unlock and remove the cover. The yams should be very soft. If they're still hard, return to Step 2 and cook them for an additional 2 to 3 minutes or until tender.
2 cups milk **Salt to taste** **2 tablespoons snipped fresh chives**	**5** Puree the soup with a hand blender in the pressure cooker (or in batches in a blender, and then pour back into the pressure cooker) until smooth. Whisk in the milk and warm over low heat. Season with salt. Sprinkle the soup with the chives.

Per serving: Calories 224 (From Fat 67); Fat 7g (Saturated 2g); Cholesterol 11mg; Sodium 150mg; Carbohydrate 35g (Dietary Fiber 4g); Protein 5g.

Note: This recipe is gluten-free.

Vary It! For a dairy-free recipe, use soy milk; for a vegetarian recipe, use vegetable rather than chicken stock. To make this recipe vegan, use soy milk and vegetable stock.

HOW TO CHOP AN ONION

Illustration by Elizabeth Kurtzman

Potato and Leek Potage

Prep time: 15 min • **Cook time:** 10 min under pressure • **Yield:** 6 servings

Ingredients	Directions
2 tablespoons butter	**1** Heat the butter in a pressure cooker over medium heat. Add the leeks and cook until soft; don't let them brown. Add the potatoes and stock. (*For Electric:* Select the Brown setting.)
4 large leeks, washed well, white and light green parts only, thinly sliced	**2** Cover and bring to high pressure over high heat. Lower the heat to stabilize the pressure. Cook for 10 minutes. (*For Electric:* Select high pressure and set the timer for 10 minutes.)
5 medium (about 2 pounds) all-purpose potatoes, peeled and thinly sliced	**3** Remove from the heat. Let the pressure drop using a quick-release method.
6 cups chicken or vegetable stock	**4** Unlock and remove the cover. The potatoes should be very soft. If they're still hard, return to Step 2 and cook them for an additional 2 to 3 minutes or until tender.
1 cup milk	
Salt and pepper to taste	**5** Puree the soup with a hand blender (or in batches in a blender, and then pour back into the pressure cooker) until smooth. Whisk in the milk and warm over low heat. Season with salt and pepper.

Per serving: Calories 247 (From Fat 85); Fat 9g (Saturated 4g); Cholesterol 21mg; Sodium 1,133mg; Carbohydrate 36g (Dietary Fiber 3g); Protein 6g.

Note: This recipe is gluten-free.

Vary It! For a dairy-free recipe, use vegetable oil instead of butter and substitute soy milk for the milk; for a vegetarian recipe, use vegetable stock instead of chicken stock. To make this a vegan recipe, implement both the dairy-free and vegetarian modifications.

Cleaning & Trimming Leeks

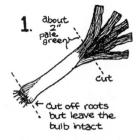
1. about 2" pale green — cut
← cut off roots but leave the bulb intact

2. slit in half
↑ still intact

3. rinse under running cold water
I'm gonna wash that grit right outta my leeks...

Illustration by Elizabeth Kurtzman

Creamy Cauliflower Soup

Prep time: 15 min • **Cook time:** 10 min under pressure • **Yield:** 6 servings

Ingredients	*Directions*
2 tablespoons olive oil **1 large onion, chopped** **1 large head cauliflower, trimmed and broken into small florets**	*1* Heat the olive oil in a pressure cooker over medium-high heat. Add the onion and cook until soft. Add the cauliflower and stock.
6 cups chicken or vegetable stock **Salt and pepper to taste**	*2* Cover and bring to high pressure over high heat. Lower the heat to stabilize the pressure. Cook for 10 minutes. (*For Electric:* Select high pressure and set the timer for 10 minutes.)
1 teaspoon caraway seeds, finely ground	*3* Remove from the heat. Let the pressure drop using a quick-release method.
	4 Unlock and remove the cover. The cauliflower should be very soft. If it's still hard, return to Step 2 and cook it for an additional 2 to 3 minutes or until tender.
	5 Puree the soup with a hand blender (or in batches in a blender, and then pour back into the pressure cooker) until smooth. Season with salt and pepper. Stir in the caraway seeds.

Per serving: Calories 127 (From Fat 80); Fat 9g (Saturated 2g); Cholesterol 5mg; Sodium 1,139mg; Carbohydrate 10g (Dietary Fiber 4g); Protein 4g.

Note: This recipe is gluten-free and dairy-free. Choose vegetable rather than chicken stock to make it vegetarian or vegan.

Split Pea Soup

Prep time: 15 min • **Cook time:** 10 min under pressure • **Yield:** 6 servings

Ingredients	Directions
2 cups (1 pound) dried green or yellow split peas, picked over	*1* Rinse the dried peas in a colander under cold water. Heat the olive oil in a pressure cooker over medium heat. Add the onion and garlic. Cook until the onion is soft. (*For Electric:* Select the Brown setting.)
2 tablespoons olive oil	
1 large onion, chopped	*2* Add the potato, carrots, celery, ham bone, marjoram, 1 teaspoon salt, and ⅛ teaspoon pepper. Cook for 2 minutes. Add the split peas and water. Stir well.
2 cloves garlic, minced	
1 large potato, peeled and diced	
2 carrots, peeled and thinly sliced	*3* Cover and bring to high pressure over high heat. Lower the heat to stabilize the pressure. Cook for 10 minutes. (*For Electric:* Select high pressure and set the timer for 10 minutes.)
1 stalk celery, thinly sliced	
1 ham bone, or 1 small ham steak, trimmed of all fat and diced	*4* Remove from the heat. Let the pressure drop using a quick-release method.
2 teaspoons dry marjoram	
1 teaspoon salt	*5* Unlock and remove the cover. Season with salt and pepper to taste. Stir well.
⅛ teaspoon pepper	
8 cups water	
Salt and pepper to taste	

Per serving: Calories 308 (From Fat 54); Fat 6g (Saturated 1g); Cholesterol 9mg; Sodium 655mg; Carbohydrate 47g (Dietary Fiber 16g); Protein 19g.

Note: This recipe is gluten-free and dairy-free.

Vary It! To make this a vegetarian or vegan recipe, use vegetable stock instead of water, eliminate the ham, and add 1 cup sliced veggie hot dogs to the soup before serving.

Beef Barley Mushroom Soup

Prep time: 15 min • **Cook time:** 20 min under pressure • **Yield:** 6 servings

Ingredients	Directions
2 tablespoons vegetable oil	*1* Heat the vegetable oil in the pressure cooker over medium-high heat. Add the onion and cook until soft. Add the meat, carrots, celery, mushrooms, barley, bay leaf, 1 teaspoon salt, ¼ teaspoon pepper, stock, and water. (*For Electric:* Select the Brown setting.)
1 large onion, chopped	
½ pound very lean beef stew meat, cut into ½-inch cubes	
3 carrots, peeled and thinly sliced	*2* Cover and bring to high pressure over high heat. Lower the heat to stabilize the pressure. Cook for 20 minutes. (*For Electric:* Select high pressure and set the timer for 20 minutes.)
3 stalks celery, thinly sliced	
¼ pound white button mushrooms, stems trimmed, quartered	
¼ pound shiitake mushrooms, stems trimmed, quartered	*3* Remove from the heat. Let the pressure drop using a quick-release method.
1 cup pearl barley, rinsed in a colander under cold water	*4* Unlock and remove the cover. Season with salt and pepper to taste. Add the parsley before serving.
1 bay leaf	
1 teaspoon salt	
¼ teaspoon black pepper	
6 cups beef or chicken stock	
2 cups water	
Salt and pepper to taste	
1 tablespoon minced flat-leaf parsley	

Per serving: Calories 281 (From Fat 70); Fat 8g (Saturated 1g); Cholesterol 24mg; Sodium 1,550mg; Carbohydrate 37g (Dietary Fiber 8g); Protein 16g.

Note: This recipe is dairy-free.

Discovering the Goodness of Grain

According to the nutrition gurus, everyone should eat 6 to 11 servings of grain each day, which isn't always an easy task. Maybe you don't have any new or exciting recipes using grains, or, more likely than not, you don't have the time it takes to cook grains until they're tender. Well, now that you know you can cook them in no time at all in your pressure cooker, you can come closer to meeting your daily requirement!

Although grains don't need to be presoaked like dried beans do (see Chapter 10), they should be picked over and rinsed in a colander under cold water before cooking. Cook them in ample water because they'll absorb a considerable amount of liquid as they hydrate during cooking. A good general rule is to use 3 to 4 cups of water for each cup of grain, and 2 cups of water for each cup of rice.

Table 7-1 tells you approximately how much cooked grain you can expect from 1 cup of uncooked grains. To find out the recommended cooking times for various types of grains, turn to Appendix A.

Table 7-1	Approximate Yields of Cooked Grains	
Uncooked Food (1 Cup)	*Cooked*	*Water, Plus 1 Tablespoon Oil*
Barley, pearl	3½ cups	4½ cups
Barley, whole (unhulled)	3½ cups	4½ cups
Bulgur wheat, whole-grain	3½ cups	4½ cups
Quinoa	3 cups	2½ cups
Rice, arborio	3 cups	2 cups
Rice, basmati	3 cups	1¾ cups
Rice, brown	2¼ cups	1¾ cups
Rice, long grain	3 cups	1¾ cups
Rice, wild	2¼ cups	3 cups
Whole wheat berries	2 cups	4½ cups

Quinoa: An Incan treat for your pressure cooker

Quinoa is a superhealthy seed from South America that has been enjoyed by the people of the Andes for generations. You can find either white or red quinoa prepackaged in most supermarkets or sold in bulk at health-food stores. High in protein, quinoa is gluten-free and can be used in place of barley or wheat berries in many recipes.

Although easy to prepare in the pressure cooker, there are a few simple rules to follow when preparing and serving quinoa:

✔ First of all, the tiny quinoa seed is covered with a bitter coating that must be rinsed away before cooking. Because the seeds are so small, be sure to rinse them in a fine mesh strainer under cold water for a minute or two.

✔ Secondly, quinoa should be served *al dente* (slightly chewy), like pasta and rice; therefore, be sure to set your timer so you don't overcook it.

✔ Like grains, quinoa absorbs lots of water, but unlike cooked grains, quinoa releases a small amount of water, so always spoon quinoa out of the pressure-cooker pot into a fine mesh strainer.

✔ Cooked quinoa benefits from resting a few minutes before using it in your recipe. Put the drained quinoa back on the hot pressure-cooker pot. Place the cover on top and let it sit for 15 minutes, but no longer. Fluff up with a fork before using.

Basic Quinoa Recipe

Prep time: 2 min • **Cook time:** 7 min under pressure • **Yield:** About 4 cups

Ingredients	*Directions*
1½ cups quinoa, rinsed and drained	*1* Combine the quinoa, water, and oil in the pressure-cooker pot.
3 cups water 1 tablespoon vegetable oil	*2* Cover and bring to high pressure over high heat. Lower the heat to stabilize the pressure. Cook for 7 minutes. (*For Electric:* Select high pressure and set the timer for 7 minutes.)
	3 Remove from the heat. Let the pressure drop using a quick-release method.
	4 Unlock and remove the cover. The quinoa should be slightly chewy. If it's hard, return to Step 2 and cook it for an additional 1 to 3 minutes or until tender.
	5 Drain the quinoa in a fine mesh strainer.

Per serving (1 cup): Calories 269 (From Fat 65); Fat 7g (Saturated 1g); Cholesterol 0mg; Sodium 13mg; Carbohydrate 44g (Dietary Fiber 4g); Protein 8g.

Note: This recipe is vegetarian, vegan, and gluten- and dairy-free.

Basic Pearl Barley Recipe

Prep time: 2 min • **Cook time:** 15 min under pressure • **Yield:** About 4 cups

Ingredients	*Directions*
1 cup pearl barley, rinsed and drained **4½ cups water** **1 tablespoon vegetable oil**	*1* Combine the pearl barley, water, and oil in the pressure-cooker pot.
	2 Cover and bring to high pressure over high heat. Lower the heat to stabilize the pressure. Cook for 15 minutes. (*For Electric:* Select high pressure and set the timer for 15 minutes.)
	3 Remove from the heat. Let the pressure drop using a quick-release method.
	4 Unlock and remove the cover. The barley should be slightly chewy. If it's hard, return to Step 2 and cook it for an additional 1 to 3 minutes or until tender.
	5 Drain the barley in a colander or strainer.

Per serving (1 cup): Calories 207 (From Fat 37); Fat 4g (Saturated 0g); Cholesterol 0mg; Sodium 5mg; Carbohydrate 39g (Dietary Fiber 8g); Protein 5g.

Note: This recipe is vegetarian, vegan, and dairy-free.

Citrusy Grain Salad

Prep time: 10 min • **Yield:** 4 servings

Ingredients	*Directions*
4 cups cooked quinoa, cooled to room temperature **3½ cups cooked pearl barley, cooled to room temperature**	**1** Combine the cooked quinoa and barley, lemon and orange zest, carrots, celery, scallions, parsley, mint, and dried cranberries in a large mixing bowl. Toss well.
Grated zest of 1 lemon **Grated zest of 1 orange**	**2** Whisk together the lemon juice, olive oil, and Dijon mustard. Season with salt and black pepper. Pour over the salad and toss. Refrigerate for 1 hour before serving.
2 carrots, coarsely grated	
2 stalks celery, diced small	
4 scallions or green onions, thinly sliced	
⅓ cup coarsely chopped flat-leaf parsley	
3 tablespoons coarsely chopped mint leaves	
⅓ cup dried cranberries	
3 tablespoons freshly squeezed lemon juice	
⅓ cup extra-virgin olive oil	
2 teaspoons Dijon mustard	
Salt and pepper to taste	

Per serving: Calories 664 (From Fat 234); Fat 26g (Saturated 3g); Cholesterol 0mg; Sodium 277mg; Carbohydrate 100g (Dietary Fiber 12g); Protein 13g.

Note: This recipe is vegetarian, vegan, and dairy-free.

Vary It! For a gluten-free recipe, substitute cooked brown rice for the barley, cooking the rice under pressure for 15 minutes.

Tip: To make pressure-cooked quinoa and barley, see the Basic Quinoa Recipe and Basic Barley Recipe in this chapter.

Basic Rice Recipe

Prep time: 2 min • **Cook time:** See Table A-3 in Appendix A • **Yield:** About 2¼–3 cups

Ingredients	*Directions*
1 cup rice, rinsed and drained	*1* Combine the rice, water, and oil in the pressure-cooker pot.
1½ cups water (for wild rice, use 3 cups)	
1 tablespoon vegetable oil	*2* Cover and bring to high pressure over high heat. Lower the heat to stabilize the pressure. Cook according to the time recommended in Table A-3 of Appendix A for the type of rice being made. (*For Electric:* Select high pressure and set the timer for 7 minutes.)
	3 Remove from the heat. Let the pressure drop using a quick-release method.
	4 Unlock and remove the cover. The rice should be slightly chewy. If it's hard, return to Step 2 and cook it for an additional 1 to 3 minutes or until tender.
	5 If necessary, drain the rice in a colander or strainer.

Per serving (½ cup): Calories 192 (From Fat 31); Fat 3g (Saturated 0g); Cholesterol 0mg; Sodium 1mg; Carbohydrate 36g (Dietary Fiber 1g); Protein 3g.

Note: This recipe is vegetarian, vegan, and gluten- and dairy-free.

Arroz con Pollo

Prep time: 15 min • **Cook time:** 7 min under pressure • **Yield:** 6 servings

Ingredients	Directions
Salt and pepper	*1* Generously salt and pepper the chicken pieces.
3-pound chicken, skin removed, cut into eighths	*2* Heat 2 tablespoons of the olive oil in a pressure cooker over medium-high heat. Brown the chicken in batches. Set aside on a large plate. Add the chorizo, if desired, and cook for 1 minute. (*For Electric:* Select the Brown setting.)
3 tablespoons olive oil	
1 chorizo sausage, thinly sliced (optional)	
½ cup white wine	*3* Return the browned chicken to the pressure cooker. Add the wine and cook for 2 minutes. Remove to a plate with any juices and set aside.
1 small onion, chopped	
2 cloves garlic, peeled and minced	
1 red bell pepper, cored, seeded, and diced	*4* Heat the remaining 1 tablespoon olive oil in the pressure cooker. Add the onion, garlic, bell pepper, and tomato. Cook until the onion is soft. Add the rice and cook for 1 minute. Add the peas, stock, salt, chicken, and chorizo, with any accumulated juices. Stir well.
1 large ripe tomato, peeled, or 2 canned plum tomatoes, seeded and coarsely chopped	
1 cup uncooked long-grain white rice	*5* Cover and bring to high pressure over high heat. Lower the heat to stabilize the pressure. Cook for 7 minutes. (*For Electric:* Select high pressure and set the timer for 7 minutes.)
½ cup frozen peas	
3 cups chicken stock	*6* Remove from the heat. Let the pressure drop using a quick-release method.
1 teaspoon salt	
	7 Unlock and remove the cover. Fluff the rice and serve.

Per serving: Calories 396 (From Fat 141); Fat 16g (Saturated 3g); Cholesterol 80mg; Sodium 1,075mg; Carbohydrate 32g (Dietary Fiber 2g); Protein 30g.

Note: This recipe is gluten-free and dairy-free.

Spanish Rice

Prep time: 15 min • **Cook time:** 7 min under pressure • **Yield:** 6 servings

Ingredients	*Directions*
2 tablespoons olive oil	*1* Heat the olive oil in a pressure cooker over medium-high heat. Add the onion, garlic, and bell pepper. Cook until the onion is soft. Add the rice and cook for 1 minute. (*For Electric:* Select the Brown setting.)
1 large onion, chopped	
2 cloves garlic, minced	
1 green bell pepper, cored, seeded, and diced	*2* Add the tomato sauce, water, salt, black pepper, and chipotle pepper, if desired.
2 cups uncooked long-grain white rice	
Three 8-ounce cans tomato sauce	*3* Cover and bring to high pressure over high heat. Lower the heat to stabilize the pressure. Cook for 7 minutes. (*For Electric:* Select high pressure and set the timer for 7 minutes.)
2 cups water	
2 teaspoons salt	
⅛ teaspoon black pepper	*4* Remove from the heat. Let the pressure drop using a quick-release method.
1 chipotle pepper (optional)	
	5 Unlock and remove the cover. Remove the chipotle pepper, if used, before serving.

Per serving: Calories 338 (From Fat 48); Fat 5g (Saturated 1g); Cholesterol 0mg; Sodium 1,465mg; Carbohydrate 66g (Dietary Fiber 3g); Protein 7g.

Note: This recipe is vegetarian, vegan, and gluten- and dairy-free.

Yellow Split Pea and Basmati Pilaf

Prep time: 15 min • **Cook time:** 8 min under pressure • **Yield:** 4 servings

Ingredients	Directions
1 cup basmati rice **½ cup yellow split peas** **2 tablespoons vegetable oil** **1 large onion, chopped** **½ teaspoon grated fresh gingerroot** **1 teaspoon cumin seeds** **2 cups chicken or vegetable stock** **¼ cup water** **¾ teaspoon salt** **⅛ teaspoon pepper** **2 tablespoons minced cilantro** **½ cup chopped dry-roasted cashews**	*1* Rinse the rice and split peas under cold water. Place in a bowl and cover with cold water. Soak for 10 minutes. *2* Heat the vegetable oil in a pressure cooker over medium-high heat. Add the onion, gingerroot, and cumin seeds. Cook until the onion is soft. (*For Electric:* Select the Brown setting.) *3* Drain the rice mixture, rinse, and add to the pressure cooker with the stock, water, salt, and pepper. Stir well. *4* Cover and bring to high pressure over high heat. Lower the heat to stabilize the pressure. Cook for 8 minutes. (*For Electric:* Select high pressure and set the timer for 8 minutes.) *5* Remove from the heat. Let the pressure drop using a quick-release method. *6* Unlock and remove the cover. *7* Add the cilantro and fluff the rice. Spoon into a serving dish and sprinkle with the cashews.

Per serving: Calories 450 (From Fat 156); Fat 17g (Saturated 3g); Cholesterol 3mg; Sodium 1,049mg; Carbohydrate 68g (Dietary Fiber 8g); Protein 11g.

Note: This recipe is vegetarian and vegan if you use vegetable rather than chicken stock. It's also gluten- and dairy-free.

Tip: I like to serve this pilaf with the Indian Butter Chicken in Chapter 8 or the Moroccan Chicken in Chapter 9.

Bulgur Pilaf

Prep time: 10 min • **Cook time:** 10 min under pressure • **Yield:** 4 servings

Ingredients	Directions
2 tablespoons olive oil 1 cup whole-grain bulgur wheat, picked over 1 large red onion, chopped 2 cloves garlic, peeled and minced 2 carrots, scraped and diced small 1 stalk celery, diced small 8 ounces mushrooms, sliced 3 cups chicken, beef, or vegetable stock 1 teaspoon salt ¼ teaspoon black pepper 1 cup cooked green peas	**1** Heat the olive oil in a pressure cooker over medium-high heat. Add the bulgur wheat, onion, and garlic. Cook until the onion is soft. (*For Electric:* Select the Brown setting.) **2** Add the carrots, celery, and mushrooms. Cook for 2 minutes. Add the stock, salt, and black pepper. **3** Cover and bring to high pressure over high heat. Lower the heat to stabilize the pressure. Cook for 10 minutes. (*For Electric:* Select high pressure and set the timer for 10 minutes.) **4** Remove from the heat. Let the pressure drop using a quick-release method. **5** Open and remove the cover. Taste the wheat. If it's still hard, return to Step 2 and cook it for an additional 1 to 3 minutes or until tender. **6** Fluff the pilaf. Add the peas and serve.

Per serving: Calories 295 (From Fat 95); Fat 11g (Saturated 2g); Cholesterol 4mg; Sodium 1,374mg; Carbohydrate 44g (Dietary Fiber 11g); Protein 10g.

Note: This recipe is vegetarian and vegan when you use vegetable stock rather than beef or chicken. It's also dairy-free.

Vary It! To make this recipe gluten-free, replace the bulgur wheat with brown rice, cooking the rice under pressure for 15 minutes.

Tip: Bulgur comes in four different sizes: fine, medium, coarse, and whole. If you can't find it in your local supermarket, try a health-food store.

Chapter 8

Fork-Tender Stews

In This Chapter

▶ Loading your stews with flavor

▶ Enjoying the convenience of stew

▶ Trying out some savory stew recipes

Stews are an economical way of stretching a pound or two of inexpensive cuts of meat or poultry — along with garden-fresh veggies, herbs, and spices — into dinner for eight. Because the objective is to have a melding of flavors, choose ingredients that complement each other as their flavors come together while cooking.

Although stews are usually considered a slow-simmered food, you'll be amazed at how you can get the same results in the pressure cooker in less than half the time — without sacrificing flavor or appearance. The trick is coaxing the optimum flavor from each ingredient. In this chapter, I show you how to do just that, and I share a sampling of my favorite stew recipes.

Flavor, Flavor, Flavor: The Makings of a Great Stew!

Nothing is worse than a watery, tasteless stew, especially when it's so easy to make when done right! Making stew is like building a house. First, you have to build the foundation by choosing the main ingredient, be it meat, poultry, or even root vegetables. Then you need the structure to bring it all together — perhaps a flavorful broth, some vegetable puree, or hearty wine or malt-flavored beer. Next, you need to add some decorative yet essential touches in the form of vibrant, colorful, flavor-packed vegetables such as carrots, peas, and string beans, or perhaps some starchy potatoes for added body. Finally, you can spark things up with a sprinkling of herbs and spices, both dried and fresh. By the time you're done, you'll have the tastiest, best-smelling stew around!

A cut above the rest: Selecting your meat

Choosing the right cut of meat is as important when making a stew as it is when making a braised roast. And the more expensive cuts aren't necessarily the best!

I always avoid purchasing prepackaged stew meat. I find that what appears on the top of the package is not always representative of what's on the bottom. Resourceful supermarkets have been known to conceal gristle and fatty pieces under better ones. For best results, do like I do and purchase a nice top round London broil or roast. Remove all the visible fat and cut the meat into uniform-sized pieces. You can do the same thing with pork and lamb. A nice center cut piece of pork loin or a small boneless leg of lamb turns into great stew meat.

If you want to use chicken, boneless chicken thighs make a great stew as long as you remove the excess fat. Boneless white breast meat can be dry, and the flavor can cook out. To prevent this from happening, use breast meat only in recipes that have an intense, powerful flavor.

Browning your meat

Browning the meat or poultry is one of the first steps when preparing stews in a pressure cooker. Browning in hot oil seals in the natural juices and caramelizes the exterior so that the meat or poultry looks and tastes better. For best results, follow these suggestions:

- ✔ **Make sure that the oil is very hot.** Don't add the meat or poultry until it is.
- ✔ **Dry the meat or poultry.** Pat it with paper towels before browning. This step prevents the hot oil from dropping dramatically in temperature when the raw food is added.
- ✔ **Brown in batches.** If you put too much raw meat or poultry into the hot oil, the oil has a hard time coming back up to the correct temperature. The food will sputter rather than sizzle as it steams, releasing its natural juices rather than browning and sealing them in.

Sautéing and deglazing

Sautéed onions, garlic, gingerroot, and peppers add tremendous flavor to a stew. These ingredients need to be cooked until soft and perhaps a bit browned.

Don't cook with what you wouldn't drink!

Purchasing wine to drink can be, at best, intimi- dating for the uninitiated. Buying wine for cook- ing can also cause some anxiety. Here's a good rule to follow: If you wouldn't drink it, don't cook with it! Never use cooking wine that's marketed as such and sold in grocery stores. These wines are loaded with sodium and are of poor quality that can mask the fresh flavor of your ingredi- ents. If you're uncertain about what wine to pur- chase, go a local, reputable liquor store and ask for some advice, and remember, a good bottle of wine shouldn't set you back more than $8 to $10.

Cook onions, garlic, gingerroot, and peppers only to the golden brown stage — never deeper — or they'll make the stew bitter.

After the food is done browning, you need to deglaze the pan, as shown in Figure 8-1. *Deglazing* means loosening up and dissolving all the caramelized juices from browning the meat, poultry, or other ingredients. Here's how to do it:

1. **Remove the browned item from the pan.**

2. **Add liquid such as chopped or pureed tomatoes, wine, beer, broth, or even water to the pan.**

3. **Bring this liquid to a boil and quickly stir and scrape the bottom of the pot with a large kitchen spoon.**

   The aroma will be heavenly!

4. **Boil the sauce until it's reduced by half.**

DEGLAZING A PAN.....

Figure 8-1:
Steps for deglazing a pan.

1. ONCE YOU ARE DONE BROWNING, YOU NEED TO DEGLAZE THE PAN. (YOU WANT TO LOOSEN UP/DIS- SOLVE ALL OF THE CARAMELIZED JUICES FROM BROWNING MEAT, POULTRY, ONIONS, ETC...

2. DO SO, BY ADDING LIQUID (CHOPPED OR PUREED TOMATOES, WINE, BEER, BROTH OR WATER).

★ REMOVE THE BROWNED ITEM FROM THE PAN.

RAISE HEAT AND QUICKLY BRING TO A BOIL.

3. QUICKLY... STIR AND SCRAPE THE BOTTOM OF THE POT WITH A LARGE KITCHEN SPOON. BOIL UNTIL THE SAUCE...

THE AROMA SHOULD BE HEAVENLY

...IS REDUCED BY HALF.

SPOON OVER COOKED MEAT, POULTRY OR FISH !

Illustration by Elizabeth Kurtzman

Season away!

Well-seasoned food makes for delectable, delicious food. By just having a few herbs and spices on hand, you'll be amazed how easy it is to transform plain food into a culinary masterpiece!

✔ **Salt and black pepper:** I usually like to generously salt and pepper the meat or poultry after I pat it dry, right before browning it in the hot oil. Doing so seems to intensify the flavor immensely.

I always use kosher salt. Because it doesn't contain any of the additives found in table salt, it tastes better. Table salt contains free-flowing agents, so it doesn't stick to food as well as kosher salt.

If you don't have a pepper mill already, do yourself a favor and pick one up. Nothing beats the flavor of freshly ground black pepper. Preground pepper lacks all the intensity of the freshly ground stuff and should be banned from cooking!

If you season the meat or poultry before browning, you probably won't have to add any additional salt and pepper. As with all recipes, however, always taste the food before serving to make sure that it's well seasoned.

✔ **Bay leaf:** A member of the evergreen family, this aromatic herb imparts wonderful flavor to almost everything. Fresh bay leaves aren't always readily available, but dried leaves are. A leaf or two is usually all you need.

✔ **Dried thyme:** This is one of my favorite herbs to use in cooking. A bit more subtle than oregano, with tones of mint, thyme provides a well-rounded flavor to most dishes when used judiciously.

✔ **Sage:** With a pungent, almost musty taste and aroma, sage goes well with most poultry and pork. Fresh sage leaves can be found in the produce section of most supermarkets.

✔ **Fresh parsley:** I like to finish some stews with a healthy sprinkling of minced parsley. If added at the beginning of the recipe, the parsley loses its flavor and bright green color. Therefore, always add it right before serving. Never use curly parsley. I prefer the flat-leaf, or Italian, variety, which is easier to mince and is more flavorful.

Adding the veggies

Although tough cuts of meat cook up fork-tender in the pressure cooker, they do need to cook longer than most vegetables. Therefore, you need to cook the meat under pressure until it's almost ready before adding the vegetables 4 to 8 minutes before the stew is done cooking. For example, look at My Favorite Beef Stew recipe in this chapter. You first cook the meat for 15 minutes under pressure. After releasing the pressure, you add all the vegetables except the mushrooms, and cook them under pressure for 8 minutes. Then you release the pressure again, add the mushrooms, and cook them for 1 minute. Our rich-tasting, delicious stew is ready from start to finish in less than 45 minutes! (See Chapter 5 for more information on stop-and-go cooking.)

Stews: Meals of Convenience

For me, stew is synonymous with convenience. A combination of meat or poultry, vegetables, and other ingredients brought together in a flavorful sauce or gravy, these one-pot meals are usually quick and easy to make, especially in the pressure cooker. Following are some of my favorite stew recipes for your cooking and dining pleasure:

- **My Favorite Beef Stew:** I'm of Italian descent, so I believe that beef stew should be red with tomatoes and red wine. It also needs to be full of great vegetables and served over egg noodles.

- **Vegetable Tagine with Couscous:** Tagine (pronounced "ta-*jean*") is a type of thick Moroccan stew. Usually made with meats like lamb and goat, or chicken, tagine also can be made with only vegetables, as it is in this recipe. Serve it with couscous.

- **Meatball Stew:** When I was growing up, my mother used to make a meatball stew very similar to this one. You can substitute prepared frozen meatballs from the supermarket. The cooking time under pressure won't be affected, only the time it takes to reach pressure.

- **Irish Lamb Stew:** A peasant dish made with readily available ingredients, authentic Irish lamb stew is simplicity at its best. A true meat-and-potatoes dish, you can also add 3 large carrots, cut lengthwise and then into 1-inch pieces, along with the potatoes.

- **Pork and Mustard Stew:** This is a wonderfully flavored stew, perfect for a fall or winter meal. The addition of whole-seed mustard right before serving gives this stew an added taste punch.

- **Pork Stew with Green Beans and Mushrooms:** A combination of meat, green beans, and mushrooms in a light, flavorful sauce, this stew is special enough to be served to company with parsleyed potatoes or buttered noodles.

- **Indian Butter Chicken:** After having eaten this dish more than a few times at my local Indian restaurant, I decided to adapt the recipe so that it can be made in the pressure cooker. The contrast of smooth and spicy makes this dish an all-time favorite.

- **Sweet-and-Sour Chicken:** This pressure-cooker adaptation of a Chinese restaurant favorite is one of the easiest and quickest recipes I know for getting dinner on the table in 30 minutes or less from start to finish.

My Favorite Beef Stew

Prep time: 20 min • **Cook time:** 24 min under pressure • **Yield:** 6 servings

Ingredients

Salt and pepper

1½ pounds top round or chuck, trimmed of all fat and cut into 1-inch cubes

3 tablespoons olive oil, divided

1 large onion, chopped

3 cloves garlic, minced

¾ cup red wine

One 14½-ounce can diced tomatoes

½ teaspoon dried thyme

1 bay leaf

8 ounces green beans, ends trimmed and cut into 1-inch pieces

8 ounces baby carrots

2 stalks celery, cut into 1-inch pieces

1 large potato, peeled and cut into 1-inch chunks

8 ounces white button mushrooms, quartered

2 tablespoons flat-leaf parsley, minced

8 ounces cooked broad egg noodles

Directions

1 Generously salt and pepper the meat. Heat 2 tablespoons of the olive oil in a pressure cooker over high heat. Brown the meat in two batches. Remove and set aside in a large bowl. (*For Electric:* Select the Brown setting.)

2 Add the remaining 1 tablespoon of olive oil. Add the onion and garlic. Cook until the onion is soft. Return the browned meat to the pressure cooker. Add the wine. Bring to a boil and cook for 2 minutes. Add the tomatoes, dried thyme, and bay leaf.

3 Cover and bring to high pressure over high heat. Lower the heat to stabilize the pressure. Cook for 15 minutes. (*For Electric:* Select high pressure and set the timer for 15 minutes.)

4 Remove from the heat. Let the pressure drop using a quick-release method. Unlock and remove the cover.

5 Add the green beans, carrots, celery, and potato.

6 Cover and bring to high pressure over high heat. Lower the heat to stabilize the pressure. Cook for 8 minutes. (*For Electric:* Select high pressure and set the timer for 8 minutes.)

7 Remove from the heat. Let the pressure drop using a quick-release method. Unlock and remove the cover.

8   Season to taste with salt and pepper. Add the mushrooms.

9   Cover and bring to high pressure over high heat. Lower the heat to stabilize the pressure. Cook for 1 minute. (*For Electric:* Select high pressure and set the timer for 1 minute.)

10   Remove from the heat. Let the pressure drop using a quick-release method.

11   Unlock and remove the cover. Stir in the parsley before serving. Serve with the noodles.

Per serving: *Calories 426 (From Fat 115); Fat 13g (Saturated 3g); Cholesterol 101mg; Sodium 277mg; Carbohydrate 44g (Dietary Fiber 6g); Protein 34g.*

Note: This recipe is dairy-free.

Vary It! To make this recipe gluten-free, substitute gluten-free noodles for the egg noodles.

Mincing Garlic

HEY! Crush the garlic clove under the blade of a knife.

Pull away the paper-like skin.

Put the clove on the cutting board. Make slices through the clove in one direction, then slice crosswise, to mince!

Illustration by Elizabeth Kurtzman

Vegetable Tagine with Couscous

Prep time: 10 min • **Cook time:** 35 min under pressure • **Yield:** 4 servings

Ingredients	*Directions*
2 tablespoons olive oil	**1** Heat the olive oil in a pressure cooker over medium-high heat. Add the onion and garlic. Cook until the onion is soft. Add the cumin, paprika, cinnamon, 2 teaspoons salt, and black pepper. Cook for 2 minutes. (*For Electric:* Select the Brown setting.)
1 large red onion, coarsely chopped	
2 cloves garlic, crushed	
1½ teaspoons ground cumin	**2** Add the tomatoes and the red and green peppers. Cook for 2 minutes. Add the carrots, celery, squash, chickpeas, green beans, and stock.
1 teaspoon paprika	
½ teaspoon ground cinnamon	
2 teaspoons salt	**3** Cover and bring to high pressure over high heat. Lower the heat to stabilize the pressure. Cook for 5 minutes. (*For Electric:* Select high pressure and set the timer for 5 minutes.)
¼ teaspoon black pepper	
One 14½-ounce can diced tomatoes	
1 red bell pepper, cored, seeded, and diced	**4** Remove from the heat. Let the pressure drop using a quick-release method.
1 green bell pepper, cored, seeded, and diced	**5** Unlock and remove the cover.
2 carrots, peeled and cut into ½-inch pieces	**6** Taste the vegetables. If they're still hard, return to Step 2 and cook them for an additional 1 to 3 minutes or until tender.
2 stalks celery, cut into ½-inch pieces	
2 cups peeled, cubed butternut squash	**7** Season to taste with salt. Add the parsley. Serve with the couscous, prepared according to package instructions.
1 cup cooked chickpeas	
8 ounces green beans, trimmed and cut into 1-inch pieces	

1½ cups vegetable or chicken stock

Salt to taste

2 tablespoons minced flat-leaf parsley

One 10-ounce package couscous

Per serving: Calories 527 (From Fat 84); Fat 9g (Saturated 1g); Cholesterol 0mg; Sodium 1,733mg; Carbohydrate 97g (Dietary Fiber 16g); Protein 18g.

Note: This recipe is vegetarian and vegan when made with vegetable stock rather than chicken stock. It's also dairy-free.

Vary It! For a gluten-free recipe, substitute 2 cups cooked rice for the couscous.

Couscous: From Morocco to mainstream

Over the past 10 to 20 years, as ethnic dining has expanded beyond take-out Chinese and pizza, Americans have been exposed to many new and exotic foods and ingredients used in other parts of the world. Ingredients such as cilantro and tofu have become as common in our pantries and fridges as spaghetti and ketchup. Couscous is one of these foods; formerly unheard of, it's now commonplace.

A staple of North Africa, *couscous* is a type of pasta made with semolina flour. When making couscous in the traditional manner, Arabic women mix the semolina with a small amount of water to make a paste. They then rub the paste through a fine mesh screen. The resulting pellets are sun-dried and stored for later use. Fortunately for us, commercially made couscous can be purchased at most supermarkets, usually in the aisle with the rice and noodle mixes.

Meatball Stew

Prep time: 20 min • **Cook time:** 10 min under pressure • **Yield:** 4 servings

Ingredients	*Directions*
1 pound lean ground beef 2 large eggs 1½ cups plain breadcrumbs 4 tablespoons grated pecorino Romano cheese 1 teaspoon salt ⅛ teaspoon pepper 4 tablespoons minced flat-leaf parsley, divided 3 tablespoons olive oil 1 medium onion, chopped 4 cloves garlic, minced One 10-ounce package frozen peas and carrots 2 large potatoes, peeled and cut into 2-inch chunks One 29-ounce can tomato sauce 1 teaspoon dried Italian seasoning Salt and pepper to taste	*1* Combine the ground beef, eggs, breadcrumbs, cheese, 1 teaspoon salt, ⅛ teaspoon pepper, and 2 tablespoons of the parsley in a large mixing bowl. Do not overmix. Shape into 8 meatballs. *2* Heat the olive oil in a pressure cooker over high heat. Brown the meatballs. (*For Electric:* Select the Brown setting.) *3* Remove the meatballs and pour out all but 1 tablespoon of the cooking oil. Add the onion and garlic. Cook over medium-high heat until the onion is soft. Add the peas and carrots, potatoes, tomato sauce, and Italian seasoning. Drop in the meatballs, one at a time. *4* Cover and bring to high pressure over high heat. Lower the heat to stabilize the pressure. Cook for 10 minutes. (*For Electric:* Select high pressure and set the timer for 10 minutes.) *5* Remove from the heat. Let the pressure drop using a quick-release method. *6* Unlock and remove the cover. Season with salt and pepper to taste. Stir in the remaining 2 tablespoons parsley before serving.

Per serving: Calories 604 (From Fat 251); Fat 28g (Saturated 8g); Cholesterol 118mg; Sodium 2,319mg; Carbohydrate 56g (Dietary Fiber 8g); Protein 36g.

Vary It! To make this recipe gluten-free and dairy-free, use gluten-free breadcrumbs and eliminate the grated cheese.

Irish Lamb Stew

Prep time: 20 min • **Cook time:** 28 min under pressure • **Yield:** 8 servings

Ingredients	*Directions*
Salt and pepper	**1** Generously salt and pepper the lamb. Heat 2 tablespoons of the olive oil in a pressure cooker over high heat. Brown the meat in three batches. Remove and set aside in a large bowl. (*For Electric:* Select the Brown setting.)
2 pounds boneless lamb shoulder, trimmed of all fat and cut into 2-inch cubes	
3 tablespoons olive oil, divided	
2 large onions, chopped	**2** Add the remaining 1 tablespoon olive oil. Add the onions and cook until soft. Return the browned meat with any accumulated juices to the pressure cooker. Add the water and 1 teaspoon salt.
1¼ cups water	
2 pounds all-purpose potatoes, peeled and cut into 2-inch chunks	
3 tablespoons minced flat-leaf parsley	**3** Cover and bring to high pressure over high heat. Lower the heat to stabilize the pressure. Cook for 20 minutes. (*For Electric:* Select high pressure and set the timer for 20 minutes.)
	4 Remove from the heat. Let the pressure drop using a quick-release method. Unlock and remove the cover.
	5 Add the potatoes. Cover and bring to high pressure over high heat. Lower the heat to stabilize the pressure. Cook for 8 minutes. (*For Electric:* Select high pressure and set the timer for 8 minutes.)
	6 Remove from the heat. Let the pressure drop using a quick-release method. Unlock and remove the cover.
	7 If the stew is very liquidy, bring it to a boil, uncovered, and cook until the sauce thickens. Season to taste with salt and pepper. Stir in the parsley before serving.

Per serving: Calories 395 (From Fat 161); Fat 18g (Saturated 5g); Cholesterol 147mg; Sodium 108mg; Carbohydrate 23g (Dietary Fiber 3g); Protein 34g.

Note: This recipe is gluten-free and dairy-free.

Pork and Mustard Stew

Prep time: 20 min • **Cook time:** 18 min under pressure • **Yield:** 6 servings

Ingredients	*Directions*
Salt and pepper	*1* Generously salt and pepper the pork loin. Set aside.
2 pounds lean pork loin, cut into 1-inch cubes	
2 tablespoons olive oil	*2* Heat the olive oil in a pressure cooker over medium-high heat. Add the onions and garlic. Cook until the onion is soft. Raise the heat to high. Add the pork and cook until golden. Sprinkle with the flour. Stir well. Add the wine, broth, and sage and stir to combine. (*For Electric:* Select the Brown setting.)
2 large onions, chopped	
2 cloves garlic, chopped	
1 tablespoon all-purpose flour	
¾ cup dry red wine	*3* Cover and bring to high pressure over high heat. Lower the heat to stabilize the pressure. Cook for 10 minutes. (*For Electric:* Select high pressure and set the timer for 10 minutes.)
¾ cup beef or chicken broth	
5 fresh sage leaves, chopped	
8 small red or new potatoes, scrubbed, peeled, and quartered	*4* Remove from the heat. Let the pressure drop using a quick-release method. Unlock and remove the cover. Add the potatoes and carrot.
1 large carrot, thinly sliced	
1½ tablespoons whole-seed mustard	*5* Cover and bring to high pressure over high heat. Lower the heat to stabilize the pressure. Cook for 8 minutes. (*For Electric:* Select high pressure and set the timer for 8 minutes.)
2 tablespoons minced flat-leaf parsley	
	6 Remove from the heat. Let the pressure drop using a quick-release method. Unlock and remove the cover. Season to taste with salt and pepper. Stir in the mustard and parsley before serving.

Per serving: Calories 467 (From Fat 138); Fat 15g (Saturated 4g); Cholesterol 86mg; Sodium 488mg; Carbohydrate 43g (Dietary Fiber 5g); Protein 36g.

Note: This recipe is dairy-free.

Vary It! For a gluten-free recipe, leave out the all-purpose flour.

Pork Stew with Green Beans and Mushrooms

Prep time: 20 min • **Cook time:** 14 min under pressure • **Yield:** 6 servings

Ingredients	*Directions*
Salt and pepper	*1* Generously salt and pepper the pork loin. Set aside.
2 pounds lean pork loin, cut into 1-inch cubes	*2* Heat the olive oil in the pressure cooker over medium-high heat. Add the onion and garlic. Cook until the onion is soft. Raise the heat to high. Add the pork loin and cook for 6 minutes. Sprinkle with the flour. Stir well. Add the beer, broth, and thyme and stir to combine. (*For Electric:* Select the Brown setting.)
2 tablespoons olive oil	
1 large onion, chopped	
2 cloves garlic, peeled and chopped	
2 tablespoons all-purpose flour	*3* Cover and bring to high pressure over high heat. Lower the heat to stabilize the pressure. Cook for 10 minutes. (*For Electric:* Select high pressure and set the timer for 10 minutes.)
¾ cup beer or dry white wine	
¾ cup chicken broth	
½ teaspoon dried thyme	*4* Remove from the heat. Let the pressure drop using a quick-release method. Unlock and remove the cover. Add the green beans and mushrooms.
Two 10-ounce packages frozen French-cut green beans	
¾ pound fresh white button mushrooms, quartered	*5* Cover and bring to high pressure over high heat. Lower the heat to stabilize the pressure. Cook for 4 minutes. (*For Electric:* Select high pressure and set the timer for 4 minutes.) Remove from the heat. Let the pressure drop using a quick-release method.
2 tablespoons minced flat-leaf parsley	
	6 Unlock and remove the cover. Add salt and pepper to taste. If there's too much liquid, bring it to a boil and reduce until the sauce is thick. Stir in the parsley before serving.

Per serving: *Calories 274 (From Fat 94); Fat 10g (Saturated 3g); Cholesterol 85mg; Sodium 288mg; Carbohydrate 12g (Dietary Fiber 3g); Protein 33g.*

Note: This recipe is dairy-free.

Vary It! For a gluten-free recipe, leave out the all-purpose flour.

Indian Butter Chicken

Prep time: 15 min • **Cook time:** 8 min under pressure • **Yield:** 6 servings

Ingredients	Directions
Salt and pepper	**1** Generously salt and pepper the chicken. Heat the vegetable oil in a pressure cooker over high heat. Add the onion, gingerroot, jalapeño, and garam masala. Cook for 3 minutes. Add the chicken and cook until no longer pink on the outside (chicken will still be raw on the inside). Add the tomato paste and chicken broth. Stir well. (*For Electric:* Select the Brown setting.)
1½ pounds boneless chicken breast, cut into ¾-inch cubes	
2 tablespoons vegetable oil	
1 large onion, minced	
1 tablespoon minced or grated gingerroot	**2** Cover and bring to high pressure over high heat. Lower the heat to stabilize the pressure. Cook for 8 minutes. (*For Electric:* Select high pressure and set the timer for 8 minutes.)
1 small jalapeño, seeded and minced	
2 teaspoons garam masala spice blend	
One 6-ounce can tomato paste	**3** Remove from the heat. Let the pressure drop using a quick-release method. Unlock and remove the cover.
2 cups chicken broth	
½ cup heavy cream	**4** Over low heat, stir in the heavy cream. Add the cilantro and butter. Stir until the butter melts. Serve with white rice, squeezing juice from the lime wedges over the servings.
2 tablespoons minced cilantro	
3 tablespoons butter, cut into small pieces	
3 cups cooked white rice	
1 lime, cut into 6 pieces	

Per serving: Calories 448 (From Fat 297); Fat 33g (Saturated 15g); Cholesterol 137mg; Sodium 520mg; Carbohydrate 11g (Dietary Fiber 2g); Protein 27g.

Note: This recipe is gluten-free.

Tip: Garam masala spice blend is readily available at most Indian and specialty food stores. You can make your own by combining ¾ teaspoon ground cumin, ½ teaspoon paprika, ¼ teaspoon ground cinnamon, ⅛ teaspoon ground cayenne, ⅛ teaspoon ground cloves, and 1 bay leaf, crumbled, in a small bowl. Store in an airtight jar.

Vary It! Try serving over Yellow Split Pea and Basmati Pilaf (see Chapter 7) instead of rice.

Sweet-and-Sour Chicken

Prep time: 15 min • **Cook time:** 10 min under pressure • **Yield:** 6 servings

Ingredients	*Directions*
1 tablespoon vegetable oil 1 large onion, chopped 1 large red bell pepper, cored, seeded, and diced 1 large green bell pepper, cored, seeded, and diced 2 pounds boneless chicken thighs, trimmed of all visible fat and cut into 1-inch pieces 2 tablespoons soy sauce 1½ cups prepared sweet-and-sour or duck sauce 1 tablespoon apple cider vinegar 3 tablespoons water 1 teaspoon garlic powder 2 scallions, white and green parts, thinly sliced 2 cups cooked white rice	*1* Heat the oil in a pressure cooker over medium-high heat. Add the onion and the red and green bell peppers. Cook for 2 minutes. Add the chicken and soy sauce. Cook for 3 minutes. Add the sweet-and-sour sauce, vinegar, water, and garlic powder. Stir well. (*For Electric:* Select the Brown setting.)
	2 Cover and bring to high pressure. Lower the heat to stabilize the pressure. Cook for 10 minutes. (*For Electric:* Select high pressure and set the timer for 10 minutes.)
	3 Remove from the heat. Let the pressure drop using a quick-release method.
	4 Unlock and remove the cover.
	5 Transfer to a serving dish and garnish with the scallions. Serve with the rice.

Per serving: Calories 450 (From Fat 172); Fat 19g (Saturated 5g); Cholesterol 94mg; Sodium 769mg; Carbohydrate 39g (Dietary Fiber 2g); Protein 29g.

Note: This recipe is dairy-free.

Vary It! For a gluten-free version, use gluten-free soy sauce.

Chapter 9

Enjoying Roasts and Prime Poultry Any Day of the Week

Roasts and large cuts of meat and poultry are usually reserved for occasions such as a family celebration, a holiday, or a leisurely Sunday dinner around the table with family and friends. Roasts are an easy way to feed a group of people, but they also take two to three hours to cook. The long cooking time may be the real reason why they're served only occasionally. That's too bad, because my favorite part of a roast is the delicious leftovers enjoyed the next day!

In this chapter, I show you how using your pressure cooker speeds up the required cooking time so any day of the week can be a special occasion. I also help you choose the right cuts of meat, make use of accessories like steaming baskets and racks for the best results, and determine when a particular dish is safely done. Last but not least, I share some of my favorite recipes for roasting beef, pork, and poultry.

Producing Fabulous Results in Half the Time

A few years ago, I decided to try my hand at adapting a basic, favorite pot roast recipe for the pressure cooker. First, I made sure that the meat would fit comfortably in the pressure cooker, which is about 8½ inches in diameter. I determined that a 3- to 3½-pound roast was perfect. Because I already knew that the pressure cooker tenderizes as it cooks, I purchased an inexpensive cut of beef, a rump roast from the hindquarter.

I followed the original recipe by generously seasoning the meat with salt and freshly ground black pepper. I then browned and seared it in the pressure cooker over high heat to seal in the juices. To build on the flavor, I added some onion, which I cooked quickly for a minute or two. With all of these great caramelized flavors on the bottom of the pot, I added some red wine to deglaze and scrape up any cooked-on particles. I then increased the liquid with some homemade beef broth. I didn't really want the meat to boil, so I placed it in a steaming basket on top of a trivet in the pressure cooker. The moment of truth came about an hour later — about 90 minutes less than it would have taken in an oven — when I opened the pressure cooker and cut into the meat. The meat was fork-tender and succulent! The gravy, ambrosial!

I was then inspired to try other cuts of meat, such as pork loin, quartered chicken, and, yes, even a whole turkey breast, all of which cooked perfectly in my pressure cooker. Before I knew it, come mealtime, every day was like Sunday!

Recognizing That Not All Cuts Are Created Equal

Some cuts of meat are better suited for cooking in the pressure cooker than others, especially tougher, less-expensive ones and cuts that are very lean, because they cook up tender under pressure. A basic cooking method for preparing large cuts of meat and poultry is braising. When you braise, you first brown the food over medium-high heat in a small amount of oil. You then cover the browned food and cook it over low heat in a small amount of cooking liquid for an extended period of time until it's fork-tender.

The following sections highlight different cuts of meat and poultry that I particularly like to make in the pressure cooker.

Making the most of beef

All cuts of beef that come from the front and hindquarter are ideal for the pressure cooker because cattle develop a lot of muscle here — and not much fat — from lumbering around. Some good choices are chuck and brisket from the front of the steer, and round and rump from, well, the rump or rear of the animal. Other good choices are flank and skirt steak from the belly area.

Picking pork

Pork really is the other white meat. Much leaner today than ever before, it can also dry out quickly when cooked. The loin is very lean white meat and is ideal for roasting and braising in the pressure cooker. To maximize flavor and to ensure that the pork is juicy, I like to rub it with a paste of garlic and spices before browning it on all sides in a small amount of oil in the pressure cooker. Lots of vegetables and some cooking liquid are sure to keep the meat tender.

Looking at lamb

A boneless, tied leg of lamb stuffed with pieces of garlic and rosemary, browned in olive oil, and braised with dry white wine is a superb piece of meat for the pressure cooker, especially when company is coming and you want to impress your guests. Less-expensive lamb shanks are also delectable when braised in the pressure cooker, with the now-tender meat falling off the bone.

Perusing poultry

From a cook's standpoint, chickens and turkeys are poorly designed creatures. Getting a whole bird, with its juicier dark meat and drier white meat, to cook evenly without something coming out dry and stringy is almost impossible. But when made in the pressure cooker, chicken — whole or quartered — comes out succulent. Although you may not be able to fit a whole turkey into even an 8-quart pressure cooker, a 4- to 5-pound whole breast fits perfectly in a 6-quart pressure cooker and cooks up juicy, as do turkey legs and wings.

Keeping Meats Out of Hot Water (Or Other Liquids)

When braising large cuts of meat such as chuck and rump roasts and boneless legs of lamb in the pressure cooker, I've found the results to be better if the meat doesn't sit directly in the cooking liquid, where it has a tendency to boil, but rather in a steaming basket or on a rack.

- **A steaming basket** is made of metal and is usually about 7 inches in diameter and 2 to 3 inches deep, with small round cutouts along the bottom, for, well, steaming. The basket usually comes with a metal wire trivet. The trivet is placed in the pressure cooker first and the basket goes on top.

- **A steaming rack** looks like a 7-inch-diameter lid with small round cut-outs on top. It sits directly in the pressure cooker.

Steaming baskets and racks serve the same purpose: to keep the food out of contact with the cooking liquid. If your pressure cooker doesn't have either of these two steaming devices, you can always purchase an inexpensive, collapsible, metal steaming basket at any housewares store. Regardless of the type you use, the steaming basket or rack is placed in the pressure cooker after the meat is browned, as detailed in the recipe.

Besides a steaming basket, some pressure cookers also come with an insert dish or pan. The same diameter and depth as the basket, these dishes and pans differ from steaming baskets in that they don't have any holes in the bottom. They can be used to make casseroles and desserts.

Is It Done Yet?

For the most part, meat is roasted or braised in the pressure cooker until fork-tender. Because cooking also kills harmful bacteria, cooking meat thoroughly is important in order to ensure that the bacteria are killed off.

An instant-read thermometer is a good way to determine whether meat or poultry is adequately cooked. Place the probe into the thickest part of the meat, inserting it about halfway down without touching the bone or pot. Table 9-1 provides you with safe cooking temperatures for cooked meat and poultry.

Table 9-1	Safe Cooking Temperatures for Meat and Poultry
Food	*Safe Cooking Temperature*
Beef	170° (well done)
Chicken	180°
Ground meat or poultry	165°
Ham (cured pork)	140°
Lamb	170° (well done)
Pork	160°
Turkey	180°

To get an idea of when your meat and poultry may reach the correct temperature, turn to Appendix A, which lists recommended cooking times for meat and poultry prepared in a pressure cooker.

A Roast in Every Pot

In this section are a few of my favorite roast recipes for the pressure cooker that I want to share with you. For the most part, they require very little preparation, and I know that you'll be pleased by how quick and easy they are to make — and how delicious they are, too!

Following are some recommended go-withs to turn the recipes in this chapter into complete meals. You can find the recipes for the side dishes noted here in Chapter 11.

- What would Sunday Pot Roast be without Grandma's Mashed Potatoes and tender Carrots and Onions? Two perfect sides that will turn any meal into a special occasion.

- Tangy Warm French-Style Potato Salad holds its own when served with "Barbecued" Beef or "Barbecued" Chicken.

- Caraway Pork Roast with Sauerkraut and Pickled Beets are the perfect autumn combination when the weather starts getting cooler.

- Be sure to serve the Pulled Pork with Greens in Pot Likker and lots of homemade cornbread to sop up all the juices and sauce.

- Steamed Lemon Artichokes as a first course and Ratatouille on the side are excellent Mediterranean accompaniments for Chicken Cacciatore.

- Braised Turkey Breast served with Cauliflower and Broccoli Custard makes an elegant, yet simple to put together, dinner.

Sunday Pot Roast

Prep time: 20 min • **Cook time:** 60 min under pressure • **Yield:** 6 servings

Ingredients	Directions
2 tablespoons all-purpose flour	*1* Combine the flour, 2 teaspoons salt, and ¼ teaspoon pepper. Rub into the roast. Heat the olive oil in a pressure cooker over high heat. Add the roast and brown all sides evenly. Add the onion and cook for 1 minute. Add the bay leaf. (*For Electric:* Select the Brown setting.)
2 teaspoons salt	
¼ teaspoon pepper	
3- to 4-pound boneless, trimmed chuck or rump roast	*2* Remove the meat to a steaming basket and then place the basket in the pressure cooker. Add the stock, wine, and/or water.
1 tablespoon olive oil	
1 small onion, sliced	
1 bay leaf	*3* Cover and bring to high pressure over high heat. Lower the heat to stabilize the pressure. Cook for 60 minutes. (*For Electric:* Select high pressure and set the timer for 60 minutes.)
1½ cups beef stock, red wine, water, or any combination thereof	
Salt and pepper to taste	*4* Remove from the heat. Release the pressure with a quick-release method. Unlock and remove the cover. Test the roast with a fork; it should penetrate easily. If the meat isn't tender, replace the cover and cook the meat under pressure for an additional 10 minutes.
	5 Remove the roast and the steaming basket. Cover and let sit for 10 minutes before slicing it against the grain.
	6 To make gravy, bring the liquid to a boil, uncovered, and cook to desired consistency. Season with salt and pepper to taste. Remove and discard the bay leaf.

Per serving: Calories 549 (From Fat 363); Fat 40g (Saturated 17g); Cholesterol 146mg; Sodium 1,112mg; Carbohydrate 3g (Dietary Fiber 0g); Protein 41g.

Note: This recipe is dairy-free.

Vary It! Use gluten-free flour in Step 1 to make this recipe gluten-free.

"Barbecued" Beef

Prep time: 20 min • **Cook time:** 60 min under pressure • **Yield:** 8 servings

Ingredients	*Directions*
1 tablespoon vegetable oil 3- to 4-pound boneless, trimmed chuck or rump roast	*1* Heat the oil in a pressure cooker over medium-high heat. Add the roast and brown evenly on all sides. (*For Electric:* Select the Brown setting.)
1 large onion, sliced 2 stalks celery, finely chopped 1½ cups prepared barbecue sauce One 12-ounce can beer 1½ teaspoons chili powder	*2* Add the onion and celery. Cook for 1 minute. Remove the roast to a plate. Add the barbecue sauce, beer, and chili powder. Stir well. Place the steaming basket in the pressure cooker. Place the browned roast in the steaming basket.
	3 Cover and bring to high pressure over high heat. Lower the heat to stabilize the pressure. Cook for 60 minutes. (*For Electric:* Select high pressure and set the timer for 60 minutes.)
	4 Remove from the heat. Release the pressure using the natural-release method. When the pressure has dropped, unlock and remove the cover.
	5 Test the roast with a fork; the fork should penetrate easily. If the meat isn't tender, cover and cook under pressure for an additional 10 minutes.
	6 Remove the roast. Let the meat sit for at least 15 minutes before slicing it thinly and against the grain. Serve with the barbecue sauce.

Per serving: *Calories 463 (From Fat 301); Fat 34g (Saturated 13g); Cholesterol 114mg; Sodium 471mg; Carbohydrate 8g (Dietary Fiber 1g); Protein 30g.*

Note: This recipe is dairy-free.

Ropa Vieja with Fried Plantains

Prep time: 20 min • **Cook time:** 50 min under pressure • **Yield:** 8 servings

Ingredients	Directions
1 large onion, cut into ¼-inch-thick slices **2 pounds beef brisket or flank steak, trimmed of all fat** **Salt and black pepper to taste** **1 carrot, peeled and cut into 1-inch pieces** **1 stalk celery, cut into 1-inch pieces** **1 sprig parsley** **About 4 cups water** **2 tablespoons olive oil** **1 medium onion, chopped** **2 cloves garlic, minced** **1 green bell pepper, cored, seeded, and chopped** **One 14½-ounce can tomato sauce** **¼ teaspoon dried oregano** **1 bay leaf** **1 tablespoon red wine vinegar** **3 cups cooked white rice** **Fried Plantains (optional; see the following recipe)**	**1** Place the onion slices on the bottom of a pressure cooker, overlapping if necessary. Cut the brisket to fit flat in the pressure cooker and place the brisket on top of the onion. Generously salt and pepper the brisket. **2** Add the carrot, celery, and parsley. Add just enough water to cover the meat, about 4 cups. **3** Cover and bring to high pressure over high heat. Lower the heat to stabilize the pressure. Cook for 50 minutes. (*For Electric:* Select high pressure and set the timer for 50 minutes.) **4** Remove from the heat. Let the pressure drop using a quick-release method. Unlock and remove the cover. **5** Remove the brisket from the cooking liquid. Discard the vegetables and strain the stock. Measure 1 cup of the stock and set aside. Shred the meat and set aside. Wash and dry the pressure cooker. **6** Heat the olive oil in the pressure cooker over medium-high heat. Add the chopped onion, garlic, and green pepper and cook until the onion is soft. Add the tomato sauce, reserved stock, oregano, bay leaf, and vinegar. Stir in the shredded meat.

7 Cover and bring to high pressure over high heat. Lower the heat to stabilize the pressure. Cook for 5 minutes. (*For Electric:* Select high pressure and set the timer for 5 minutes.)

8 Remove from the heat. Let the pressure drop using a quick-release method. Unlock and remove the cover.

9 Season with salt and black pepper to taste. Serve with the rice and, if desired, Fried Plantains.

Fried Plantains

Vegetable oil

3 large very ripe plantains (black skin), peeled and cut on a diagonal into ½-inch slices

1 Heat 1 inch of oil in a large skillet over medium-high heat.

2 Fry the plantain slices in batches on both sides until deep brown.

3 Drain on paper towels and serve.

Per serving: *Calories 434 (From Fat 160); Fat 17g (Saturated 5g); Cholesterol 59mg; Sodium 171mg; Carbohydrate 43g (Dietary Fiber 4g); Protein 27g.*

Note: This recipe is gluten-free and dairy-free.

Caraway Pork Roast with Sauerkraut

Prep time: 20 min • **Cook time:** 35 min under pressure • **Yield:** 6 servings

Ingredients	_Directions_
4 cloves garlic, minced	**1** Combine the garlic, caraway seeds, salt, and pepper in a small bowl to form a paste. With a knife, score the top and bottom of the roast, all over, about ⅛ inch deep. Rub the garlic mixture into the cuts.
1½ teaspoons caraway seeds	
1 teaspoon salt	
¼ teaspoon pepper	
2½- to 3-pound boneless pork loin roast	**2** Heat the olive oil in a pressure cooker over high heat. Add the roast and brown evenly on all sides. Remove the roast. (_For Electric:_ Select the Brown setting.)
1 tablespoon olive oil	
1 large onion, thinly sliced	**3** Add the onion and cook for 1 minute. Add the beer. Cook for 1 minute. Add the sauerkraut, bay leaf, and chicken stock. Place the roast on top of the sauerkraut.
One 12-ounce can beer	
1 pound sauerkraut, drained and rinsed under cold water	**4** Cover and bring to high pressure over high heat. Lower the heat to stabilize the pressure. Cook for 35 minutes. (_For Electric:_ Select high pressure and set the timer for 35 minutes.)
1 bay leaf	
½ cup chicken stock	
	5 Remove from the heat. Release the pressure with a quick-release method. Unlock and remove the cover. Test the roast with a fork; the fork should penetrate easily. If not tender, cover and cook under pressure for an additional 10 minutes.
	6 Remove the roast and let sit for 10 minutes before slicing.

Per serving: Calories 395 (From Fat 203); Fat 23g (Saturated 8g); Cholesterol 115mg; Sodium 832mg; Carbohydrate 6g (Dietary Fiber 3g); Protein 40g.

Note: This recipe is dairy-free. To make this recipe gluten-free, use gluten-free beer.

Pulled Pork

Prep time: 20 min • **Cook time:** 15 min under pressure • **Yield:** 6 servings

Ingredients	Directions
1 tablespoon olive oil	*1* Heat the olive oil in a pressure cooker over high heat. Add the onion and cook 3 minutes or until soft. Add the remaining ingredients except the pork and rolls. Cook for 5 minutes. Remove from heat. *(For Electric: Select the Brown setting.)*
1 medium onion, chopped	
3 cloves garlic, minced	
One 14½-ounce can diced tomatoes	
1 tablespoon tomato paste	*2* Using an immersion blender, puree the mixture in the pot until smooth, or transfer the mixture to a blender, puree until smooth, and pour back into the pot.
2 tablespoons apple cider vinegar	
1 tablespoon brown sugar	*3* Add the sliced pork tenderloin.
1 tablespoon Worcestershire sauce	*4* Cover and bring to high pressure over high heat. Lower the heat to stabilize the pressure. Cook for 15 minutes. *(For Electric: Select high pressure and set the timer for 15 minutes.)*
2 tablespoons prepared adobo seasoning	
⅓ cup water	
1 chipotle chili in adobo, seeded and chopped	*5* Remove from the heat. Release the pressure with a quick-release method. Unlock and remove the cover. Remove pork slices to a large cutting board and, while still warm, shred the meat with two forks.
Salt and pepper to taste	
2½- to 3-pound pork tenderloin, cut into 1½-inch slices	*6* Return the meat to the sauce in the pot and bring to a simmer over medium heat. Cook 10 minutes, uncovered, until sauce thickens. *(For Electric: Select Warm and simmer meat 10 minutes.)*
6 soft rolls	
	7 Serve over split soft rolls.

Per serving: Calories 403 (From Fat 107); Fat 12g (Saturated 3g); Cholesterol 106mg; Sodium 1,950mg; Carbohydrate 30g (Dietary Fiber 3g); Protein 42g.

Note: This recipe is dairy-free.

New England Boiled Dinner

Prep time: 15 min • **Cook time:** 24 min under pressure • **Yield:** 4 servings

Ingredients	Directions
2 cups water	**1** Add the water, bay leaf, garlic, and peppercorns to the pressure cooker. Place a steaming basket in the pressure cooker. Place the pork butt in the basket.
1 bay leaf	
4 cloves garlic, crushed	
½ teaspoon whole black peppercorns	**2** Cover and bring to high pressure over high heat. Lower the heat to stabilize the pressure. Cook for 20 minutes. (*For Electric:* Select high pressure and set the timer for 20 minutes.)
2-pound smoked pork butt, netting or covering removed	
1 pound small red or new potatoes, cut in half	**3** Remove from the heat. Release the pressure with a quick-release method. Unlock and remove the cover. Add the potatoes, carrots, leeks or scallions, and cabbage.
2 large carrots, peeled and cut into 1-inch pieces	
2 leeks, or 8 scallions, cleaned well and cut into 1-inch pieces	**4** Reposition the cover and bring to high pressure over high heat. Lower the heat to stabilize the pressure. Cook for 4 minutes. (*For Electric:* Select high pressure and set the timer for 4 minutes.)
1 small head green cabbage, cored and quartered	
	5 Remove from the heat. Release the pressure with a quick-release method. Unlock and remove the cover.
	6 Remove the meat and vegetables with a slotted spoon to a large serving platter. Slice the pork as thinly as possible. Spoon some of the cooking liquid over the meat and vegetables.

Per serving: Calories 642 (From Fat 367); Fat 41g (Saturated 14g); Cholesterol 130mg; Sodium 2,687mg; Carbohydrate 36g (Dietary Fiber 8g); Protein 36g.

Note: This recipe is gluten-free and dairy-free.

Moroccan Chicken

Prep time: 10 min • **Cook time:** 15 min under pressure • **Yield:** 4 servings

Ingredients	Directions
4 tablespoons olive oil	*1* Heat the olive oil in a pressure cooker over medium-high heat. Add the onion, garlic, 1 tablespoon of the parsley, cilantro, salt, pepper, and, if desired, saffron. Stir well and cook 3 minutes or until onions are soft. (*For Electric:* Select the Brown setting.)
1 large onion, sliced	
1 clove garlic, thinly sliced	
2 tablespoons minced flat-leaf parsley, divided	
1 tablespoon minced cilantro	*2* Add the chicken. Stir to coat with the onion mixture. Pour the stock over the chicken; do not stir. Place the lemon slices on top of the chicken.
1 teaspoon salt	
½ teaspoon black pepper	*3* Cover and bring to high pressure over high heat. Lower the heat to stabilize the pressure. Cook for 15 minutes. (*For Electric:* Select high pressure and set the timer for 15 minutes.)
4 threads saffron (optional)	
3- to 4-pound chicken, quartered, with or without skin	
1 cup chicken stock	*4* Remove from the heat. Let the pressure drop using a quick-release method. Unlock and remove the cover.
1 large lemon, thinly sliced	
8 large green Sicilian olives	*5* Remove the chicken with a slotted spoon to a platter. Cover to keep warm.
One 10-ounce package couscous	
	6 Reduce the cooking liquid over high heat until the sauce is thick. (*For Electric:* Select the Brown setting.) Add the olives and cook until warmed through. Pour the sauce over the chicken. Sprinkle with the remaining 1 tablespoon parsley.
	7 Serve with cooked couscous, prepared according to package directions.

Per serving: Calories 791 (From Fat 335); Fat 37g (Saturated 8g); Cholesterol 167mg; Sodium 1,142mg; Carbohydrate 59g (Dietary Fiber 5g); Protein 52g.

Note: This recipe is dairy-free.

Vary It! For a gluten-free recipe, substitute 2 cups cooked rice for the couscous.

Chicken Cacciatore

Prep time: 20 min • **Cook time:** 10 min under pressure • **Yield:** 4 servings

Ingredients	Directions
2 tablespoons olive oil	**1** Heat the olive oil in a pressure cooker over medium-high heat. Brown the chicken pieces in batches and set them aside on a large plate. (*For Electric:* Select the Brown setting.)
4-pound chicken, skin and excess fat removed, cut into serving pieces	
1 large onion, chopped	**2** Add the onion, garlic, cherry pepper (if desired), and mushrooms. Cook for 2 minutes. Return the browned chicken to the pressure cooker. Add the wine, tomatoes, salt, and black pepper. Cook for 2 minutes.
2 cloves garlic, peeled and very thinly sliced	
1 small pickled cherry or jalapeño pepper, seeded and coarsely chopped (optional)	
8 ounces white mushrooms, thinly sliced	**3** Cover and bring to high pressure over high heat. Lower the heat to stabilize the pressure. Cook for 10 minutes. (*For Electric:* Select high pressure and set the timer for 10 minutes.)
⅓ cup dry white wine	
One 28-ounce can crushed tomatoes	**4** Remove from the heat. Release the pressure with a quick-release method. Unlock and remove the cover.
1 teaspoon salt	
¼ teaspoon black pepper	**5** Transfer to a serving dish and garnish with the parsley. Serve with the white rice.
1 tablespoon minced parsley	
2 cups cooked white rice	

Per serving: Calories 470 (From Fat 174); Fat 19g (Saturated 4g); Cholesterol 93mg; Sodium 1,280mg; Carbohydrate 38g (Dietary Fiber 3g); Protein 34g.

Note: This recipe is gluten-free and dairy-free.

"Barbecued" Chicken

Prep time: 20 min • **Cook time:** 15 min under pressure • **Yield:** 4 servings

Ingredients	Directions
3 pounds chicken pieces, skin and excess fat removed	*1* Rub the chicken pieces with salt.
Salt	*2* Heat the vegetable oil in a pressure cooker over medium-high heat. Brown the chicken pieces in batches and set them aside on a large plate. (*For Electric:* Select the Brown setting.)
2 tablespoons vegetable oil	
1 large green bell pepper, cored, seeded, and diced	
1 large onion, chopped	*3* Add the green pepper, onion, and garlic. Cook for 2 minutes. Return the browned chicken to the pressure cooker. Add the barbecue and chili sauces.
2 cloves garlic, peeled and minced	
⅔ cup jarred barbecue sauce	*4* Cover and bring to high pressure over high heat. Lower the heat to stabilize the pressure. Cook for 15 minutes. (*For Electric:* Select high pressure and set the timer for 15 minutes.)
⅔ cup jarred tomato chili sauce	
	5 Remove from the heat. Release the pressure with a quick-release method. Unlock and remove the cover.
	6 Transfer to a serving dish.

Per serving: Calories 419 (From Fat 158); Fat 18g (Saturated 3g); Cholesterol 116mg; Sodium 1,887mg; Carbohydrate 24g (Dietary Fiber 2g); Protein 39g.

Note: This recipe is dairy-free.

Vary It! For a gluten-free recipe, use gluten-free barbecue and chili sauces.

Braised Turkey Breast

Prep time: 15 min • **Cook time:** 40 min under pressure • **Yield:** 6 servings

Ingredients	*Directions*
Salt and pepper	*1* Generously salt and pepper the turkey breast.
4- to 5-pound whole turkey breast, wings removed, rinsed under cold water and patted dry	*2* Heat the oil in a pressure cooker over medium-high heat. Add the turkey breast and brown on all sides. Remove and set aside. (*For Electric:* Select the Brown setting.)
2 tablespoons vegetable oil	
1 onion, thinly sliced	*3* Add the onion, garlic, carrots, and celery. Cook until the onion is soft. Add the stock and wine. Cook for 2 minutes. Place the turkey breast in the pressure cooker.
2 garlic cloves, crushed	
2 carrots, peeled and thinly sliced	*4* Cover and bring to high pressure over high heat. Lower the heat to stabilize the pressure. Cook for 40 minutes. (*For Electric:* Select high pressure and set the timer for 40 minutes.)
2 stalks celery, thinly sliced	
1 cup chicken stock	
1 cup dry red wine	*5* Remove from the heat. Release the pressure with a quick-release method.
1 tablespoon cornstarch	
2 tablespoons water	*6* Unlock and remove the cover. Carefully remove the turkey and place on a large plate. Cover with foil.
	7 Strain the cooking liquid. Pour it back into the pressure cooker and boil it down by a third. (*For Electric:* Select the Brown setting.) Combine the cornstarch and water. Add to the liquid and whisk until thickened. Season to taste with salt and pepper.
	8 Slice the turkey off the carcass. Serve with the gravy.

Per serving: Calories 433 (From Fat 180); Fat 20g (Saturated 5g); Cholesterol 149mg; Sodium 390mg; Carbohydrate 1g (Dietary Fiber 0g); Protein 58g.

Note: This recipe is gluten-free and dairy-free.

Chapter 10

Dried Beans and the Pressure Cooker: A Match Made in Heaven!

In This Chapter

▶ Discovering the benefits of beans

▶ Soaking beans before cooking

▶ Cooking beans to perfection

▶ Using beans in a variety of ways

This chapter contains a lot of recipes, and rightfully so. If ever a food was created to be made in the pressure cooker, it has to be the dried bean. Beans usually require up to 2 hours of slow simmering, but by using a pressure cooker, you reduce the cooking time by well over 70 minutes, a time savings of more than 50 percent!

Beans have been a food staple around the world for more than 7,000 years. With your super-rapid pressure cooker and the recipes that follow, they'll soon become a staple ingredient in your kitchen, too! To make you a convert, I give you some great, well-known, popular recipes. Some call for cooked beans that you prepare beforehand, while others start off with dried beans after they've been soaked.

Beans: A Powerhouse of Good Things

Packed with more protein than any other legume or vegetable, beans are a protein powerhouse. Fat- and cholesterol-free, they are high in fiber and provide eight out of the nine amino acids essential for good health. Beans are also high in iron and calcium and are an excellent source of complex carbohydrates, which are slowly released into our body for energy. A complete source of nutrients, beans are a key dietary component in a vegetarian diet.

If beans are so good for us, why aren't we eating them every day? Unfortunately, many people consider beans to be too labor intensive to prepare, based on the fact that they must be soaked before cooking. Other people think of beans as "un-chic." Yet, as a plant product, beans have sustained the poor of the world for thousands of years.

As people and countries become more affluent, bean consumption as a source of protein diminishes, being replaced by meat. In the 1960s, bean consumption in the United States was 7½ pounds per person, only to decline to 5 pounds in 1984. That trend may be reversing, however. Because people today are much more aware of the importance of a balanced diet, including the need for fiber, beans are beginning to once again play an important role in people's food choices.

"Dried" Doesn't Mean "All Dried Up"

All beans grow enclosed in a pod. Some are picked when they're still "green" or fresh. Others are picked after they've dried on the plant. Regardless, for easy and long-term storage, most beans are dried and then packaged to be sold.

Because dried beans have all the water removed from them, they won't rot and spoil. This doesn't mean that they'll last forever. Dried beans less than a year old cook better than older ones. They hydrate quicker and are more tender; old beans just never seem to get tender enough. Most companies don't put an expiration date on the package, so I recommend that you buy your beans either in bulk from a retailer who sells them loose by the pound or at a supermarket that has a high turnover.

A good indicator as to whether dried beans are fresh is their appearance. They should be well shaped and not shriveled, always whole and never cracked. They should also be bright in color and shiny. If not, purchase them elsewhere.

To Soak or Not to Soak? That Is the Question

There are many theories about whether, and for how long, you should soak dried beans before you cook them. Soaking beans gets them hydrating sooner. Because you can never be certain how old the beans are, I recommend that you always soak them before cooking for the best results and to sort of give them a jump-start. I share with you the two most commonly used soaking methods in the following sections.

I personally think that the flavor and texture are better when beans are well hydrated overnight before being cooked, but that may just be me. Nevertheless, in the event that you don't have time to soak the beans by either of the following methods, you can and should still cook them. Cook them as the recipe calls for, although you'll probably have to increase the cooking time by 5 to 10 minutes, depending on the type of bean and how old it is.

Regardless of whether you soak the beans or which soaking method you choose, always pick through the dried beans to remove any foreign particles, such as pebbles, dirt, or twigs, and then rinse them in a colander with cold water.

Overnight soaking

Use the overnight soak method if you want beans the next day. Place the beans in a large bowl. Pour in enough room-temperature water to cover the beans by about 2 inches. Let them sit overnight. The next day, drain the beans and cook them.

Quick soaking

The quick-soak method is best when you're short on time, but you still have an hour for the beans to hydrate. Place the beans in a pressure cooker or another large pot. Add enough water to cover the beans by 2 inches. Bring the water to a boil over high heat. Boil as you normally would boil water, not under pressure. Boil for 2 minutes. Remove from the heat and let the beans sit for 1 hour to hydrate. Drain the beans and cook them.

Getting the Hang of Cooking Beans

Because all beans are different, even within the same type, providing exact cooking times is difficult. (For approximate cooking times, see Appendix A.) The times I provide in this chapter's recipes are approximate, based on my years of experience. The type, brand, and age of the beans used determines how long the beans need to cook. If the beans aren't tender enough after you cook them for the amount of time a recipe specifies, simply cook them a couple minutes longer under pressure until you're satisfied.

Table 10-1 tells you approximately how many cups of cooked beans you can expect to get for each cup of dried beans that you cook. A good general rule when cooking dried, soaked beans is to use 2 cups of water for each cup of dried beans.

Table 10-1	Cooked Yields of Dried Beans and Legumes	
Food	**Uncooked (dry)**	**Cooked**
Azuki beans	1 cup	2 cups
Black beans	1 cup	2 cups
Black-eyed peas	1 cup	2¼ cups
Chickpeas (garbanzos)	1 cup	2½ cups
Cranberry beans	1 cup	2¼ cups
Gandules (pigeon peas)	1 cup	3 cups
Great Northern beans	1 cup	2¼ cups
Kidney beans, red or white	1 cup	2 cups
Lentils, green, brown, or red	1 cup	2 cups
Navy or pea beans	1 cup	2 cups
Peas, split green or yellow	1 cup	2 cups
Pinto beans	1 cup	2¼ cups

Beans have a tendency to foam when cooking. Therefore, never fill the pressure cooker more than half full when cooking dried beans. Foam created by the cooking beans floats to the top of the pot. It's possible for small pieces of bean skin or other small particles to float up with the foam and block one of the safety valves. Even though your pressure cooker is 100 percent safe to use, for maximum benefit and use, you never want to block any of the valves.

You can add a tablespoon of oil to the water to reduce the foaming that beans often cause.

I recommend using the cold-water release method when the beans are done cooking. This method, which I describe in Chapter 4, eliminates sputtering and foaming of cooking liquid out of the pressure regulator valve or vent pipe, which may occur if you use a quick-release method.

Never add salt to the soaking or cooking water when initially preparing beans. Salt inhibits the capability of the skin to soften, making for a tough, not-too-tender bean. Always season the beans after they're done cooking. Like little sponges, they'll absorb the salt quite quickly and be flavorful.

A Potful of Beans Is a Cook's Best Friend

Beans can be used in preparing all types of dishes, including dips, soups, stews, and chili. They're a cook's best friend and the best convenience food I know. A batch of cooked beans in the refrigerator means that dinner's just minutes away from being served.

Even though beans are available in cans, I prefer cooked, dried beans whenever possible. To save time, however, beans can be prepared beforehand and used when needed. For example, cook up a pound or two, season with salt, and store them in their cooking liquid in the fridge for up to a week.

To get you started, I provide two master recipes — the Master Bean Recipe and the Master Chickpea Recipe — for cooking beans in the pressure cooker. I also give you 11 quick and easy nonpressure-cooker recipes that call for 2 to 4 cups of cooked beans made from one or the other of the master recipes. The following list tells you which of the nonpressure-cooker recipes call for which master recipe:

- ✔ Use the beans from the Master Bean Recipe to prepare the Tuscan Bean Salad, Pasta Fazool, Italian Sausages and Beans, Black Beans and Rice, Refried Beans, Prairie Fire Bean Dip, and Bean Burritos with Fresh Tomato Salsa.

- ✔ Use the beans from the Master Chickpea Recipe to prepare the Spicy Indian Chickpea Stew, Three-Bean Salad, Garlicky Chickpeas and Cabbage Soup, and Hummus.

I also give you several recipes for bean dishes that you can prepare in your pressure cooker, including bean-heavy soups and chilis.

Master Bean Recipe

Prep time: 5 min, plus soaking time • **Cook time:** 12 min under pressure • **Yield:** About 4–5 cups

Ingredients	*Directions*
2 cups (1 pound) dried kidney beans, pinto beans, or black beans, picked over	*1* Rinse the beans in a colander under cold water. Soak the beans.
1 medium onion, whole, peeled	*2* Place the beans in a pressure cooker. Add the onion, garlic, green bell pepper, bay leaf, and water.
1 clove garlic, peeled	
½ green bell pepper, cored, seeded, and cut in half	*3* Cover and bring to high pressure over high heat. Lower the heat to stabilize the pressure. Cook for 12 minutes. (*For Electric:* Select high pressure and set the timer for 12 minutes.)
1 bay leaf	
4 cups water	
Salt to taste	*4* Remove from the heat. Release the pressure with a quick-release method.
	5 Unlock and remove the cover. Taste the beans. If they're still hard, return to Step 3 and cook for an additional 2 to 4 minutes or until tender.
	6 Remove and discard the onion, garlic, green bell pepper, and bay leaf. Season with salt.
	7 If not using the cooked beans right away, store them in their cooking liquid, in a covered container in the refrigerator, up to a week.

Per serving (1 cup): Calories 298 (From Fat 11); Fat 1g (Saturated 0g); Cholesterol 0mg; Sodium 151mg; Carbohydrate 55g (Dietary Fiber 15g); Protein 20g.

Note: This recipe is vegetarian, vegan, gluten-free, and dairy-free.

Tuscan Bean Salad

Prep time: 15 min • **Yield:** 4 servings

Ingredients	Directions
Center heart of a bunch of celery, light yellow part only, with leaves	*1* Remove all the pale yellow leaves from the celery ribs and finely mince. Slice the celery into thin pieces. Place in a large mixing bowl with the cooked beans and tomatoes. Set aside.
4 cups cooked white kidney beans, cooled to room temperature	
1 pint cherry or grape tomatoes	*2* Heat the olive oil in a small skillet over medium heat. Add the garlic. Cook until golden brown and crisp, taking care not to burn it. Pour the oil and garlic over the beans and tomatoes.
4 tablespoons olive oil	
5 large cloves garlic, peeled and very thinly sliced	
4 tablespoons sherry or red wine vinegar	*3* Add the vinegar and oregano. Toss well. Season with salt and pepper.
1 teaspoon dried oregano, crumbled	*4* Line a serving plate with a few lettuce leaves. Spoon the bean salad on top of the lettuce and serve.
Salt and pepper to taste	
Boston or leaf lettuce	

Per serving: Calories 370 (From Fat 132); Fat 15g (Saturated 2g); Cholesterol 0mg; Sodium 176mg; Carbohydrate 47g (Dietary Fiber 13g); Protein 16g.

Note: This recipe is vegetarian, vegan, gluten-free, and dairy-free.

Pasta Fazool

Prep time: 10 min • **Cook time:** 4 min • **Yield:** 4 servings

Ingredients	*Directions*
3 tablespoons olive oil	*1* Heat the olive oil in a pressure cooker over medium-high heat. Add the onion and garlic. Cook until the onion is soft. Add the tomato, carrot, celery, oregano, 1½ teaspoons salt, and ¼ teaspoon pepper. Cook for 2 minutes. Add the beans and stock. Stir well. (*For Electric:* Select the Brown setting.)
1 small onion, chopped	
1 clove garlic, crushed	
1 plum tomato, fresh or canned, coarsely chopped	
1 carrot, diced small	*2* Cover and bring to high pressure over high heat. Lower the heat to stabilize the pressure. Cook for 4 minutes. (*For Electric:* Select high pressure and set the timer for 4 minutes.)
1 stalk celery, diced small	
1 teaspoon dried oregano	
1½ teaspoons salt	
¼ teaspoon pepper	*3* Remove from the heat. Release the pressure with a quick-release method.
2 cups cooked white kidney or pinto beans	
4 cups chicken or vegetable stock	*4* Unlock and remove the cover. Season with salt and pepper to taste.
Salt and pepper to taste	
8 ounces dried ditalini (small, tube-shaped pasta), cooked al dente	*5* Add the cooked ditalini. Stir and scoop into serving bowls.
Extra-virgin olive oil and grated pecorino Romano or Parmesan cheese	*6* Drizzle each serving with the olive oil. Serve with the cheese.

Per serving: Calories 510 (From Fat 123); Fat 14g (Saturated 2g); Cholesterol 18mg; Sodium 983mg; Carbohydrate 75g (Dietary Fiber 10g); Protein 22g.

Vary It! To make this a vegetarian recipe, use vegetable stock rather than chicken stock. For a gluten-free recipe, in place of the dried ditalini pasta, use a small, similarly shaped, gluten-free pasta. For a vegan or dairy-free version, substitute vegetable stock for the chicken stock and use a soy-based product for the cheese.

Italian Sausages and Beans

Prep time: 5 min • **Cook time:** 25 min • **Yield:** 4 servings

Ingredients	Directions
2 tablespoons olive oil	*1* Heat the olive oil over medium-high heat in a deep 10- or 12-inch covered skillet. Add the garlic and cook for 1 minute. Add the sausage links. Brown on both sides. Prick the sausage links with a fork.
4 cloves garlic, crushed	
8 links Italian sausage with fennel, sweet or hot	
½ cup water	*2* Add the water. Cover and cook for 5 to 8 minutes or until the sausage is no longer pink in the center. Remove the cover and cook over high heat until the water evaporates.
½ cup red or white wine	
One 14½-ounce can or 2 cups diced tomatoes, coarsely chopped	*3* Add the wine and cook for 1 minute over medium heat. Add the tomatoes and beans. Cover and cook for 15 minutes. Season with salt and pepper. Sprinkle with the parsley before serving.
4 cups cooked white kidney or pinto beans	
Salt and black pepper to taste	
2 tablespoons minced flat-leaf parsley	

Per serving: Calories 498 (From Fat 203); Fat 23g (Saturated 6g); Cholesterol 45mg; Sodium 814mg; Carbohydrate 47g (Dietary Fiber 13g); Protein 28g.

Note: This is a gluten- and dairy-free recipe.

Vary It! For a vegetarian or vegan version of this recipe, substitute veggie sausage links for the pork sausage. Proceed from Step 1 directly to Step 3, skipping Step 2.

Black Beans and Rice with Pickled Red Onions

Prep time: 5 min • **Cook time:** 25 min • **Yield:** 4 servings

Ingredients	Directions
3 tablespoons olive oil	**1** Heat the olive oil in a large, deep skillet over medium heat. Add the bell pepper, onion, and garlic and cook until soft. Add the cumin and oregano and cook for 1 minute longer.
1 green bell pepper, cored, seeded, and finely chopped	
1 large onion, minced	
6 cloves garlic, minced	**2** Add the beans and stock. Lower the heat to a simmer and cook, covered, for 15 minutes. Mash some of the beans against the side of the skillet to thicken the cooking liquid. Season with salt and pepper.
1 teaspoon ground cumin	
1 teaspoon dried oregano	
4 cups cooked black beans	**3** Serve over the white rice. Spoon some of the pickled red onions on top of the beans.
2 cups chicken or vegetable stock	
Salt and black pepper to taste	
2 cups cooked white rice	
Pickled Red Onions (see the following recipe)	

Pickled Red Onions

1 large red onion, cut in half and very thinly sliced	**1** Combine the onion, lime juice, olive oil, and cilantro leaves in a small serving bowl. Season with salt and black pepper.
Juice from 2 fresh limes	
3 tablespoons olive oil	**2** Let sit at room temperature for at least 30 minutes before serving.
4 sprigs cilantro, leaves only, coarsely chopped	
Salt and pepper to taste	

Per serving: Calories 529 (From Fat 168); Fat 19g (Saturated 3g); Cholesterol 3mg; Sodium 724mg; Carbohydrate 73g (Dietary Fiber 17g); Protein 19g.

Note: This recipe is dairy-free. For a gluten-free, vegetarian, or vegan version, choose vegetable stock rather than chicken stock.

Refried Beans

Prep time: 5 min • **Cook time:** 15 min • **Yield:** About 3 cups

Ingredients	Directions
2 tablespoons olive oil **1 large onion, minced** **1 clove garlic, minced** **4 cups cooked red kidney or pinto beans, drained, 1 cup cooking liquid reserved** **1 teaspoon dried marjoram leaves** **Salt and pepper to taste**	*1* Heat the olive oil over medium-high heat in a large skillet. Add the onion and garlic and cook until soft. *2* Add the beans, marjoram, and ½ cup of the cooking liquid. Over low heat, begin to gently mash the beans with the back of a large kitchen spoon or potato masher. *3* Continue cooking, stirring continuously, until you obtain a thick, somewhat creamy mixture that begins to pull away from the sides of the pan. If the mixture appears too dry, add additional cooking liquid, a couple tablespoons at a time. *4* Season with salt and pepper.

Per serving (½ cup): Calories 201 (From Fat 46); Fat 5g (Saturated 1g); Cholesterol 0mg; Sodium 100mg; Carbohydrate 29g (Dietary Fiber 8g); Protein 11g.

Note: This recipe is vegetarian, vegan, gluten-free, and dairy-free.

Tip: Most recipes for refried beans are made with lard; however, I've found olive oil to be a good, healthy substitute.

Tip: Serve these beans as a side dish or use them in the following recipes for Prairie Fire Bean Dip or Bean Burritos with Fresh Tomato Salsa.

Prairie Fire Bean Dip

Prep time: 5 min • **Cook time:** 15 min • **Yield:** About 4 cups

Ingredients	*Directions*
4 ounces deli provolone or Asiago cheese, shredded	**1** Add the cheese, butter, chiles, onion, and garlic to the refried beans.
4 tablespoons butter or margarine, cut into small cubes	**2** Cook over low heat, stirring continuously until the cheese and butter are melted.
One 3½-ounce can roasted jalapeños or green chiles, chopped, 1 teaspoon juice reserved	**3** Serve dip hot with tortilla chips or crackers.
2 tablespoons minced onion	
1 clove garlic, minced	
About 3 cups refried beans, still hot in the skillet	
Tortilla chips or crackers	

Per serving (¼ cup): *Calories 130 (From Fat 63); Fat 7g (Saturated 3g); Cholesterol 14mg; Sodium 143mg; Carbohydrate 12g (Dietary Fiber 4g); Protein 6g.*

Note: This recipe is vegetarian and gluten-free.

Bean Burritos with Fresh Tomato Salsa

Prep time: 10 min • **Cook time:** 15–20 min • **Yield:** 6 burritos

Ingredients	*Directions*
About 3 cups refried beans	*1* Preheat the oven to 400 degrees. Spoon approximately ½ cup refried beans down the center one-third of a tortilla, stopping 1 inch from the top and bottom edges. Sprinkle with 2 tablespoons of cheese and a couple jalapeño slices, if desired.
Six 10-inch flour tortillas	
1¼ cups shredded sharp cheddar cheese	
Pickled jalapeño slices (optional)	*2* Fold about 1 inch of the bottom and the top of the tortilla over the filling. Roll the filling into the tortilla. Place the burritos on a baking pan.
Fresh Tomato Salsa (see the following recipe)	*3* Cover with foil and bake until the filling is heated through and the cheese melts, approximately 15 to 20 minutes.
Sour cream (optional)	
	4 Carefully remove with a spatula to serving plates. Serve with Fresh Tomato Salsa and/or, if desired, the sour cream.

Fresh Tomato Salsa

2 large ripe tomatoes, cut into eighths	*1* Place the tomatoes, scallions, garlic, cilantro, and lime juice in a food processor bowl or blender jar. Pulse 2 or 3 times until finely chopped. Do not puree.
2 scallions, white and light green parts only, cut into eighths	
2 cloves garlic, peeled and quartered	*2* Season with salt and hot sauce.
8 sprigs cilantro, leaves only	
1 tablespoon lime juice	
Salt and hot sauce to taste	

Per serving: Calories 546 (From Fat 164); Fat 18g (Saturated 7g); Cholesterol 25mg; Sodium 494mg; Carbohydrate 74g (Dietary Fiber 11g); Protein 24g.

Note: This recipe is vegetarian.

Master Chickpea Recipe

Prep time: 5 min, plus soaking time • **Cook time:** 25 min under pressure • **Yield:** About 5 cups

Ingredients	Directions
2 cups (1 pound) dried chickpeas, picked over	*1* Rinse the chickpeas in a colander under cold water. Soak the chickpeas.
1 medium onion, peeled	
6 dried cloves	*2* Place the chickpeas in a pressure cooker. Stick the onion with the cloves. Add the onion with cloves, garlic, bay leaf, and water.
2 cloves garlic, peeled	
1 bay leaf	*3* Cover and bring to high pressure over high heat. Lower the heat to stabilize the pressure. Cook for 25 minutes. (*For Electric:* Select high pressure and set the timer for 25 minutes.)
4 cups water	
Salt to taste	
	4 Remove from the heat. Release the pressure with the cold-water-release method. Taste the beans. If they're still hard, return to Step 3 and cook them for an additional 2 to 3 minutes.
	5 Remove and discard the onion, garlic, and bay leaf. Season with salt.

Per serving (½ cup): Calories 140 (From Fat 19); Fat 3g (Saturated 0g); Cholesterol 0mg; Sodium 64mg; Carbohydrate 23g (Dietary Fiber 6g); Protein 7g.

Note: This recipe is vegetarian, vegan, gluten-free, and dairy-free.

The chickpea: Neither chicken nor pea

Chickpeas have been a dietary staple for more than 7,000 years. Originally grown in Asia, they were spread throughout the Mediterranean region by the Phoenicians and brought to the Americas by the Spanish. These round, golden beans maintain their shape well when cooked. They're a favorite in soups, stews, salads, and dips, so it's well worth having a batch on hand in the refrigerator.

Spicy Indian Chickpea Stew

Prep time: 5 min • **Cook time:** 15 min • **Yield:** 4 servings

Ingredients	Directions
2 tablespoons olive oil	**1** Heat the olive oil in a large skillet over medium-high heat. Add the onion and garlic and cook until soft. Add the coriander, cumin, turmeric, and cayenne pepper. Cook for 1 minute.
1 medium onion, chopped	
1 clove garlic, minced	
1 teaspoon ground coriander	
½ teaspoon ground cumin	**2** Stir in the chickpeas, salt, and black pepper. Cook until the chickpeas are heated through.
⅛ teaspoon turmeric	
Pinch of cayenne pepper	**3** Remove from the heat and stir in the lemon juice and cilantro. Serve with basmati rice.
2 cups cooked chickpeas	
½ teaspoon salt	
¼ teaspoon black pepper	
1 teaspoon freshly squeezed lemon juice	
2 tablespoons minced cilantro	
Cooked basmati rice	

Per serving: Calories 207 (From Fat 82); Fat 9g (Saturated 1g); Cholesterol 0mg; Sodium 298mg; Carbohydrate 25g (Dietary Fiber 7g); Protein 8g.

Note: This recipe is vegetarian, vegan, gluten-free, and dairy-free.

Three-Bean Salad

Prep time: 5 min, plus marinating time • **Yield:** 8 servings

Ingredients	Directions
2 cups cooked red kidney beans	*1* Combine the kidney beans, chickpeas, green beans, green bell pepper, and onion together in a large storage container or glass jar.
2 cups cooked chickpeas	
1 pound green beans, cut into 1-inch pieces and cooked	*2* Whisk together the vegetable oil, vinegar, sugar, salt, and black pepper.
1 small green bell pepper, cored, seeded, and finely chopped	
1 small onion, finely chopped	*3* Pour the vinaigrette over the beans and toss. Cover and refrigerate for 24 hours before serving.
¼ cup vegetable oil	
⅓ cup white vinegar	
¼ cup sugar	
½ teaspoon salt	
¼ teaspoon black pepper	

Per serving: Calories 230 (From Fat 74); Fat 8g (Saturated 1g); Cholesterol 0mg; Sodium 151mg; Carbohydrate 33g (Dietary Fiber 8g); Protein 9g.

Note: This recipe is vegetarian, vegan, gluten-free, and dairy-free.

Garlicky Chickpeas and Cabbage Soup

Prep time: 10 min • **Cook time:** 6 min under pressure • **Yield:** 6 servings

Ingredients	*Directions*
3 tablespoons olive oil	*1* Heat the olive oil in a pressure cooker over medium heat. Add the garlic and cook for 1 to 2 minutes or until golden. Add the cabbage and cook for 5 minutes. Add the chickpeas, tomato sauce, water, 1 teaspoon salt, and ¼ teaspoon pepper. (*For Electric:* Select the Brown setting.)
8 cloves garlic, minced	
4 cups shredded, cored green cabbage	
4 cups cooked chickpeas	
One 15-ounce can tomato sauce	*2* Cover and bring to high pressure over high heat. Lower the heat to stabilize the pressure. Cook for 6 minutes. (*For Electric:* Select high pressure and set the timer for 6 minutes.)
3 cups water	
1 teaspoon salt	
¼ teaspoon pepper	*3* Remove from the heat. Release the pressure with a quick-release method.
Salt and pepper to taste	
	4 Unlock and remove the cover. Season with salt and pepper to taste.

Per serving: Calories 278 (From Fat 89); Fat 10g (Saturated 1g); Cholesterol 0mg; Sodium 833mg; Carbohydrate 39g (Dietary Fiber 11g); Protein 12g.

Note: This recipe is vegetarian, vegan, gluten-free, and dairy-free.

Shredding Cabbage

First, cut the cabbage into halves, then into quarters. Start with one quarter.

Put the round side down on the cutting board and hold it by the pointed side of the wedge.

Use a big, sharp knife and cut thin slices along the angle of the wedge.

Illustration by Elizabeth Kurtzman

Hummus

Prep time: 5 min • **Yield:** About 2 cups

Ingredients	*Directions*
2 cups cooked chickpeas	*1* Place all the ingredients in a food processor bowl.
4 tablespoons olive oil	
3 tablespoons freshly squeezed lemon juice	*2* Process until smooth, scraping down the sides of the bowl. Add additional lemon juice if the hummus is too thick.
1 teaspoon salt	
1 clove garlic, quartered	
½ cup flat-leaf parsley, leaves only	

Per serving (¼ cup): Calories 130 (From Fat 71); Fat 8g (Saturated 1g); Cholesterol 0mg; Sodium 296mg; Carbohydrate 12g (Dietary Fiber 3g); Protein 4g.

Note: This recipe is vegetarian, vegan, gluten-free, and dairy-free.

Tip: Serve with toasted pita triangles, French bread, or vegetable crudités. Or, make pita pocket sandwiches by filling the pitas with hummus, chopped tomatoes, and shredded lettuce.

Black Bean and Vegetable Soup

Prep time: 10 min, plus soaking time • **Cook time:** 24 min under pressure • **Yield:** 8 servings

Ingredients	*Directions*
2 cups (1 pound) black beans, picked over	*1* Rinse the beans in a colander under cold water. Soak the beans.
2 tablespoons olive oil	*2* Heat the olive oil in a pressure cooker over medium-high heat. Add the onion, garlic, and bell pepper. Cook until the onion is soft. Add the cumin, paprika, and oregano. Cook for 1 minute. Add the tomatoes and cook for 2 minutes. Add the beans, bay leaf, and stock. (*For Electric:* Select the Brown setting.)
1 large onion, chopped	
2 cloves garlic, minced	
1 red bell pepper, cored, seeded, and diced small	
1 teaspoon ground cumin	*3* Cover and bring to high pressure over high heat. Lower the heat to stabilize the pressure. Cook for 20 minutes. (*For Electric:* Select high pressure and set the timer for 20 minutes.)
1 teaspoon paprika	
1 teaspoon dried oregano	
One 14½-ounce can diced tomatoes	*4* Remove from the heat. Release the pressure with a quick-release method. Unlock and remove the cover. Taste the beans. If they're still hard, return to Step 3 and cook them for an additional 2 to 3 minutes.
1 bay leaf	
7 cups chicken stock, vegetable stock, or water	
3 carrots, diced	*5* Remove and discard the bay leaf. Remove 4 cups of the beans with broth and puree in a blender. Return to the pressure cooker. Add the carrots, celery, and corn. Cover and bring to high pressure over high heat. Lower the heat to stabilize the pressure. Cook for 4 minutes. (*For Electric:* Select high pressure and set the timer for 4 minutes.)
2 stalks celery, diced	
1 cup fresh or frozen corn kernels	
Salt and black pepper to taste	
Sour cream (optional)	
	6 Remove from the heat. Release the pressure with a quick-release method. Unlock and remove the cover. Season with the salt and black pepper. If desired, serve with a dollop of sour cream.

Per serving: Calories 278 (From Fat 71); Fat 8g (Saturated 2g); Cholesterol 4mg; Sodium 1,045mg; Carbohydrate 41g (Dietary Fiber 13g); Protein 13g.

Note: This recipe is gluten-free.

Vary It! To make this recipe vegetarian, use vegetable stock or water; to make it dairy-free, use vegan sour cream for serving. For a vegan recipe, do both.

Senate Bean Soup

Prep time: 15 min, plus soaking time • **Cook time:** 15 min under pressure • **Yield:** About 4 servings

Ingredients	*Directions*
1 pound navy beans, picked over	*1* Rinse the beans in a colander under cold water. Soak the beans.
2 tablespoons vegetable oil	
1 large onion, chopped	*2* Heat the vegetable oil in a pressure cooker over medium-high heat. Add the onion and cook until soft and golden brown. Add the beans, ham hock, carrot, celery, and water. (*For Electric:* Select the Brown setting.)
1 smoked ham hock	
1 carrot, peeled and chopped	
1 stalk celery, chopped	*3* Cover and bring to high pressure over high heat. Lower the heat to stabilize the pressure. Cook for 15 minutes. (*For Electric:* Select high pressure and set the timer for 15 minutes.)
6 cups water	
Salt and pepper to taste	
	4 Remove from the heat. Release the pressure with a quick-release method.
	5 Unlock and remove the cover. Taste the beans. If they're still hard, return to Step 3 and cook them for 2 to 3 minutes longer.
	6 Remove the skin and meat from the ham hock. Discard the skin and bones. Chop up the meat and add it to the beans.
	7 Roughly mash the beans with a potato masher until the soup is thick but lumpy. Season with salt and pepper.

Per serving: *Calories 499 (From Fat 104); Fat 12g (Saturated 2g); Cholesterol 14mg; Sodium 183mg; Carbohydrate 75g (Dietary Fiber 18g); Protein 27g.*

Note: This recipe is gluten-free and dairy-free.

Vary It! For a vegetarian or vegan version of this recipe, substitute 2 links of veggie chorizo sausage for the smoked ham hock. Dice the sausage before serving the soup.

Drunken Beans

Prep time: 5 min, plus soaking time • **Cook time:** 20 min under pressure • **Yield:** 8 servings

Ingredients	*Directions*
2 cups (1 pound) dried black or pinto beans, picked over	*1* Rinse the beans in a colander under cold water. Soak the beans.
1 large onion, chopped	
2 cloves garlic, minced	*2* Place the beans in a pressure cooker. Add the onion, garlic, water, and beer.
2½ cups water	
One 12-ounce can beer	*3* Cover and bring to high pressure over high heat. Lower the heat to stabilize the pressure. Cook for 15 minutes. (*For Electric:* Select high pressure and set the timer for 15 minutes.)
One 14½-ounce can Mexican-style diced tomatoes with jalapeño	
1 tablespoon chili powder	*4* Remove from the heat. Release the pressure with a quick-release method. Unlock and remove the cover. Taste the beans. If they're still hard, return to Step 3 and cook the beans for an additional 2 to 3 minutes.
3 teaspoons ground cumin	
2 teaspoons salt	
½ cup prepared barbecue sauce	*5* Add the tomatoes, chili powder, ground cumin, 2 teaspoons salt, and barbecue sauce.
Salt to taste	
	6 Cover and bring to high pressure over high heat. Lower the heat to stabilize the pressure. Cook for 5 minutes. (*For Electric:* Select high pressure and set the timer for 5 minutes.)
	7 Remove from the heat. Release the pressure with a quick-release method. Unlock and remove the cover. Mash some of the beans against the side of the pressure cooker to thicken the cooking liquid. Season with salt.

Per serving: Calories 190 (From Fat 12); Fat 1g (Saturated 0g); Cholesterol 0mg; Sodium 1,032mg; Carbohydrate 34g (Dietary Fiber 11g); Protein 11g.

Note: This recipe is vegetarian, vegan, and dairy-free.

Vary It! For a gluten-free version, substitute 12 ounces of broth for the beer and use gluten-free barbecue sauce.

N'awlins Red Beans and Rice

Prep time: 15 min, plus soaking time • **Cook time:** 16 min under pressure • **Yield:** 8 servings

Ingredients	Directions
2 cups (1 pound) dried red kidney beans, picked over	**1** Rinse the beans in a colander under cold water. Soak the beans.
2 tablespoons olive oil	**2** Heat the olive oil in a pressure cooker over medium-high heat. Add the onion and garlic. Cook until the onion is soft. Add the carrots, celery, tomatoes, hot sauce, and bay leaf. Cook for 2 minutes. Add the beans, ham hock, and water. (*For Electric:* Select the Brown setting.)
1 large onion, chopped	
4 cloves garlic, minced	
2 carrots, peeled and finely chopped	
2 stalks celery, finely chopped	**3** Cover and bring to high pressure over high heat. Lower the heat to stabilize the pressure. Cook for 15 minutes. (*For Electric:* Select high pressure and set the timer for 15 minutes.)
One 14½-ounce can diced tomatoes	
1 teaspoon hot sauce	
1 bay leaf	**4** Remove from the heat. Release the pressure with a quick-release method. Unlock and remove the cover. Taste the beans. If they're still hard, return to Step 3 and cook them for an additional 2 to 3 minutes.
1 smoked ham hock	
4 cups water	
Salt and pepper to taste	
½ pound smoked andouille sausage or smoked kielbasa, thinly sliced	**5** Season with salt and pepper. Add the sausage. Cover and bring to high pressure over high heat. Lower the heat to stabilize the pressure. Cook for 1 minute. (*For Electric:* Select high pressure and set the timer for 1 minute.) Remove from the heat. Release the pressure with a quick-release method.
3 cups cooked white rice	
	6 Unlock and remove the cover. Remove the skin and meat from the ham hock. Discard the skin and bone. Chop the meat and add to the beans. Remove and discard the bay leaf. Mash some of the beans with a spoon against the side of the pressure cooker to thicken the cooking liquid.
	7 Taste and adjust for salt and pepper. Serve with the white rice.

Per serving: Calories 425 (From Fat 16); Fat 5g (Saturated 5g); Cholesterol 39mg; Sodium 489mg; Carbohydrate 50g (Dietary Fiber 9g); Protein 21g.

Note: This recipe is gluten-free and dairy-free.

Tailgate Chili

Prep time: 25 min, plus soaking time • **Cook time:** 15 min under pressure • **Yield:** 8 servings

Ingredients	*Directions*
2 cups (1 pound) pinto beans, picked over	*1* Rinse the beans in a colander under cold water. Soak the beans.
3 tablespoons olive oil	*2* Heat the olive oil in a pressure cooker over medium-high heat. Add the onion; garlic; green, red, and jalapeño peppers; carrots; and celery. Cook until the onion is soft. Add the chili powder, cumin, and oregano. Stir and cook for 1 minute. (*For Electric:* Select the Brown setting.)
1 large onion, chopped	
2 cloves garlic, minced	
1 large green bell pepper, seeded and chopped	
1 large red bell pepper, seeded and chopped	
1 jalapeño pepper, seeded and chopped	*3* Add the ground beef and cook until no longer pink, breaking up large chunks with a spoon. Add the tomatoes, beans, and water. Stir to combine.
2 carrots, peeled and chopped	*4* Cover and bring to high pressure over high heat. Lower the heat to stabilize the pressure. Cook for 15 minutes. (*For Electric:* Select high pressure and set the timer for 15 minutes.)
2 stalks celery, chopped	
2 tablespoons chili powder	
4 teaspoons ground cumin	
1 teaspoon ground oregano	*5* Remove from the heat. Release the pressure with a quick-release method.
1 pound lean ground beef	
One 28-ounce can crushed tomatoes	*6* Unlock and remove the cover. Taste the beans. If they're still hard, return to Step 3 and cook them for an additional 2 to 3 minutes.
1¾ cups water	
Salt to taste	*7* Season with salt. Serve over the white rice and garnish with the cheddar cheese.
3 cups cooked white rice	
Shredded cheddar cheese	

Per serving: Calories 455 (From Fat 121); Fat 13g (Saturated 4g); Cholesterol 35mg; Sodium 324mg; Carbohydrate 62g (Dietary Fiber 15g); Protein 24g.

Note: This recipe is gluten-free.

Vary It! For a dairy-free version, substitute a soy-based product for the cheddar cheese. For a vegetarian version of the recipe, use 16 ounces meat-flavored seitan, coarsely chopped in a food processor, in place of the ground beef. Make both substitutions for a vegan recipe.

White Bean and Chicken Chili

Prep time: 25 min, plus soaking time • **Cook time:** 15 min under pressure • **Yield:** 8 servings

Ingredients	*Directions*
1 cup white kidney beans, picked over	*1* Rinse the beans in a colander under cold water. Soak the beans.
3 tablespoons olive oil	
1 large onion, chopped	*2* Heat the olive oil in a pressure cooker over medium-high heat. Add the onion and garlic. Cook until the onion is soft. Add the chicken and cook, stirring, until no longer pink. Add the beans, chilies, cumin, and oregano. Cook 2 minutes longer. Add the stock. Stir to combine. (*For Electric:* Select the Brown setting.)
4 cloves garlic, minced	
2 pounds boneless chicken breast, cut into bite-sized pieces	
Two 4.5-ounce cans chopped green chiles, drained	*3* Cover and bring to high pressure over high heat. Lower the heat to stabilize the pressure. Cook for 15 minutes. (*For Electric:* Select high pressure and set the timer for 15 minutes.)
2 teaspoons ground cumin	
2 teaspoons ground oregano	
6 cups chicken or vegetable stock	*4* Remove from the heat. Release the pressure with a quick-release method.
Salt to taste	
1½ cups shredded white cheddar cheese	*5* Unlock and remove the cover. Taste the beans. If they're still hard, return to Step 3 and cook them for an additional 2 to 3 minutes.
½ cup chopped cilantro	
	6 Mash some of the beans with a spoon against the side of the pressure cooker to thicken the cooking liquid. Season with salt. Garnish with the cheddar cheese and cilantro when serving.

Per serving (½ cup): Calories 140 (From Fat 19); Fat 3g (Saturated 0g); Cholesterol 0mg; Sodium 64mg; Carbohydrate 23g (Dietary Fiber 6g); Protein 7g.

Note: This recipe is gluten-free.

Vary It! For a dairy-free version, substitute a soy-based product for the cheddar cheese. To make this recipe vegetarian, use 16 ounces poultry-flavored seitan, cut into bite-sized pieces, in place of the chicken. Make both substitutions for a vegan version of the recipe.

Chapter 11

Vegetables: Nature's Nourishing Bounty

In This Chapter

▶ Using the pressure cooker to save time and preserve nutrients

▶ Making fresh, delicious vegetable side dishes and salads

I've never met a vegetable I didn't like. Each one has its own unique characteristics and taste. Unfortunately, too many people have this thing against these green, yellow, orange, and red foods. Vegetables are full of vitamins and minerals and, when cooked properly, are quite tasty, too! Even a supermarket rotisserie chicken warrants a veggie side dish or two, and this is where your pressure cooker comes in. Why make powdery instant potatoes when in about the same amount of time you can have the real thing, all hot and steaming with a pat of melting butter dripping down the sides? Fresh vegetables and the pressure cooker were made for each other, especially when you're short on time.

Saving Time and Nutrients

Cooking vegetables in a pressure cooker cuts back on the cooking time by 70 percent on average. Vegetables cooked under pressure can also be more nutritious for you. When you cook or steam vegetables in a conventional pot, some of the water-soluble nutrients get washed away. When the vegetables are cooked in a pressure cooker, however, they cook so quickly that they maintain more nutrients and keep their natural, vibrant colors and flavors.

To facilitate things for you, I've compiled a table in Appendix A that gives approximate cooking times for vegetables. The cooking times begin when the pressure cooker reaches high pressure. Remember that most vegetables cook very quickly; if cooked 30 to 60 seconds too long, your crisp broccoli becomes mush! Always err on the side of being underdone. Start with the shortest cooking time; you can always continue cooking under pressure for an additional couple minutes until the desired texture is reached.

Steaming Your Vegetables

Most pressure cookers come with a trivet and steaming basket or rack, all shown in Figure 11-1. These enable you to steam vegetables in a matter of minutes as opposed to boiling them in water the old, conventional way. In fact, with a pressure cooker and steamer basket or rack, you'll never, ever have to cook vegetables by drowning them in boiling water again! If your pressure cooker didn't come with a steaming basket or rack, you can purchase an adjustable stainless-steel one in the gadget section of most housewares stores and some supermarkets. These usually don't require the use of a trivet because, depending on the design, they have their own built-in bases.

To use these nifty accessories, simply pour 2 to 3 cups of water into the pressure-cooker pot. You want the basket or rack sitting just above the water, so gauge the amount accordingly. Place the trivet in the pot. Position the steaming basket on the trivet and add the vegetables. Most steaming racks simply sit on the bottom of the pressure cooker, lip side down, and don't require a trivet. Add the veggies. Start the countdown time for cooking once the pressure cooker reaches and maintains high pressure (see Appendix A).

When you're done cooking, simply remove the vegetables by removing the steaming basket with a potholder and pulling up on the basket handle. If you're using a steaming rack, remove the vegetables with a slotted spoon.

Figure 11-1:
A standard steaming basket, trivet, and rack.

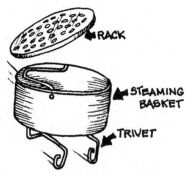

Illustration by Elizabeth Kurtzman

Eat Those Veggies!

Vegetables should be a part of every meal. In fact, you should eat at least seven servings of fruits and vegetables every day for a healthy diet. To help you get going, I share with you some of my favorite vegetable recipes for both hot and cold dishes.

Casseroles are also great when made in the pressure cooker. As an example, I include one of my favorite show-off side dishes — Cauliflower and Broccoli Custard — in this chapter. I used to make this casserole dish in the oven, in a hot water bath (see Chapter 12 for a complete description of hot water baths). One day I was really pressed for time. Because I had begun to make cheesecakes in the pressure cooker and the final "baking" steps really weren't all that different, I decided to come up with a pressure-cooker method for making custard-based casseroles, such as the one in this chapter, as well as a custardy corn pudding and others. The results were excellent, and it was great not having to turn the oven on for a single side dish.

Celebrating the seasons

I'm a true believer of buying what's in season. I also go out of my way to support local agriculture by buying as much and as often as possible from local farmers and farm stands. Even though locally grown produce may be a bit more expensive, the quality and freshness outweigh the cost.

With cherries, a summer fruit, now available in December and oranges in August, some consumers are confused as to what seasonal produce is. The following is a short but concise listing of what's in season and when as far as veggies are concerned. Take note: Some vegetables are considered cool-weather crops and are planted and harvested twice a year, like broccoli and Swiss chard, for example.

✔ **Spring:** Artichokes, asparagus, broccoli, chives, collard greens, fava beans, fennel, green beans, mustard greens, pea pods, snow peas, spinach, spring baby lettuce, sugar snap peas, sweet corn, Swiss chard, Vidalia onions, watercress

✔ **Summer:** Beets, bell peppers, cucumbers, eggplant, garlic, green beans, green peas, lima beans, okra, radishes, summer squash, sweet corn, tomatillos, tomatoes, zucchini

✔ **Fall:** Acorn squash, broccoli, Brussels sprouts, butternut squash, cauliflower, celery root, chayote squash, garlic, kohlrabi, parsnips, pumpkin, rutabagas, sweet potatoes, Swiss chard, turnips, winter squash, yams

✔ **Winter:** Brussels sprouts, cauliflower, kale, leeks, parsnips, potatoes, radicchio, rutabagas, sweet potatoes, turnips, winter squash, yams

Grandma's Mashed Potatoes

Prep time: 10 min • **Cook time:** 7 min under pressure • **Yield:** 4 servings

Ingredients	*Directions*
3 cups water	**1** Pour the water into a pressure cooker. Place the potatoes in a steaming basket and place in the pressure cooker.
4 medium-large russet potatoes, peeled and cut into 1½-inch chunks	**2** Cover and bring to high pressure over high heat. Lower the heat to stabilize the pressure. Cook for 7 minutes. (*For Electric:* Select high pressure and set the timer for 7 minutes.)
¼ to ½ cup milk	
6 tablespoons butter, divided	**3** Remove from the heat. Release the pressure with a quick-release method. Unlock and remove the cover. Taste the potatoes. If they're still hard, return to Step 2 and cook them for an additional 1 to 2 minutes.
Salt and pepper to taste	
	4 Carefully remove the steaming basket with the potatoes. Discard the cooking liquid. Place the milk and 5 tablespoons of the butter in the pressure cooker. Heat the milk, uncovered, over medium-high heat until the butter melts.
	5 Remove from the heat. Add the potatoes and mash, using a hand-held potato masher or an electric mixer, until creamy. Season with salt and pepper.
	6 Spoon into a large serving bowl. Make an indentation on top of the potatoes with a large spoon. Top with the remaining 1 tablespoon butter. Serve immediately.

Per serving: Calories 289 (From Fat 161); Fat 18g (Saturated 11g); Cholesterol 49mg; Sodium 161mg; Carbohydrate 30g (Dietary Fiber 3g); Protein 3g.

Note: This recipe is vegetarian and gluten-free.

Vary It! To make this recipe vegan or dairy-free, use soy milk and substitute vegan margarine for the butter.

Vary It! To make Garlic Mashed Potatoes, add 5 cloves of peeled, crushed garlic along with the raw potatoes. To make Cheddar Cheese and Chives Mashed Potatoes, add ½ cup of grated extra-sharp cheddar cheese and 3 tablespoons of snipped fresh chives before serving.

Mashed Potatoes with Cabbage

Prep time: 20 min • **Cook time:** 11 min under pressure • **Yield:** 6 servings

Ingredients	Directions
3 cups water	**1** Pour the water into a pressure cooker. Place the cabbage in a steaming basket and place in the pressure cooker.
½ small head green cabbage (about 1 pound), cored and coarsely chopped	**2** Cover and bring to high pressure. Lower the heat to stabilize the pressure. Cook for 4 minutes. (*For Electric:* Select high pressure and set the timer for 4 minutes.)
2 pounds (about 4 medium) all-purpose potatoes, peeled and cubed	**3** Remove from the heat. Release the pressure with a quick-release method. Unlock and remove the cover. Carefully remove the steaming basket. Place the cabbage in a bowl and set aside.
4 tablespoons butter	
8 scallions, white and light green parts, thinly sliced	**4** Place the potatoes in the steaming basket and place in the pressure cooker. Cover and bring to high pressure. Lower the heat to stabilize the pressure. Cook for 7 minutes. (*For Electric:* Select high pressure and set the timer for 7 minutes.)
1 cup milk	
Salt and pepper to taste	**5** Remove from the heat. Release the pressure with a quick-release method. Unlock and remove the cover. Taste the potatoes. If they're still hard, return to Step 4 and cook for an additional 1 to 2 minutes.
2 tablespoons minced flat-leaf parsley	**6** Carefully remove the steaming basket. Discard the cooking liquid. Rinse out the pot and dry. Melt the butter over medium heat. Add the scallions and cook until softened but not browned, about 2 minutes.
	7 Reduce the heat to low. Add the cooked potatoes. With a potato masher or fork, mash until smooth. Add the cooked cabbage and milk, stirring until heated through. Season with salt and black pepper. (*For Electric:* Select the Brown setting.)
	8 Spoon into a serving bowl and sprinkle with the parsley.

Per serving: Calories 221 (From Fat 85); Fat 9g (Saturated 6g); Cholesterol 26mg; Sodium 420mg; Carbohydrate 31g (Dietary Fiber 4g); Protein 5g.

Note: This recipe is vegetarian and gluten-free.

Vary It! To make this recipe vegan or dairy-free, use soy milk and substitute vegan margarine for the butter.

Warm French-Style Potato Salad

Prep time: 15 min • **Cook time:** 7 min under pressure • **Yield:** 4 servings

Ingredients	Directions
1½ cups dry white wine	**1** Combine the white wine, vinegar, and 1 teaspoon salt in the pressure cooker. Add the potatoes.
¼ cup white wine vinegar	
1 teaspoon salt	**2** Cover and bring to high pressure. Lower the heat to stabilize the pressure. Cook for 7 minutes. (*For Electric:* Select high pressure and set the timer for 7 minutes.)
2 pounds small red or new potatoes, scrubbed well and pricked twice with a fork	
4 tablespoons extra-virgin olive oil	**3** Remove from the heat. Release the pressure with a quick-release method.
2 tablespoons chopped flat-leaf parsley	**4** Unlock and remove the cover. Taste the potatoes. If they're still hard, return to Step 2 and cook for an additional 1 to 2 minutes.
Salt and pepper to taste	
4 scallions, white and green parts, thinly sliced	**5** Carefully remove the potatoes with a slotted spoon to a colander. Quarter the potatoes and place in a large bowl.
	6 Bring the cooking liquid to a boil and reduce by half. Pour into a small mixing bowl. Add the olive oil and parsley. Whisk together. Season with salt and pepper. Pour over the potatoes. Add the scallions and toss gently. (*For Electric:* Select the Brown setting.)

Per serving: Calories 281 (From Fat 124); Fat 14g (Saturated 2g); Cholesterol 0mg; Sodium 738mg; Carbohydrate 32g (Dietary Fiber 5g); Protein 6g.

Note: This recipe is vegetarian, vegan, gluten-free, and dairy-free.

Candied Sweet Potatoes

Prep time: 10 min • **Cook time:** 7 min under pressure • **Yield:** 8 servings

Ingredients	*Directions*
2 strips orange peel	*1* Place the orange peel in the bottom of a pressure cooker. Add the sweet potato slices in three layers, sprinkling each layer with one-third of the brown sugar and cinnamon, ending with a final layer of brown sugar and cinnamon. Sprinkle with salt and drizzle with the orange juice. Dot with the butter.
3 pounds small sweet potatoes, peeled and cut into ½-inch-thick slices	
¾ cup packed light brown sugar	*2* Cover and bring to high pressure over high heat. Lower the heat to stabilize the pressure. Cook for 7 minutes. (*For Electric:* Select high pressure and set the timer for 7 minutes.)
¾ teaspoon ground cinnamon	
Pinch of salt	*3* Remove from the heat. Release the pressure with a quick-release method.
1 cup orange juice	
1 tablespoon butter, softened	*4* Unlock and remove the cover. Taste the sweet potatoes. If they're still hard, return to Step 2 and cook for an additional 1 to 2 minutes.
	5 Carefully remove the candied sweet potatoes with a spatula to a serving bowl. Discard the orange peel.
	6 Bring the cooking liquid in the pressure cooker to a boil, and cook until the liquid is reduced by half. Pour the syrup over the yams. (*For Electric:* Select the Brown setting.)

Per serving: Calories 141 (From Fat 14); Fat 2g (Saturated 1g); Cholesterol 4mg; Sodium 30mg; Carbohydrate 32g (Dietary Fiber 1g); Protein 1g.

Note: This recipe is vegetarian, vegan, gluten-free, and dairy-free.

Mashed Butternut Squash and Parsnips

Prep time: 10 min • **Cook time:** 5 min under pressure • **Yield:** 8 servings

Ingredients	*Directions*
3 cups water	*1* Place the steaming basket and water in the pressure cooker. Place the parsnips and squash in the steaming basket.
1 pound parsnips, peeled and cut into 1-inch chunks	
2 pounds butternut squash, seeded, peeled, and cut into 1-inch chunks	*2* Cover and bring to high pressure over high heat. Lower the heat to stabilize the pressure. Cook for 5 minutes. (*For Electric:* Select high pressure and set the timer for 5 minutes.)
½ cup milk	
4 tablespoons butter	*3* Remove from the heat. Release the pressure with a quick-release method. Unlock and remove the cover. Taste the vegetables. If they're still hard, return to Step 2 and cook for an additional 1 to 2 minutes.
2 tablespoons light brown sugar	
Salt and pepper to taste	
	4 Carefully remove the steaming basket with the vegetables. Discard the cooking liquid.
	5 Place the milk, butter, and brown sugar in the pressure cooker. Heat, uncovered, over medium-high heat until the butter melts. Remove from the heat. (*For Electric:* Select the Brown setting.)
	6 Add the vegetables and mash, using a hand-held potato masher or electric mixer, until creamy. Season with salt and pepper. Serve immediately.

Per serving: Calories 160 (From Fat 58); Fat 6g (Saturated 4g); Cholesterol 17mg; Sodium 90mg; Carbohydrate 26g (Dietary Fiber 5g); Protein 3g.

Note: This recipe is vegetarian and gluten-free.

Vary It! To make this recipe vegan or dairy-free, use soy milk and substitute vegan margarine for the butter.

Carrots and Onions

Prep time: 15 min • **Cook time:** 2 min under pressure • **Yield:** 4 servings

Ingredients	*Directions*
3 cups water **2 pounds of the smallest baby carrots you can find** **1 pint white pearl onions, peeled** **2 tablespoons butter** **2 tablespoons light brown sugar** **Salt and pepper to taste** **1 tablespoon snipped fresh dill**	*1* Pour the water into a pressure cooker. Place the carrots and onions in a steaming basket and place in the pressure cooker.
	2 Cover and bring to high pressure over high heat. Lower the heat to stabilize the pressure. Cook for 2 minutes. (*For Electric:* Select high pressure and set the timer for 2 minutes.)
	3 Remove from the heat. Release the pressure with a quick-release method. Unlock and remove the cover.
	4 Carefully remove the steaming basket with the vegetables. Discard the cooking liquid. Rinse the pressure cooker and wipe it dry.
	5 Place the butter and brown sugar in the pressure cooker. Melt the butter over medium heat, stirring until the sugar is melted. Add the carrots and onions. Stir until coated with sugar. Cook until lightly caramelized and soft, about 5 minutes. (*For Electric:* Select the Brown setting.)
	6 Season with salt and pepper. Place in a serving bowl and sprinkle with the dill.

Per serving: Calories 229 (From Fat 64); Fat 7g (Saturated 4g); Cholesterol 16mg; Sodium 247mg; Carbohydrate 40g (Dietary Fiber 5g); Protein 3g.

Note: This recipe is vegetarian and gluten-free.

Vary It! To make this recipe vegan or dairy-free, substitute vegan margarine for the butter.

Tip: For a quick-and-easy way to peel small pearl onions, trim the root end and drop the onions in boiling water for 30 to 45 seconds. Immediately rinse under cold water and slip the skins off.

Cauliflower and Broccoli Custard

Prep time: 30 min • **Cook time:** 28 min under pressure • **Yield:** 8 servings

Ingredients

6 cups water, divided

1 small head cauliflower, trimmed and broken into florets

1 small bunch broccoli, trimmed and cut into florets

4 tablespoons butter

6 tablespoons flour

1½ cups milk

1 teaspoon salt

⅛ teaspoon pepper

Pinch of nutmeg

6 eggs, divided

⅔ cup grated Parmesan cheese, divided

Salt and pepper to taste

Directions

1 Pour 3 cups of the water into a pressure cooker. Place the cauliflower in a steaming basket and place in the pressure cooker.

2 Cover and bring to high pressure over high heat. Lower the heat to stabilize the pressure. Cook for 4 minutes. (*For Electric:* Select high pressure and set the timer for 4 minutes.)

3 Remove from the heat. Release the pressure with a quick-release method. Unlock and remove the cover.

4 Carefully remove the cauliflower to a large bowl. Place the broccoli in the steaming basket.

5 Cover and bring to high pressure over high heat. Lower the heat to stabilize the pressure. Cook for 4 minutes. (*For Electric:* Select high pressure and set the timer for 4 minutes.)

6 Remove from the heat. Release the pressure with a quick-release method. Unlock and remove the cover.

7 Puree the cauliflower in a food processor and place in a large mixing bowl. Puree the broccoli in a food processor and place in a large mixing bowl. Wash and dry the pressure cooker. Set aside.

8 To prepare a white sauce, melt the butter in a saucepan over medium heat. Stir in the flour and cook for 2 minutes. Whisk in the milk, 1 teaspoon salt, ⅛ teaspoon pepper, and nutmeg. Simmer for 5 minutes.

9 Add half the white sauce to each of the vegetable purees. Add 3 beaten eggs and ⅓ cup Parmesan cheese to each vegetable puree. Season with salt and pepper to taste.

10 Butter a 2-quart soufflé dish that fits in the pressure cooker. Pour the cauliflower mixture into the prepared dish. Spoon the broccoli mixture on top. With a flat knife, swirl the mixture to give it a marbleized effect. Cover the top of the dish with foil.

11 Place a metal trivet or round rack in the bottom of the pressure cooker. Pour in the remaining 3 cups of water. Fold a 24-inch length of foil in half lengthwise. Center the foil strip on the trivet, molding it on the trivet and up the sides of the pressure cooker. Place the prepared custard in the pressure cooker. Fold the ends of the aluminum foil strip on top of the dish.

12 Cover and bring to high pressure over high heat. Lower the heat to stabilize the pressure. Cook for 20 minutes. (*For Electric:* Select high pressure and set the timer for 20 minutes.)

13 Remove from the heat. Release the pressure with a quick-release method.

14 Unlock and remove the cover. Let the custard cool a few minutes. To remove the dish from the pressure cooker, pull up on the ends of the aluminum foil strips.

Per serving: Calories 223 (From Fat 124); Fat 14g (Saturated 7g); Cholesterol 188mg; Sodium 549mg; Carbohydrate 13g (Dietary Fiber 3g); Protein 13g.

Note: This recipe is vegetarian.

Vary It! To make this recipe dairy-free, use soy milk and soy-based Parmesan cheese, and substitute vegan margarine for the butter. To make this recipe gluten-free, use gluten-free flour in Step 8.

soufflé dish

Illustration by Elizabeth Kurtzman

Steamed Lemon Artichokes

Prep time: 15 min • **Cook time:** 7 min under pressure • **Yield:** 4 servings

Ingredients	*Directions*
1 cup water	**1** Pour the water into a pressure cooker. Add all but 3 tablespoons of the lemon juice, the salt, and the bay leaf. Stir until the salt dissolves. Place the reserved lemon rinds in the water.
Juice of 2 lemons, divided, rinds reserved	
1 teaspoon salt	
1 bay leaf	**2** Cut off the stems from the artichokes. Tear off and discard the top two or three layers of tough outer leaves. Cut off 1 to 1½ inches from the tops of the artichokes. Carefully open and expose the inner leaves and choke. Pull out and remove any thorny leaves. With a teaspoon, scoop out and discard any fuzzy matter from the center choke.
4 large artichokes	
1 cup mayonnaise	
1 clove garlic, peeled and minced	
2 tablespoons minced flat-leaf parsley, or snipped dill	**3** Wet artichokes in the lemon water in the pressure cooker to slow down discoloring. Place upside down in a steaming basket in the pressure cooker.
	4 Cover and bring to high pressure over high heat. Lower the heat to stabilize the pressure. Cook for 7 minutes. (*For Electric:* Select high pressure and set the timer for 7 minutes.)
	5 Remove from the heat. Release the pressure with a quick-release method. Unlock and remove the cover. Carefully remove the artichokes from the pressure cooker with a slotted spoon and cool to room temperature.
	6 In a small mixing bowl, whisk together the mayonnaise, the remaining 3 tablespoons of lemon juice, and the garlic.

7 Carefully open the center of each artichoke and fill with one-fourth of the lemon mayonnaise. Sprinkle the tops with the parsley or dill.

8 Pluck artichoke leaves from the whole artichoke. Dip them into the lemon mayonnaise. Eat by scraping the underside of the leaves along your upper teeth to remove the soft flesh; discard the leaf. The center leaves are usually tender enough to be eaten whole.

Per serving: Calories 457 (From Fat 396); Fat 44g (Saturated 7g); Cholesterol 33mg; Sodium 712mg; Carbohydrate 15g (Dietary Fiber 7g); Protein 5g.

Note: This recipe is vegetarian and gluten-free.

Vary It! To make this recipe vegan or dairy-free, use vegan mayonnaise.

PREPARING AN ARTICHOKE

1. CUT OFF STEMS FROM THE ARTICHOKES. TEAR OFF AND DISCARD THE TOP TWO OR THREE LAYERS OF TOUGH, OUTER LEAVES.

2. CAREFULLY OPEN AND EXPOSE INNER LEAVES AND 'CHOKE.' PULL OUT AND REMOVE ANY THORNY LEAVES.

3. WITH A TEASPOON, SCOOP OUT AND DISCARD ANY FUZZY MATTER FROM THE CENTER CHOKE.

4. WET ARTICHOKES IN THE LEMON WATER IN THE PRESSURE COOKER TO SLOW DOWN ANY DISCOLORING.

5. PLACE UPSIDE DOWN IN THE STEAMING BASKET IN THE PRESSURE COOKER.

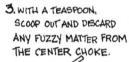

Illustration by Elizabeth Kurtzman

Greens with Salt Pork

Prep time: 10 min • **Cook time:** 5 min under pressure • **Yield:** 8 servings

Ingredients	*Directions*
4-ounce piece of salt pork	*1* Brown the salt pork in a pressure cooker over medium heat until golden. Add the greens, water, sugar, and hot pepper. (*For Electric:* Select the Brown setting.)
1 bunch (about 1 pound) of greens, such as kale, mustard, collard, turnip, or beet, rinsed very well, stems removed, coarsely chopped	*2* Cover and bring to high pressure over high heat. Lower the heat to stabilize the pressure. Cook for 5 minutes. (*For Electric:* Select high pressure and set the timer for 5 minutes.)
2 cups water	
1 teaspoon sugar	
2 pinches of crushed, hot red pepper	*3* Remove from the heat. Release the pressure with a quick-release method.
Salt and black pepper to taste	*4* Unlock and remove the cover.
	5 Season with salt and pepper. Serve the greens in a bowl with some of the pot liquid.

Per serving: Calories 121 (From Fat 100); Fat 11g (Saturated 4g); Cholesterol 12mg; Sodium 268mg; Carbohydrate 4g (Dietary Fiber 1g); Protein 2g.

Note: This recipe is gluten-free and dairy-free.

Ratatouille

Prep time: 20 min • **Cook time:** 4 min under pressure • **Yield:** 6 servings

Ingredients	*Directions*
3 tablespoons olive oil	*1* Heat the olive oil in a pressure cooker over medium-high heat. Add the onion, garlic, and the green and red bell peppers. Cook until the onion is soft. (*For Electric:* Select the Brown setting.)
1 medium onion, chopped	
2 cloves garlic, peeled and thinly sliced	
1 green bell pepper, cored, seeded, and diced	*2* Add the zucchini, tomatoes, water, thyme, 1½ teaspoons salt, and ¼ teaspoon black pepper. Cook for 2 minutes. Add the eggplant.
1 red bell pepper, cored, seeded, and diced	
1 small zucchini, trimmed, quartered lengthwise, and diced	*3* Cover and bring to high pressure over high heat. Lower the heat to stabilize the pressure. Cook for 4 minutes. (*For Electric:* Select high pressure and set the timer for 4 minutes.)
One 14½-ounce can diced tomatoes	
¼ cup water	*4* Remove from the heat. Release the pressure with a quick-release method.
½ teaspoon dried thyme	
1½ teaspoons salt	*5* Unlock and remove the cover. Add the basil and parsley. Season with salt and pepper to taste. Stir in the vinegar. Serve hot or at room temperature.
¼ teaspoon black pepper	
1 large eggplant, peeled and cut into ½-inch cubes	
2 tablespoons shredded basil	
2 tablespoons minced flat-leaf parsley	
Salt and pepper to taste	
2 tablespoons red wine vinegar	

Per serving: Calories 115 (From Fat 63); Fat 7g (Saturated 1g); Cholesterol 0mg; Sodium 383mg; Carbohydrate 13g (Dietary Fiber 4g); Protein 2g.

Note: This recipe is vegetarian, vegan, gluten-free, and dairy-free.

Sweet-and-Sour Red Cabbage

Prep time: 15 min • **Cook time:** 6 min under pressure • **Yield:** 8 servings

Ingredients	*Directions*
2 tablespoons vegetable oil	**1** Heat the vegetable oil in a pressure cooker over medium-high heat. (*For Electric:* Select the Brown setting.) Add the onion and cook until soft. Add the vinegar, chicken stock, brown sugar, and cloves. Stir well until the sugar dissolves. Add the cabbage, apple chunks, and bay leaf.
1 large red onion, chopped	
½ cup apple cider vinegar	
1 cup chicken or vegetable stock	
½ cup packed dark brown sugar	**2** Cover and bring to high pressure over high heat. Lower the heat to stabilize the pressure. Cook for 6 minutes. (*For Electric:* Select high pressure and set the timer for 6 minutes.)
¼ teaspoon ground cloves	
2-pound head red cabbage, tough outer leaves discarded, shredded	**3** Remove from the heat. Release the pressure with a quick-release method.
2 Granny Smith apples, peeled, cored, and cut into ½-inch chunks	**4** Unlock and remove the cover. Taste the cabbage. If it's not tender, return to Step 2 and cook for an additional 1 to 2 minutes.
1 bay leaf	
Salt and pepper to taste	**5** Remove and discard the bay leaf. Add salt and pepper.

Per serving: Calories 140 (From Fat 39); Fat 4g (Saturated 0g); Cholesterol 1mg; Sodium 214mg; Carbohydrate 26g (Dietary Fiber 3g); Protein 2g.

Note: This recipe is gluten- and dairy-free. To make it vegetarian or vegan, use vegetable stock rather than chicken stock.

Tip: This dish is the perfect accompaniment to many German and Northern European dishes. Have a batch on hand to serve with Sauerbraten (Chapter 6) or Caraway Pork Roast (Chapter 9).

Pickled Beets

Prep time: 20 min • **Cook time:** 3 min under pressure • **Yield:** 6 servings

Ingredients	*Directions*
1 cup water	*1* Combine the water, vinegar, brown sugar, pickling spices, and salt in the pressure cooker. Stir until the sugar dissolves. Add the beets, onions, garlic, and bay leaf.
½ cup apple cider vinegar	
⅓ cup packed dark brown sugar	
1 tablespoon pickling spices	*2* Cover and bring to high pressure. Lower the heat to stabilize the pressure. Cook for 3 minutes. (*For Electric:* Select high pressure and set the timer for 3 minutes.)
1 teaspoon salt	
2 pounds beets (about 4 large), peeled and thinly sliced	*3* Remove from the heat. Release the pressure with a quick-release method.
1 medium red onion, sliced into rings	*4* Unlock and remove the cover. Taste the beets. They should be crisp-tender. If they're too hard, return to Step 2 and cook for 1 additional minute.
1 clove garlic, peeled and sliced	
1 bay leaf	*5* Carefully remove the beets and onions with a slotted spoon to a bowl. Bring the cooking liquid to a boil and reduce by half. Pour through a strainer over the beets. Cool to room temperature before serving. (*For Electric:* Select the Brown setting.)

Per serving: Calories 117 (From Fat 3); Fat 0g (Saturated 0g); Cholesterol 0mg; Sodium 505mg; Carbohydrate 28g (Dietary Fiber 3g); Protein 3g.

Note: This recipe is vegetarian, vegan, gluten-free, and dairy-free.

Salade Niçoise

Prep time: 20 min • **Cook time:** 7 min under pressure • **Yield:** 4 servings

Ingredients	*Directions*
3 cups water 1 pound green beans, trimmed and cut into 1½-inch pieces	**1** Pour the water into a pressure cooker. Place the green beans, potatoes, and eggs, in their shells, in a steaming basket and place the basket in the pressure cooker.
1 pound small red or new potatoes, scrubbed well and pricked twice with a fork 4 eggs, in shell	**2** Cover and bring to high pressure over high heat. Lower the heat to stabilize the pressure. Cook for 7 minutes. (*For Electric:* Select high pressure and set the timer for 7 minutes.)
1 large head Boston or green leaf lettuce, washed and dried	**3** Remove from the heat. Release the pressure with a quick-release method.
Two 7-ounce cans oil-packed tuna	
1 pint cherry tomatoes 1 cucumber, peeled and cut into ¼-inch slices	**4** Unlock and remove the cover. Taste the potatoes. If they're still hard, return to Step 2 and cook for an additional 1 to 2 minutes (remove the eggs before doing so).
½ cup brine-cured black olives	**5** Carefully remove the steaming basket with the vegetables and eggs. Remove the eggs and potatoes; peel and quarter.
1 small red onion, sliced into thin rings	
4 tablespoons extra-virgin olive oil	**6** Line a serving platter with the lettuce. Mound the green beans on one half of the platter and the potatoes on the other. Mound the tuna in the center.
4 tablespoons red wine vinegar	
1 tablespoon Dijon mustard ¼ teaspoon dried thyme	**7** Place the eggs, tomatoes, cucumber, and black olives around the beans and potatoes. Place the onion slices on top of the salad.
Salt and pepper to taste	**8** Whisk together the olive oil, vinegar, mustard, and thyme. Season with the salt and pepper. Drizzle on top of the salad and serve immediately.

Per serving: Calories 485 (From Fat 281); Fat 31g (Saturated 5g); Cholesterol 232mg; Sodium 724mg; Carbohydrate 33g (Dietary Fiber 8g); Protein 22g.

Note: This recipe is vegetarian, gluten-free, and dairy-free.

Vary It! To make this a vegan recipe, eliminate the eggs.

Chapter 12

Dynamite Desserts and Fabulous Fruits

Some people shy away from making desserts because they think it takes too long. Nothing could be further from the truth when you're using a pressure cooker. Creamy cheesecakes, like the ones most people only dream about, are ready from start to finish in 35 minutes. Smooth egg custard and homey apple crisp are ready in even less time. Get the picture? Now get going and start turning out your own post-dinner extravaganzas!

As you probably expect, all of the recipes in this chapter are vegetarian as written, so they don't include notes to that effect. Other special-diet accommodations (dairy-free, gluten-free, and/or vegan) are noted following the recipes.

Using the Pressure Cooker as a Hot Water Bath

You've likely made a recipe or two in your lifetime that called for a *bain-marie,* which is French for "hot water bath." Certain desserts, such as cheesecake and baked custard, should not brown as they cook. To prevent browning, they're baked at a moderately high temperature with the cake or baking pan sitting in a larger pan of simmering water.

Well, imagine your pressure cooker as an enclosed *bain-marie* that cooks up to 70 percent faster than your oven. By placing a cheesecake or pudding, for example, on a trivet sitting over simmering water in the steam bath environment of the pressure cooker, you can make some great desserts.

You should know a couple things about this technique before trying your hand at it. Some pressure cookers come with a steamer basket and trivet set or a steamer plate. The trivet or steamer plate is essential when "baking" in your pressure cooker. If you don't have one, purchase a 6- to 7-inch round, wire, metal cooling rack with legs at your favorite housewares store.

You probably have different-sized casserole and baking dishes in your kitchen. Always make sure that the baking dish or pan you use is heatproof and small enough to fit in your pressure cooker. Small, deep, round ones work the best when making dishes such as bread pudding and crisps. The best type of pan to use when making a cheesecake in your pressure cooker is a 7-inch spring-form pan with removable sides. So that you don't run the risk of water leaking into the pan, cover the bottom and sides with one sheet of aluminum foil. To prevent wet tops on baked goods, securely cover the pan or baking dish with a sheet of aluminum foil before placing it in the pressure cooker.

To make it easier to position and later remove the dish or pan from the pressure cooker, make an aluminum foil sling to assist you, as shown in Figure 12-1. The sling is simply made from a 24-inch-long sheet of aluminum foil, folded in half lengthwise. Once the foil is folded, you center the prepared, covered pan of food on the sling. Holding the ends of the sling, carefully lower the pan into the pressure cooker onto the trivet (the one that came with the steaming basket) or onto a small, round, metal wire cooling rack (7 inches in diameter or smaller to fit into the pressure cooker). The ends of the sling are folded down on top of the pan of food. To remove the cooked pan of food, carefully pull up on the ends of the sling.

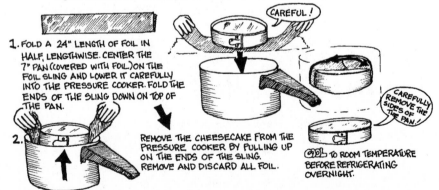

FOIL-WRAPPED CAKE PAN WITH FOIL SLING AND TRIVET

1. FOLD A 24" LENGTH OF FOIL IN HALF, LENGTHWISE. CENTER THE 7" PAN (COVERED WITH FOIL) ON THE FOIL SLING AND LOWER IT CAREFULLY INTO THE PRESSURE COOKER. FOLD THE ENDS OF THE SLING DOWN ON TOP OF THE PAN.

CAREFUL!

CAREFULLY REMOVE SIDES OF THE PAN!

2. REMOVE THE CHEESECAKE FROM THE PRESSURE COOKER BY PULLING UP ON THE ENDS OF THE SLING. REMOVE AND DISCARD ALL FOIL.

COOL TO ROOM TEMPERATURE BEFORE REFRIGERATING OVERNIGHT.

Figure 12-1: Making and using an aluminum foil sling.

Illustration by Elizabeth Kurtzman

Cheesecakes, Custards, and Other Tasty Treats

Cheesecakes, custards, and puddings were made for the pressure cooker. Although these desserts are usually baked in the oven in a hot water bath, they bake wonderfully in the hot water bath atmosphere that the pressure cooker creates. The addition of hot, intense steam adds greater benefit because everything winds up cooking at least 50 percent faster, too.

Following are tidbits about each of the recipes you can find in this section:

- **Chocolate Sandwich Cookie Cheesecake:** This recipe combines America's favorite cookie with one of its favorite desserts — cheesecake.

- **Key Lime Cheesecake:** Yellow in color, key limes are much smaller than the more common green Persian lime. If you can't find key limes, regular green limes will do, with equally delicious results.

- **Double Chocolate Cheesecake:** With a chocolate cookie crust and smooth chocolate filling, this dessert is sure to satisfy the most powerful of chocolate cravings.

- **Italian Ricotta Cheesecake:** Made with ricotta (rather than cream cheese) and traditionally flavored with orange, this cheesecake is the perfect ending to an Italian meal.

- **Flan:** What makes this smooth-yet-dense egg custard from Spain unique is that it cooks in a baking dish on a coating of hardened burnt sugar, which melts into a delicious, caramel-flavored liquid that coats the dessert when you invert it onto a serving plate.

- **Apple Crisp:** Reminiscent of baked granola with fruit, this dessert is just as tasty the next day for breakfast.

- **Cinnamon Raisin Bread Pudding:** Originally a frugal cook's solution for using up stale bread, bread pudding is a popular, easy-to-prepare dessert.

- **Creamy Rice Pudding:** Rice pudding is the queen of comfort desserts. Enjoyed around the world in infinite versions, it's always creamy and soothing and has just enough chew.

Chocolate Sandwich Cookie Cheesecake

Prep time: 15 min • **Cook time:** 20 min under pressure • **Yield:** 6 servings

Ingredients	*Directions*
¾ **cup crushed chocolate sandwich cookies**	**1** Lightly butter a 7-inch springform pan. Cover the outside bottom and sides of the pan with a single sheet of aluminum foil. Combine the cookie crumbs and melted butter and press into the bottom and 1 inch up the sides of the pan.
2 tablespoons butter, melted	
Two 8-ounce packages cream cheese, softened	
½ cup sugar	**2** In a large mixing bowl, mix the cream cheese, sugar, and vanilla with an electric mixer on medium speed until fluffy. Add the eggs, one at a time, mixing on low speed just until well blended. Gently stir in the quartered cookies. Pour over the crust. Cover tightly with aluminum foil.
½ teaspoon vanilla	
2 eggs	
10 chocolate sandwich cookies, quartered	
2½ cups water	**3** Place a metal trivet or rack in the pressure cooker pot. Pour in the water. Fold a 24-inch length of foil in half lengthwise. Center the pan on the foil sling and carefully lower it into the pressure cooker. Fold the ends of the sling down on top of the pan.
	4 Cover and bring to high pressure over high heat. Lower the heat to stabilize the pressure. Cook for 20 minutes. (*For Electric:* Select high pressure and set the timer for 20 minutes.)
	5 Remove from the heat. Let sit undisturbed for 10 minutes. Release any remaining pressure with a quick-release method.
	6 Unlock and remove the cover. Remove the cheesecake from the pressure cooker by pulling up on the ends of the aluminum foil sling. Remove and discard all foil. Cool to room temperature before refrigerating overnight. Before serving, carefully remove the sides of the springform pan.

Per serving: Calories 547 (From Fat 344); Fat 38g (Saturated 21g); Cholesterol 164mg; Sodium 497mg; Carbohydrate 43g (Dietary Fiber 1g); Protein 10g.

Key Lime Cheesecake

Prep time: 15 min • **Cook time:** 20 min under pressure • **Yield:** 6 servings

Ingredients	*Directions*
¾ **cup graham cracker crumbs** ½ **cup plus 2 tablespoons sugar, divided** **2 tablespoons butter, melted**	*1* Lightly butter a 7-inch springform pan. Cover the outside bottom and sides with a single sheet of aluminum foil. Combine the graham cracker crumbs, the 2 tablespoons sugar, and the melted butter and press into the bottom and 1 inch up the sides of the pan.
Two 8-ounce packages cream cheese, softened **2 eggs** **3 tablespoons freshly squeezed Key or Persian lime juice** **2 teaspoons grated lime zest**	*2* In a large mixing bowl, mix the cream cheese and the ½ cup sugar with an electric mixer on medium speed until fluffy. Add the eggs, one at a time, mixing on low speed. Add the lime juice and lime zest and mix until well blended. Pour over the crust. Cover tightly with aluminum foil.
2½ cups water	*3* Place a metal trivet or rack in the pressure cooker. Pour in the water. Fold a 24-inch length of foil in half lengthwise. Center the pan on the foil sling and carefully lower it into the pressure cooker. Fold the ends of the sling down on top of the pan.
	4 Cover and bring to high pressure over high heat. Lower the heat to stabilize the pressure. Cook for 20 minutes. (*For Electric:* Select high pressure and set the timer for 20 minutes.)
	5 Remove from the heat. Let sit undisturbed 10 minutes. Release any remaining pressure with a quick-release method.
	6 Unlock and remove the cover. Remove the cheesecake from the pressure cooker by pulling up on the ends of the aluminum foil sling. Remove and discard all foil. Cool to room temperature before refrigerating overnight. Before serving, carefully remove the sides of the springform pan.

Per serving: Calories 469 (From Fat 301); Fat 33g (Saturated 20g); Cholesterol 164mg; Sodium 336mg; Carbohydrate 35g (Dietary Fiber 1g); Protein 9g.

Double Chocolate Cheesecake

Prep time: 15 min • **Cook time:** 20 min under pressure • **Yield:** 6 servings

Ingredients	Directions
¾ **cup chocolate wafer cookie crumbs**	*1* Lightly butter a 7-inch springform pan. Cover the outside bottom and sides with a single sheet of aluminum foil. Combine the cookie crumbs and melted butter and press into the bottom and 1 inch up the sides of the pan.
2 tablespoons butter, melted	
Two 8-ounce packages cream cheese, softened	
½ **cup sweetened condensed milk**	*2* In a large mixing bowl, mix the cream cheese and condensed milk with an electric mixer on medium speed until fluffy. Add the eggs, one at a time, mixing on low speed. Add the melted chocolate and vanilla and mix until well blended. Pour over the crust. Cover tightly with aluminum foil.
3 eggs	
1½ **cups semisweet chocolate chips, melted in the microwave**	
1 teaspoon vanilla	*3* Place a metal trivet or rack in the pressure cooker. Pour in the water. Fold a 24-inch length of foil in half lengthwise. Center the pan on the foil sling and carefully lower it into the pressure cooker. Fold the ends of the sling down on top of the pan.
2½ **cups water**	
	4 Cover and bring to high pressure over high heat. Lower the heat to stabilize the pressure. Cook for 20 minutes. (*For Electric:* Select high pressure and set the timer for 20 minutes.)
	5 Remove from the heat. Let sit undisturbed for 10 minutes. Release any remaining pressure with a quick-release method.
	6 Unlock and remove the cover. Remove the cheesecake from the pressure cooker by pulling up on the ends of the aluminum foil sling. Remove and discard all foil. Cool to room temperature before refrigerating overnight. Before serving, carefully remove the sides of the springform pan.

Per serving: Calories 698 (From Fat 446); Fat 50g (Saturated 28g); Cholesterol 208mg; Sodium 375mg; Carbohydrate 55g (Dietary Fiber 1g); Protein 12g.

Italian Ricotta Cheesecake

Prep time: 15 min • **Cook time:** 20 min under pressure • **Yield:** 6 servings

Ingredients	Directions
¾ cup graham cracker crumbs	**1** Lightly butter a 7-inch springform pan. Cover the outside bottom and sides with a single sheet of aluminum foil. Combine the graham cracker crumbs, the 2 tablespoons sugar, and the melted butter and press into the bottom of the pan.
⅔ cup plus 2 tablespoons sugar, divided	
2 tablespoons butter, melted	
One 15-ounce container whole-milk ricotta cheese	**2** In a large mixing bowl, mix the ricotta cheese, orange zest, vanilla, flour, the ⅔ cup sugar, and salt with an electric mixer on medium speed until creamy. Add the eggs, one at a time, mixing on low speed until well blended. Stir in the candied orange peel. Pour over the crust. Cover tightly with aluminum foil.
1 tablespoon grated orange zest	
1 teaspoon vanilla	
2 tablespoons all-purpose flour	
Pinch of salt	**3** Place a metal trivet or rack in the pressure cooker. Pour in the water. Fold a 24-inch length of foil in half lengthwise. Center the pan on the foil sling and carefully lower it into the pressure cooker. Fold the ends of the sling down on top of the pan.
3 eggs	
¼ cup diced candied orange peel	
2½ cups water	**4** Cover and bring to high pressure over high heat. Lower the heat to stabilize the pressure. Cook for 20 minutes. (*For Electric:* Select high pressure and set the timer for 20 minutes.)
Confectioners' sugar	
	5 Remove from the heat. Let sit undisturbed for 10 minutes. Release any remaining pressure with a quick-release method.
	6 Unlock and remove the cover. Remove the cheesecake from the pressure cooker by pulling up on the ends of the aluminum foil sling. Remove and discard all foil. Cool to room temperature before refrigerating overnight. Before serving, carefully remove the sides of the springform pan. Sprinkle liberally with confectioners' sugar.

Per serving: Calories 398 (From Fat 154); Fat 17g (Saturated 9g); Cholesterol 152mg; Sodium 206mg; Carbohydrate 49g (Dietary Fiber 1g); Protein 12g

Flan (Caramel Custard)

Prep time: 10 min • **Cook time:** 10 min under pressure • **Yield:** 6 servings

Ingredients	*Directions*
½ cup sugar	**1** Heat the sugar in a small skillet over medium heat until it melts and becomes a golden brown syrup. Immediately pour the syrup into a 5-cup baking dish that will fit in the pressure cooker, tilting the dish so that the sugar coats the entire bottom. Work quickly because the syrup will harden.
1 cup milk	
One 14-ounce can sweetened condensed milk	
1 teaspoon vanilla	
⅛ teaspoon salt	**2** Combine the milk, condensed milk, vanilla, and salt in a bowl. Add the eggs and whisk until smooth. Pour into the prepared dish. Cover tightly with aluminum foil.
4 eggs, lightly beaten	
2½ cups water	
	3 Place a metal trivet or rack in the pressure cooker pot. Pour in the water. Fold a 24-inch length of foil in half lengthwise. Center the baking dish on the foil sling and carefully lower it into the pressure cooker. Fold the ends of the sling down on top of the dish.
	4 Cover and bring to high pressure over high heat. Lower the heat to stabilize the pressure. Cook for 10 minutes. (*For Electric:* Select high pressure and set the timer for 10 minutes.)
	5 Remove from the heat. Release the pressure using the natural-release method, which should take about 15 to 20 minutes.
	6 Unlock and remove the cover. Remove the flan from the pressure cooker by pulling up on the ends of the aluminum foil sling. Remove and discard all foil. Cool to room temperature before refrigerating overnight.
	7 To serve, cut around the edge of the dish with a sharp knife. Place a shallow bowl on top of the dish and turn over. Cut into wedges.

Per serving: Calories 353 (From Fat 94); Fat 10g (Saturated 6g); Cholesterol 170mg; Sodium 195mg; Carbohydrate 55g (Dietary Fiber 0g); Protein 11g.

Apple Crisp

Prep time: 10 min • **Cook time:** 20 min under pressure • **Yield:** 6 servings

Ingredients	*Directions*
4 Granny Smith apples, peeled and thinly sliced	*1* Sprinkle the apples with the lemon juice.
1 tablespoon lemon juice	*2* Combine the oats, flour, brown sugar, cinnamon, salt, and butter.
1 cup old-fashioned oats	
¼ cup flour	*3* Layer the apples and the oat mixture, beginning and ending with the apples, in a 7-inch springform pan or a 2-quart soufflé dish that fits in the pressure cooker. Cover the dish tightly with aluminum foil.
½ cup packed light brown sugar	
1 teaspoon ground cinnamon	
½ teaspoon salt	*4* Place a metal trivet or rack in the pressure cooker. Pour in the water. Fold a 24-inch length of foil in half lengthwise. Center the baking dish on the foil sling and carefully lower it into the pressure cooker. Fold the ends of the sling down on top of the dish.
4 tablespoons melted butter	
2½ cups water	
	5 Cover and bring to high pressure over high heat. Lower the heat to stabilize the pressure. Cook for 20 minutes. (*For Electric:* Select high pressure and set the timer for 20 minutes.)
	6 Remove from the heat. Release the pressure using a quick-release method.
	7 Unlock and remove the cover. Remove the apple crisp from the pressure cooker by pulling up on the ends of the aluminum foil sling. Remove and discard all foil. Serve warm.

Per serving: Calories 283 (From Fat 103); Fat 11g (Saturated 6g); Cholesterol 27mg; Sodium 308mg; Carbohydrate 45g (Dietary Fiber 3g); Protein 3g.

Vary It! To make this recipe vegan or dairy-free, substitute vegan margarine for the butter.

Vary It! You can easily substitute about 1½ pounds ripe peaches or pears for the apples, with equally delicious results.

Cinnamon Raisin Bread Pudding

Prep time: 10 min • **Cook time:** 15 min under pressure • **Yield:** 6 servings

Ingredients	*Directions*
4 slices cinnamon raisin bread, torn into small pieces	**1** Butter a 5-cup baking dish that fits in your pressure cooker. Place the bread pieces in the baking dish.
2 eggs	
One 12-ounce can evaporated milk	**2** Whisk the eggs, milk, vanilla, salt, and sugar together to make a custard. Pour over the bread and let set until the custard is absorbed.
½ teaspoon vanilla	
¼ teaspoon salt	**3** Dot the top with the butter. Sprinkle with cinnamon. Cover tightly with aluminum foil.
¼ cup sugar	
1 teaspoon butter	**4** Place a metal trivet or rack in the pressure cooker. Pour in the water. Fold a 24-inch length of foil in half lengthwise. Center the baking dish on the foil sling and carefully lower it into the pressure cooker. Fold the ends of the sling down on top of the dish.
Ground cinnamon	
2 cups water	
	5 Cover and bring to high pressure over high heat. Lower the heat to stabilize the pressure. Cook for 15 minutes. (*For Electric:* Select high pressure and set the timer for 15 minutes.)
	6 Remove from the heat. Release the pressure using a quick-release method.
	7 Unlock and remove the cover. Remove the pudding from the pressure cooker by pulling up on the ends of the aluminum strip. Remove and discard all foil. Serve warm, or cool to room temperature.

Per serving: Calories 333 (From Fat 108); Fat 12g (Saturated 6g); Cholesterol 144mg; Sodium 451mg; Carbohydrate 42g (Dietary Fiber 1g); Protein 13g.

Vary It! To make this recipe gluten-free, use gluten-free cinnamon raisin bread. For a dairy-free or vegan version, use 12 ounces soy or almond milk instead of evaporated milk, and substitute vegan margarine for the butter.

Tip: For best results, let the bread absorb as much of the liquid custard as possible before cooking.

Creamy Rice Pudding

Prep time: 10 min • **Cook time:** 10 min under pressure • **Yield:** 6 servings

Ingredients	*Directions*
2 tablespoons butter	*1* Melt the butter in a pressure cooker over medium-high heat. Add the milk and bring to a boil. Stir in the rice. (*For Electric:* Select the Brown setting.)
3 cups milk	
1 cup long-grain rice	
⅓ cup sugar	*2* Cover and bring to high pressure over high heat. Lower the heat to stabilize the pressure. Cook for 10 minutes. (*For Electric:* Select high pressure and set the timer for 10 minutes.)
1 teaspoon vanilla	
Ground cinnamon	
	3 Remove from the heat. Release the pressure using the natural-release method, which should take about 15 to 25 minutes.
	4 Unlock and remove the cover. Stir in the sugar and vanilla. Sprinkle with cinnamon and serve warm or at room temperature.

Per serving: Calories 302 (From Fat 86); Fat 10g (Saturated 6g); Cholesterol 32mg; Sodium 81mg; Carbohydrate 46g (Dietary Fiber 0g); Protein 8g.

Note: This recipe is gluten-free.

Vary It! For a vegan or dairy-free version of this recipe, use soy, almond, or coconut milk and substitute vegan margarine for the butter.

Fruit Sauces, Chutneys, and Sparkling Jars of Fruit

Years ago, people would "put up" jars of fruit purees and preserves to take advantage of an abundant harvest and to prepare for the long winter months ahead when fresh fruit wouldn't be available. Even though you can now enjoy fresh fruits year-round, a pint of homemade jam is still always a welcome gift.

Although most fresh fruit preserves require slow simmering, those made with flavor-concentrated dried fruits do exceptionally well in the pressure cooker, as do the fruits I paired up in my jam recipes.

The pressure cooker also makes fantastic applesauce. Apples are usually very abundant by September or October, so if you haven't had homemade applesauce in a while, reacquaint yourself next autumn and make a batch of my easy-to-make pink applesauce. In fact, don't let yourself be limited by apples and dried fruits. Use the recommended cooking times in Appendix A and experiment with whatever ripe fruits catch your eye at your local farmers' market.

Your 4-, 6-, or 8- quart pressure cooker was designed and manufactured for cooking food and not large, bulk canning. Much larger than pressure cookers (10 quarts and up), pressure canners are wider in diameter, come with wire baskets for holding canning jars so that they don't rattle and bang into each other, and usually have a dial pressure regulator gauge on the cover that gives you the exact pounds per square inch (psi) as you pressure-can food. If you plan to do a lot of pressure canning, I strongly recommend that you use a pressure canner rather than your regular pressure cooker. On the other hand, if you happened to find a great sale on strawberries at the local Piggly Wiggly and bought way too many to eat before they'll spoil, by all means, take out your stainless-steel 6- to 8-quart pressure cooker (as long as it reaches and maintains 15 psi) and put up a few jars of jam. Check out the information on pressure canning in Chapter 5.

Autumn Harvest Applesauce

Prep time: 10 min • **Cook time:** 5 min under pressure • **Yield:** 8 servings

Ingredients	*Directions*
3 pounds apples, such as Jonathan, Golden Delicious, or Jonagold, peeled, cored, and quartered	*1* Place the apples, cranberries, cinnamon stick, cider, maple syrup, and salt in a pressure cooker. Stir well.
1½ cups fresh or frozen cranberries	*2* Cover and bring to high pressure. Lower the heat to stabilize the pressure and cook for 5 minutes. (*For Electric:* Select high pressure and set the timer for 5 minutes.)
1 cinnamon stick	
1 cup apple cider or apple juice	*3* Remove from the heat. Release the pressure using a quick-release method.
½ cup real maple syrup	
Pinch of salt	*4* Unlock and remove the cover. The apples should be very soft. Remove and discard the cinnamon stick.
	5 Puree the apples with a hand-held potato masher or process with a hand blender in the pressure-cooker pot. Taste and add additional maple syrup or sugar, if desired. Refrigerate when cool.

Per serving: Calories 159 (From Fat 5); Fat 1g (Saturated 0g); Cholesterol 0mg; Sodium 23mg; Carbohydrate 41g (Dietary Fiber 3g); Protein 0g.

Note: This recipe is vegan, gluten-free, and dairy-free.

Tip: Fresh cranberries are available from September through early winter. Because they freeze well for up to a year, buy a few extra bags and store them in your freezer to have a ready supply year-round. Use the crispest apples for the best flavor and texture.

Apricot-Pineapple Jam

Prep time: 10 min • **Cook time:** 5 min under pressure • **Yield:** About 4 cups

Ingredients	*Directions*
1½ cups water	*1* Bring the water and lemon juice to a boil in a pressure cooker. Add the sugar and stir until dissolved. Add the apricots and pineapple. (*For Electric:* Select the Brown setting.)
2 tablespoons lemon juice	
1 cup sugar	
1 pound dried apricots	*2* Cover and bring to high pressure over high heat. Lower the heat to stabilize the pressure. Cook for 5 minutes. (*For Electric:* Select high pressure and set the timer for 5 minutes.)
One 20-ounce can crushed pineapple, with juice	
	3 Remove from the heat. Release the pressure using a quick-release method.
	4 Unlock and remove the cover. Spoon the fruit mixture into a food processor bowl. Process until it's the consistency, from chunky to smooth, that you want. Refrigerate when cool.

Per serving (1 tablespoon): Calories 39 (From Fat 0); Fat 0g (Saturated 0g); Cholesterol 0mg; Sodium 2mg; Carbohydrate 10g (Dietary Fiber 1g); Protein 0g.

Note: This recipe is vegan, gluten-free, and dairy-free.

Cherry-Plum Jam

Prep time: 10 min • **Cook time:** 5 min under pressure • **Yield:** About 5 cups

Ingredients	*Directions*
1½ **cups water**	**1** Bring the water and orange juice to a boil in a pressure cooker. Add the sugar and stir until dissolved. Add the dried cherries and prunes. (*For Electric:* Select the Brown setting.)
½ **cup orange juice**	
½ **cup sugar**	
¼ **pound dried pitted cherries**	**2** Cover and bring to high pressure over high heat. Lower the heat to stabilize the pressure. Cook for 5 minutes. (*For Electric:* Select high pressure and set the timer for 5 minutes.)
1 **pound (about 3 cups) pitted prunes, cut in half**	
	3 Remove from the heat. Release the pressure using a quick-release method.
	4 Unlock and remove the cover. Using a hand-held potato masher, gently mash the cooked fruit. Stir well. Refrigerate when cool.

Per serving (1 tablespoon): Calories 31 (From Fat 0); Fat 0g (Saturated 0g); Cholesterol 0mg; Sodium 1mg; Carbohydrate 8g (Dietary Fiber 1g); Protein 0g.

Note: This recipe is vegan, gluten-free, and dairy-free.

Cranberry-Orange Chutney

Prep time: 10 min • **Cook time:** 5 min under pressure • **Yield:** About 8 cups

Ingredients	*Directions*
½ cup orange juice	**1** Combine the orange juice, vinegar, marmalade, sugar, brown sugar, ginger, cayenne pepper, and salt in a pressure cooker. Bring to a boil and stir until the sugar dissolves. (*For Electric:* Select the Brown setting.)
⅓ cup white wine vinegar	
½ cup orange marmalade	
1 cup sugar	
½ cup packed light brown sugar	**2** Add the walnuts, fresh cranberries, dried cranberries, onion, orange zest, cinnamon stick, and bay leaf. Stir together.
½ teaspoon ground ginger	
¼ teaspoon cayenne pepper	**3** Cover and bring to high pressure over high heat. Lower the heat to stabilize the pressure. Cook for 5 minutes. (*For Electric:* Select high pressure and set the timer for 5 minutes.)
½ teaspoon salt	
1 cup toasted chopped walnuts	
One 12-ounce bag fresh or frozen cranberries	**4** Remove from the heat. Release the pressure using a quick-release method.
1 cup dried cranberries	
1 small red onion, finely chopped	**5** Unlock and remove the cover. Remove the cinnamon stick and bay leaf and stir well. Cool to room temperature and refrigerate.
2 tablespoons grated orange zest	
1 cinnamon stick	
1 bay leaf	

Per serving (1 tablespoon): Calories 25 (From Fat 6); Fat 1g (Saturated 0g); Cholesterol 0mg; Sodium 10mg; Carbohydrate 5g (Dietary Fiber 0g); Protein 0g.

Note: This recipe is vegan, gluten-free, and dairy-free.

Tip: To toast walnuts, place them in a dry skillet over medium heat and cook, stirring or shaking the pan often so they don't burn, about 3 to 4 minutes.

Vary It! For a thicker, more relishlike consistency, spoon the chutney mixture into the bowl of a food processor and pulse a couple times until coarsely chopped.

Chapter 13

Recipes for Special Diets

In This Chapter

▶ Understanding vegetarian, vegan, gluten-free, and dairy-free diets

▶ Looking at the protein power of beans

▶ Adapting recipes to special diets by making substitutions

▶ Trying out some recipes that meet special needs

*D*o food allergies and dietary restrictions have you itching? According to the Food Allergy & Anaphylaxis Network (FAAN), as many as 15 million Americans have food allergies, including approximately 6 million children. Common food allergens include milk, eggs, nuts, and shellfish. Although food allergies can be inconvenient at mealtime, for some people they can also be life threatening and must be addressed on a daily basis through a carefully managed diet.

Food allergies aren't the only reason for special diets, though. Some people have medical conditions that call for a dietary overhaul. Other individuals embrace special diets as a matter of personal preference or as part of an overall change in lifestyle.

As with most topics of interest, a lot has been written and discussed over the past few years regarding special diets. At times, this proliferation of information leads to confusion and great expense on the part of consumers as they adapt from a traditional diet of meat, dairy, and carbohydrates to one that depends primarily on plant-based protein and/or making substitutions for mainstream carbs and dairy products.

Although I don't pretend to be a dietary expert on the subject and strongly suggest that you seek professional medical and nutritional advice and input, I *do* want to take this time to share with you how your pressure cooker can be your new best friend as you adapt to dietary restrictions.

Exploring Some Common Special Diets

Special diets of particular interest these days are the vegetarian diet, the vegan diet, the gluten-free diet, and the dairy-free diet. But just what do these labels actually mean?

- **Vegetarian:** *Vegetarians* eat a plant-based diet. Although they avoid beef, pork, poultry, fish, shellfish, and animal flesh of any kind, they do eat eggs and dairy products.

- **Vegan:** *Vegans* don't eat meat and fish of any kind. Nor do they eat eggs, dairy products, or processed foods containing these or other animal-derived ingredients (such as gelatin).

- **Gluten-free:** A *gluten-free* diet requires its adherents to steer clear of ingredients derived from gluten-containing foods, such as wheat, barley, rye, and oats, as well as the use of gluten as a food additive in the form of a flavoring, stabilizing, or thickening agent. Most people who follow a gluten-free diet do so because their body cannot tolerate and process gluten during digestion. This genetic aliment is called *celiac disease.*

- **Dairy-free:** A *dairy-free* diet is free of animal milk products. Vegans opt for a dairy-free diet, as do people who are *lactose-intolerant,* allergic to some of the chemical components of milk and milk-based products such as butter, yogurt, cheese, and so forth.

Discovering the Protein Punch of Beans

If you're moving away from an animal protein-based diet, you need to sub-stitute plant-based proteins for meat, poultry, and, in some cases, dairy. The easiest substitution comes in the form of legumes: kidney beans, black beans, chickpeas, lentils, and so forth. Beans are high in protein and low in fat. They're a great source of soluble fiber, which helps remove harmful choles-terol from your body before it's absorbed. They can also help lower overall cholesterol levels and reduce the risk for heart disease.

Although available in the canned variety at all food stores, canned beans are high in sodium, which is a silent killer and bad for your health when con-sumed in large quantities. Dried beans are very low in sodium; ½ cup contains just 2 to 10 milligrams, whereas canned beans can contain as much as 600 milligrams per ½ cup, a quarter of the recommended daily limit! So what's a budding vegetarian/vegan to do? Pressure-cook! In fact, dried beans are the best source of protein ounce for ounce, and they're your best bet dollar for dollar too, costing, on average, just $2 for six cups of cooked beans!

As I mention in Chapter 2, the pressure cooker cooks up to 70 percent faster than conventional cooking methods, with beans cooking in approximately 15 to 20 minutes. That means a pot of cooked beans is like money in the bank. You can use those cooked beans to make soups, stews, sandwich spreads (think hummus), and even salads.

Adapting Existing Recipes

Almost any recipe can become vegetarian or vegan by simply replacing animal products, such as meat, with an equal quantity of cooked beans. A good example of this is the recipe for Chili without the Carne in this chapter. Made with three different types of beans, even the most carnivorous of eaters will be satisfied by this dish. (See the preceding section for the lowdown on beans.)

Additionally, a wide variety of dairy-free and gluten-free products are available at most supermarkets and health-food stores, making substitution a breeze. You can find examples of substitutions for all four diets in Table 13-1.

Table 13-1	Dietary Substitutes	
If You Can't Eat This	*Substitute an Equal Amount of This*	*When Making This*
Meat/poultry	Winter squash, such as butternut, or sweet potatoes, peeled and cut into bite-sized pieces	Stews, curries, soups
	Cooked beans and legumes	Stews, soups
	Extra-firm tofu, cut into bite-sized pieces	Stews
Ground meat	Cooked, mashed lentils	Meatballs
	Finely chopped vegetables such as carrots, celery, and zucchini	Sauces
Sausage or sausage patties	Veggie sausage or patties	Casseroles, breakfast sides
Bread, pita, breadcrumbs	Gluten-free bread and bread products	Sandwich fixings, casseroles
Pasta and macaroni	Gluten-free pasta and macaroni	Pasta dishes
Wheat berries, oatmeal	Quinoa	Salads, hot breakfast cereals
Hard or soft cheese	Soy or rice-based cheese	General cooking, garnishes
Dairy products such as milk, yogurt, sour cream, or butter	Soy, coconut, or rice-based versions	General cooking, desserts, garnishes

Pressure Cooking for Special Diets

When you start out with recipes that are already designed to be gluten-free, dairy-free, vegetarian, or vegan, you don't have to concern yourself with substitutions. And better yet, you can easily use your pressure cooker to whip up dishes that work for any of these special diets.

Following are 16 recipes designed for the pressure cooker. All of them are gluten-free, dairy-free, vegetarian, and vegan. So if you're searching for a salad, soup, or main dish that tastes delicious *and* fits with your dietary approach, look no further than the next several pages.

Peruvian Quinoa Salad

Prep time: 20 min • **Yield:** 4 servings

Ingredients	Directions
4 cups cooked quinoa **1 cup cooked frozen peas** **1 cup cooked frozen corn kernels** **1 small jalapeño pepper, cored, seeded, and finely minced** **4 green onions, white and green parts, thinly sliced** **1 pint cherry or grape tomatoes, cut in half** **¾ cup coarsely chopped cilantro leaves and stems** **6 tablespoons extra-virgin olive oil** **4 tablespoons red wine vinegar** **1 tablespoon Dijon mustard** **2 cloves garlic, minced** **1 tablespoon chopped mint leaves** **Salt and pepper to taste**	*1* Combine the cooked quinoa, peas, corn, jalapeño pepper, green onions, tomatoes, and cilantro in a large mixing bowl. Toss well. *2* Whisk together the olive oil, vinegar, Dijon mustard, garlic, and mint. Season with salt and black pepper. Pour over the salad and toss. *3* Let rest 1 hour at room temperature before serving.

Per serving: *Calories 554 (From Fat 259); Fat 29g (Saturated 4g); Cholesterol 0mg; Sodium 308mg; Carbohydrate 66g (Dietary Fiber 9g); Protein 13g.*

Tip: For pressure-cooked quinoa, see my Basic Quinoa Recipe in Chapter 7.

Mediterranean Lentil Salad

Prep time: 15 min • **Cook time:** 10 min under pressure • **Yield:** 4 servings

Ingredients	Directions
1 cup brown or green lentils, picked over	*1* Rinse the lentils in a colander under cold water.
3 cups water 1 bay leaf	*2* Place the lentils in a pressure cooker. Add the water and bay leaf.
1 large red bell pepper, cored, seeded, and diced	*3* Cover and bring to high pressure over high heat. Lower the heat to stabilize the pressure. Cook 10 minutes. (*For Electric:* Select high pressure and set the timer for 10 minutes.)
½ red onion, chopped	
2 tablespoons chopped mint leaves	*4* Remove from the heat. Release the pressure with a quick-release method.
2 tablespoons chopped flat-leaf parsley	*5* Unlock and remove the cover. Taste the lentils. If they're still hard, return to Step 3 and cook for an additional 1 to 3 minutes or until tender.
7 tablespoons extra-virgin olive oil, divided	
4 tablespoons lemon juice	
Salt and black pepper to taste	*6* Drain the lentils and place them in a large mixing bowl. Discard the bay leaf.
1 large ripe tomato, seeded and diced	
Homemade Vegan "Feta" (see the following recipe) or 1 cup crumbled feta cheese	*7* Add the red pepper, onion, mint, parsley, 6 tablespoons of the olive oil and the lemon juice. Season with salt and pepper. Top with the diced tomato and Homemade Vegan "Feta" (see the following recipe) or feta cheese.
¼ cup toasted pine nuts or toasted chopped hazelnuts	*8* Drizzle the remaining tablespoon of olive oil over the tomato and cheese. Garnish the salad with toasted hazelnuts.

Homemade Vegan "Feta"

1 pound extra-firm tofu	**1** Cut the tofu into ½-inch cubes. Place the tofu in a large, rectangular, glass baking dish. Set aside.
2 tablespoons water	
2 teaspoons yellow miso paste	**2** In a mixing bowl, whisk together the water, miso paste, vinegar, lemon juice, and salt. Pour the mixture over the tofu and mix well to coat. Let sit 15 minutes.
¼ cup white vinegar	
1 tablespoon lemon juice	
1 teaspoon salt	**3** Sprinkle 1 tablespoon of the nutritional yeast over the tofu and mix together. Taste and adjust for salt. Add an additional 1 tablespoon of yeast, if desired.
1 to 2 tablespoons nutritional yeast	

Per serving: Calories 574 (From Fat 325); Fat 36g (Saturated 5g); Cholesterol 0mg; Sodium 854mg; Carbohydrate 41g (Dietary Fiber 15g); Protein 29g.

Tip: When stored in an airtight plastic container, homemade vegan "feta" will keep fresh in the refrigerator for up to one week.

Roasted Tomato Soup

Prep time: 15 min • **Cook time:** 10 min under pressure • **Yield:** 4 servings

Ingredients

2 tablespoons olive oil

1 large onion, chopped

2 cloves garlic, minced

1 large carrot, peeled and chopped

1 stalk celery, chopped

1 tablespoon fresh chopped thyme, or 1 teaspoon dried

¼ teaspoon crushed hot red pepper flakes

Salt and pepper to taste

One 28-ounce can roasted diced tomatoes

2 cups vegetable stock

2 teaspoons sugar

Dairy or vegan sour cream, or Greek yogurt

2 tablespoons chopped basil

Directions

1 Heat the olive oil in a pressure cooker over medium-high heat. Add the onion and garlic. Cook until the onion is soft. Add the carrot, celery, thyme, and red pepper flakes. Cook for 2 minutes. Season with salt and pepper. (*For Electric:* Select the Brown setting.)

2 Add the tomatoes, stock, and sugar. Bring to a boil.

3 Cover and bring to high pressure over high heat. Lower the heat to stabilize the pressure. Cook for 10 minutes. (*For Electric:* Select high pressure and set the timer for 10 minutes.)

4 Remove from the heat. Release the pressure with a quick-release method. Unlock and remove the cover.

5 Puree the soup with a hand blender or in batches in a blender, until smooth. Pour back into the pressure cooker. Simmer the soup over low heat 5 minutes. (*For Electric:* Select Warm setting.)

6 Taste and adjust for salt and pepper. Remove from heat. Stir in the sour cream or yogurt and basil. Serve immediately.

Per serving: Calories 195 (From Fat 107); Fat 12g (Saturated 3g); Cholesterol 9mg; Sodium 1,120mg; Carbohydrate 19g (Dietary Fiber 3g); Protein 2g.

Red Lentil Soup

Prep time: 20 min • **Cook time:** 6 min under pressure • **Yield:** 6 servings

Ingredients	*Directions*
2 tablespoons olive oil 1 medium onion, chopped 3 cloves garlic, minced 2 large carrots, peeled and chopped 3 stalks celery, chopped	*1* Heat the olive oil in a pressure cooker over medium-high heat. Add the onion, garlic, carrots, and celery. Cook until the onion is soft. (*For Electric:* Select the Brown setting.)
1 teaspoon ground cumin ½ teaspoon ground coriander ½ teaspoon ground cayenne pepper	*2* Add the cumin, coriander, and cayenne pepper; cook 2 minutes. Add the tomatoes and cook 2 minutes. Season with salt and pepper.
One 14-ounce can diced tomatoes Salt and pepper to taste	*3* Add the lentils and stock. Cover and bring to high pressure over high heat. Lower the heat to stabilize the pressure. Cook for 6 minutes. (*For Electric:* Select high pressure and set the timer for 6 minutes.)
2 cups red lentils, rinsed under cold water 8 cups vegetable stock or water	*4* Remove from the heat. Release the pressure with a quick-release method. Unlock and remove the cover.
	5 Puree the soup with a hand blender, or in batches in a blender, until smooth. Pour back into the pressure cooker. Simmer soup over low heat 5 minutes. (*For Electric:* Select Warm setting.)
	6 Taste and adjust for salt and pepper. Remove from the heat. Serve immediately.

Per serving: Calories 321 (From Fat 60); Fat 7g (Saturated 1g); Cholesterol 0mg; Sodium 1,558mg; Carbohydrate 50g (Dietary Fiber 17g); Protein 21g.

Tip: Try serving this soup with dairy or vegan Greek yogurt, lemon wedges, and wheat or gluten-free pita bread, in accordance with the restrictions of your particular diet.

Moroccan Chickpea and Vegetable Soup

Prep time: 15 min, plus soaking time • **Cook time:** 25 min under pressure • **Yield:** 6 servings

Ingredients	*Directions*
1 cup dried chickpeas, picked over	*1* Rinse the chickpeas in a colander under cold water. Soak the chickpeas.
2 tablespoons olive oil	*2* Heat the olive oil in a pressure cooker over medium-high heat. Add the onion, garlic, carrots, and celery. Cook until the onion is soft. Add the cumin and flour; cook 1 minute. (*For Electric:* Select the Brown setting.)
1 medium onion, chopped	
1 clove garlic, minced	
2 large carrots, peeled and chopped	
2 stalks celery, chopped	*3* Add the water, stirring rapidly with a wire whisk. Add the tomatoes, stock, and bay leaf. Season with salt and pepper.
1 teaspoon ground cumin	
¼ cup flour (eliminate for gluten-free recipe)	*4* Add the soaked, drained chickpeas. Cover and bring to high pressure over high heat. Lower the heat to stabilize the pressure. Cook for 20 minutes. (*For Electric:* Select high pressure and set the timer for 20 minutes.)
4 cups water	
One 14½-ounce can diced tomatoes	
2 cups vegetable stock	*5* Remove from the heat. Release the pressure with a quick-release method. Unlock and remove the cover. Taste the chickpeas. If they're still hard, return to Step 3 and cook for an additional 5 minutes or until tender. Taste and adjust for salt and pepper.
1 bay leaf	
Salt and pepper to taste	
½ cup uncooked white rice	
2 tablespoons chopped flat-leaf parsley	*6* Add the rice. Cover and bring to high pressure over high heat. Lower the heat to stabilize the pressure. Cook for 5 minutes. (*For Electric:* Select high pressure and set the timer for 5 minutes.)
Lemon wedges	
	7 Remove from the heat. Release the pressure with a quick-release method. Unlock and remove the cover. Garnish with parsley. Serve immediately with lemon wedges.

Per serving: Calories 208 (From Fat 53); Fat 6g (Saturated 1g); Cholesterol 0mg; Sodium 455mg; Carbohydrate 34g (Dietary Fiber 5g); Protein 6g.

Tip: If you eliminate the flour from Step 2, thicken the cooked soup by mashing some of the beans along the side of the pot with a large metal or wooden spoon.

Black Bean and Salsa Soup

Prep time: 15 min • **Cook time:** 20 min under pressure • **Yield:** 6 servings

Ingredients	*Directions*
2 cups (1 pound) dried black beans, picked over	*1* Rinse the beans in a colander under cold water. Soak the beans.
6 cups vegetable stock	
One 12-ounce jar your favorite brand of prepared salsa	*2* Place the beans in a pressure cooker. Add the stock, salsa, and bay leaf.
1 bay leaf	*3* Cover and bring to high pressure over high heat. Lower the heat to stabilize the pressure. Cook 15 minutes. (*For Electric*: Select high pressure and set the timer for 15 minutes.)
Salt and pepper to taste	
	4 Remove from the heat. Release the pressure with a quick-release method.
	5 Unlock and remove the cover. Taste the beans. If they're still hard, return to Step 3 and cook for an additional 3 to 5 minutes or until tender.
	6 Season with salt and pepper.

Per serving: Calories 262 (From Fat 17); Fat 2g (Saturated 0g); Cholesterol 0mg; Sodium 1,458mg; Carbohydrate 47g (Dietary Fiber 13g); Protein 18g.

Tip: Try serving this soup with a dollop of sour cream or Greek yogurt, depending on your dietary restrictions.

Portuguese Kale and Potatoes

Prep time: 10 min • **Cook time:** 12 min under pressure • **Yield:** 4 servings

Ingredients	Directions
3 tablespoons olive oil 2 onions, chopped 4 cloves garlic, crushed 6 peeled and diced medium potatoes 1 teaspoon smoked Spanish paprika Salt and pepper to taste 2 veggie chorizo sausages (about 4 ounces) 2 bay leaves 8 cups vegetable stock 6 cups coarsely chopped kale leaves and stems 2 cups cooked pinto, red, or white kidney beans	**1** Heat the olive oil in a pressure cooker over medium-high heat. Add the onions and garlic. Cook until the onions are soft. Add the potatoes and paprika. Season with salt and pepper. Cook for 2 minutes. Add the chorizo, bay leaves, and stock. (*For Electric:* Select the Brown setting.) **2** Cover and bring to high pressure over high heat. Lower the heat to stabilize the pressure. Cook for 10 minutes. (*For Electric:* Select high pressure and set the timer for 10 minutes.) **3** Remove from the heat. Release the pressure with a quick-release method. **4** Unlock and remove the cover. Taste and adjust for salt and pepper. **5** Add the chopped kale and beans. Cover and bring to high pressure over high heat. Lower the heat to stabilize the pressure. Cook for 2 minutes. (*For Electric:* Select high pressure and set the timer for 2 minutes.) **6** Remove from the heat. Release the pressure with a quick-release method. **7** Unlock and remove the cover. Remove the chorizo and slice thin. Return to soup. Serve immediately.

Per serving: Calories 543 (From Fat 144); Fat 16g (Saturated 2g); Cholesterol 0mg; Sodium 2,313mg; Carbohydrate 89g (Dietary Fiber 15g); Protein 22g.

Chili without the Carne

Prep time: 25 min • **Cook time:** 8 min under pressure • **Yield:** 8 servings

Ingredients	Directions
2 tablespoons olive oil	*1* Heat the olive oil in a pressure cooker over medium-high heat. Add the onion; garlic; green, red, and jalapeño peppers; carrots; and celery. Cook until the onion is soft.
1 large onion, chopped	
2 cloves garlic, minced	
1 large green bell pepper, cored, seeded, and chopped	*2* Add the chili powder, cumin, and oregano. Stir and cook 1 minute. Add the cooked beans and tomatoes. Season with salt and pepper. Stir to combine. (*For Electric:* Select the Brown setting.)
1 large red bell pepper, cored, seeded, and chopped	
1 jalapeño pepper, cored, seeded, and chopped	*3* Cover and bring to high pressure over high heat. Lower the heat to stabilize the pressure. Cook for 8 minutes. (*For Electric:* Select high pressure and set the timer for 8 minutes.)
2 carrots, peeled and chopped	
2 stalks celery, chopped	
2 tablespoons chili powder	*4* Remove from the heat. Release the pressure with a quick-release method.
4 teaspoons ground cumin	
1 teaspoon ground oregano	*5* Unlock and remove the cover.
2 cups cooked pinto beans	
2 cups cooked red kidney beans	*6* Taste and adjust for salt and pepper.
2 cups cooked black beans	
One 28-ounce can crushed roasted tomatoes	
Salt and pepper to taste	

Per serving: Calories 262 (From Fat 43); Fat 5g (Saturated 1g); Cholesterol 0mg; Sodium 342mg; Carbohydrate 44g (Dietary Fiber 14g); Protein 13g.

Tip: Try serving this recipe over white or brown rice and top with shredded dairy or vegan cheddar cheese, depending on your particular dietary restrictions.

One-Pot Pasta Dinner

Prep time: 15 min • **Cook time:** 15 min under pressure • **Yield:** 2 servings

Ingredients	Directions
1 tablespoon olive oil	*1* Heat the olive oil in a pressure cooker over medium-high heat. Add the onion and garlic. Cook until the onion is soft. Add the tomato sauce, vegetable stock, and Italian seasoning. Add the pasta. Stir well. (*For Electric:* Select the Brown setting.)
1 medium onion, chopped	
1 clove garlic, minced	
2 cups your favorite tomato sauce	
1½ cups vegetable stock	*2* Cover and bring to high pressure over high heat. Lower the heat to stabilize the pressure. Cook for 15 minutes. (*For Electric:* Select high pressure and set the timer for 15 minutes.)
1 teaspoon Italian seasoning	
8 ounces wheat or gluten-free penne or ziti pasta	
2 tablespoons chopped basil	*3* Remove from the heat. Let the pressure drop using a quick-release method.
Dairy or soy-based Parmesan cheese, grated	*4* Unlock and remove the cover. Stir in the chopped basil. Serve immediately with the grated cheese.

Per serving: Calories 610 (From Fat 96); Fat 11g (Saturated 2g); Cholesterol 4mg; Sodium 2,210mg; Carbohydrate 107g (Dietary Fiber 7g); Protein 24g.

Pasta Pomarola

Prep time: 40 min • **Cook time:** 25 min under pressure • **Yield:** 8 servings

Ingredients	*Directions*
3 tablespoons olive oil **4 large onions, chopped small** **8 carrots, chopped small** **8 stalks celery, chopped small** **One 28-ounce can whole tomatoes with liquid** **2 tablespoons chopped fresh thyme leaves** **Salt and pepper to taste** **16 ounces dried pasta, wheat or gluten-free, cooked al dente** **Dairy or soy-based Parmesan cheese, grated**	**1** Heat the olive oil in a pressure cooker over medium-high heat. Add the onions, carrots, and celery. Cook 2 minutes, stirring constantly. Reduce the heat to low and cook 30 minutes, stirring frequently so the vegetables don't stick. (*For Electric:* Select the Brown setting initially; after 2 minutes, switch to Warm.) **2** Add the tomatoes and thyme. Season with salt and pepper. **3** Cover and bring to high pressure over high heat. Lower the heat to stabilize the pressure. Cook for 15 minutes. (*For Electric:* Select high pressure and set the timer for 15 minutes.) **4** Remove from the heat. Release the pressure with a quick-release method. Unlock and remove the cover. **5** Puree the sauce with a hand blender, or in batches in a blender, until smooth. Pour back into the pressure cooker. Cover and bring to high pressure over high heat. Lower the heat to stabilize the pressure. Cook for 10 minutes. (*For Electric*: Select high pressure and set the timer for 10 minutes.) **6** Remove from the heat. Release the pressure with a quick-release method. Unlock and remove the cover. **7** Taste and adjust for salt and pepper. Serve over pasta cooked al dente with the grated Parmesan cheese.

Per serving: *Calories 369 (From Fat 69); Fat 8g (Saturated 2g); Cholesterol 4mg; Sodium 408mg; Carbohydrate 64g (Dietary Fiber 7g); Protein 13g.*

Tip: Depending on the brand and composition, gluten-free pasta may take longer to cook than traditional wheat pasta. Read and follow the package instructions for cooking times.

Minestra with Creamy Polenta

Prep time: 20 min • **Cook time:** 5 min under pressure • **Yield:** 6 servings

Ingredients

4 tablespoons olive oil, divided

1 large onion, chopped

2 cloves garlic, peeled and thinly sliced

1 green bell pepper, cored, seeded, and diced

1 red bell pepper, cored, seeded, and diced

1 yellow bell pepper, cored, seeded, and diced

1 medium eggplant, peeled and diced

1 small zucchini, trimmed, quartered lengthwise, and diced

Salt and pepper to taste

One 14½-ounce can diced tomatoes

¼ cup water

1 teaspoon dried thyme

1½ teaspoons salt

½ teaspoon black pepper

2 cups cooked pinto, red, or white kidney beans

2 tablespoons shredded fresh basil

2 tablespoons minced fresh flat-leaf parsley

Creamy Polenta (see the following recipe)

Dairy or soy-based Parmesan cheese, grated

Directions

1 Heat 2 tablespoons of the olive oil in a pressure cooker over medium-high heat. Add the onion, garlic, and the green, red, and yellow bell peppers. Cook until the onion is soft. (*For Electric:* Select the Brown setting.)

2 Add the remaining 2 tablespoons of oil and the eggplant and zucchini. Season with salt and pepper. Cook 5 minutes. Add the tomatoes, water, thyme, 1½ teaspoons salt, and ½ teaspoon black pepper. Cook for 2 minutes. Add the beans.

3 Cover and bring to high pressure over high heat. Lower the heat to stabilize the pressure. Cook for 5 minutes. (*For Electric:* Select high pressure and set the timer for 5 minutes.)

4 Remove from the heat. Release the pressure with a quick-release method.

5 Unlock and remove the cover. Taste and adjust for salt and pepper. Add the basil and parsley.

6 Serve over Creamy Polenta with grated Parmesan cheese.

Creamy Polenta

2 cups vegetable stock

2 cups dairy or soy milk

1 cup polenta, or yellow medium-coarse cornmeal

½ cup grated dairy or soy-based Parmesan cheese

1 tablespoon dairy or vegan butter

½ teaspoon salt

1 In a medium-sized saucepan, bring the stock and milk to a boil. Add the polenta or cornmeal. Cook over low heat, stirring constantly with a whisk, until the liquid is absorbed and the polenta is creamy and smooth, about 10 minutes.

2 Remove from the heat and stir in the cheese, butter, and salt. Serve immediately.

Per serving: Calories 391 (From Fat 156); Fat 17g (Saturated 6g); Cholesterol 21mg; Sodium 1,367mg; Carbohydrate 48g (Dietary Fiber 11g); Protein 15g.

Braised Eggplant

Prep time: 20 min • **Cook time:** 6 min under pressure • **Yield:** 6 servings

Ingredients	Directions
One 28-ounce can crushed tomatoes	*1* In a mixing bowl, combine the crushed tomatoes and water.
½ cup water	
4 tablespoons olive oil	*2* Drizzle 1 tablespoon of the olive oil in the bottom of the pressure cooker. Spoon ½ cup of the tomato mixture over the bottom of the pot and spread evenly.
2 medium eggplants, cut into ½-inch cubes	
Salt and black pepper to taste	*3* Evenly spread ⅓ of the cubed eggplant in the pot. Spoon ⅓ of the remaining tomato mixture over the eggplant. Season with salt and pepper. Drizzle with 1 tablespoon of the olive oil and add ½ teaspoon of the Italian seasoning, ⅛ teaspoon of the hot red pepper flakes, 1 clove of sliced garlic, ⅓ of the parsley or basil, and ¼ cup of the grated cheese.
1½ teaspoons dried Italian seasoning	
⅜ teaspoon crushed hot red pepper flakes	
3 cloves garlic, peeled and thinly sliced	
4 tablespoons chopped flat-leaf parsley or basil	*4* Repeat Step 3 two times.
¾ cup grated dairy or soy-based Parmesan cheese	*5* Cover and bring to high pressure over high heat. Lower the heat to stabilize the pressure. Cook 6 minutes. (*For Electric:* Select high pressure and set the timer for 6 minutes.)
	6 Remove from the heat. Release the pressure with a quick-release method.
	7 Unlock and remove the cover. Serve.

Per serving: Calories 203 (From Fat 115); Fat 13g (Saturated 3g); Cholesterol 8mg; Sodium 463mg; Carbohydrate 18g (Dietary Fiber 6g); Protein 8g.

Tip: Serve this recipe with gluten-free hearty Italian bread or spoon it over gluten-free spaghetti cooked al dente.

Cauliflower and Potato Curry

Prep time: 30 min • **Cook time:** 25 min under pressure • **Yield:** 8 servings

Ingredients	*Directions*
½ cup dried chickpeas, picked over	*1* Rinse the chickpeas in a colander under cold water. Soak the chickpeas.
4 tablespoons olive oil	*2* Heat the olive oil in a pressure cooker over medium-high heat. Add the onions, garlic, gingerroot, and jalapeño. Cook until the onion is soft. Add the curry powder and garam masala and cook 1 minute. Add the tomato paste, diced tomatoes, and water. Season with salt and pepper. (*For Electric:* Select the Brown setting.)
2 medium onions, chopped	
3 cloves garlic, minced	
1 tablespoon minced gingerroot	
1 jalapeño pepper, cored, seeded, and chopped fine	
2 tablespoons mild curry powder	*3* Add the soaked, drained chickpeas. Cover and bring to high pressure over high heat. Lower the heat to stabilize the pressure. Cook for 20 minutes. (*For Electric*: Select high pressure and set the timer for 25 minutes.)
1½ teaspoons garam masala	
1 tablespoon tomato paste	
One 14½-ounce can diced tomatoes	*4* Remove from the heat. Release the pressure with a quick-release method. Unlock and remove the cover. Taste the chickpea s. If they're still hard, return to Step 3 and cook for an additional 5 minutes or until tender. Taste and adjust for salt and pepper.
3½ cups water	
Salt and pepper to taste	
1 small head cauliflower, trimmed and broken into florets	*5* Add the cauliflower and potatoes. Cover and bring to high pressure over high heat. Lower the heat to stabilize the pressure. Cook for 6 minutes. (*For Electric:* Select high pressure and set the timer for 6 minutes.)
3 large red potatoes, peeled and diced	
1 cup frozen peas	*6* Remove from the heat. Release the pressure with a quick-release method. Unlock and remove the cover. Add the peas and coconut milk and simmer over low heat 5 minutes. (*For Electric:* Select Warm setting.)
¼ cup unsweetened coconut milk	
¼ cup coarsely chopped cilantro leaves and stems	*7* Taste and adjust for salt and pepper. Remove from the heat. Stir in cilantro.

Per serving: *Calories 272 (From Fat 88); Fat 10g (Saturated 3g); Cholesterol 0mg; Sodium 181mg; Carbohydrate 40g (Dietary Fiber 8g); Protein 8g.*

Tip: Try serving this dish over basmati rice and top with dollops of plain dairy or vegan Greek-style yogurt.

Cumin-Scented Beans with Greens

Prep time: 15 min • **Cook time:** 15 min • **Yield:** 6 servings

Ingredients	Directions
1 cup uncooked basmati rice	*1* Prepare the rice according to the Basic Rice Recipe in Chapter 7. Set aside to use when serving.
1 tablespoon olive oil	
1 medium onion, diced	*2* Heat the olive oil in a large skillet over medium-high heat. Add the onion and cook until soft. Add the cumin; cook, stirring, 1 minute. Add the chickpeas. Cook, stirring, 2 minutes. Add the lemon zest and water. Season with salt and pepper. Bring the mixture to a simmer. (*For Electric:* Select the Brown setting.)
1 teaspoon cumin	
1 cup cooked chickpeas	
Grated zest of one lemon	
2 tablespoons water	
Salt and black pepper to taste	*3* Stir in the spinach or kale. Cook, stirring, until the spinach or kale wilts. Remove from the heat.
One 10-ounce bag baby spinach or baby kale leaves	
	4 Divide the rice among four dinner plates. Top with the chickpeas and greens.

Per serving: Calories 211 (From Fat 28); Fat 3g (Saturated 0g); Cholesterol 0mg; Sodium 175mg; Carbohydrate 44g (Dietary Fiber 6g); Protein 6g.

Tip: Try serving this dish with dairy or plain, vegan, Greek-style yogurt and wheat or gluten-free pita bread.

Note: To cook the chickpeas, see my Master Chickpea Recipe in Chapter 10.

Meatless Monday Veggie Stew

Prep time: 20 min • **Cook time:** 8 min under pressure • **Yield:** 6 servings

Ingredients	*Directions*
2 tablespoons olive oil **2 medium onions, chopped** **2 cloves garlic, peeled and sliced** **1 small butternut squash, peeled, seeded, and diced** **2 carrots, peeled and cut into 1-inch pieces** **1 large russet potato, peeled and diced** **1½ teaspoons dried thyme** **½ teaspoon cayenne pepper** **1 tablespoon curry powder** **One 14-ounce can diced tomatoes, with liquid** **8 ounces string beans, cut into 1-inch pieces** **1 small head of cauliflower, trimmed and broken into florets** **1 cup cooked chickpeas** **4 cups vegetable stock** **Salt and pepper to taste** **Juice of one lemon** **4 tablespoons minced flat-leaf parsley**	*1* Heat the olive oil in a pressure cooker over medium-high heat. Add the onions, garlic, squash, carrots, potato, thyme, cayenne, and curry. Cook, stirring often, for 5 minutes. (*For Electric:* Select the Brown setting.) *2* Add the tomatoes and cook 2 minutes. Add the string beans, cauliflower, chickpeas, and stock. Season with salt and pepper. *3* Cover and bring to high pressure over high heat. Lower the heat to stabilize the pressure. Cook for 8 minutes. (*For Electric*: Select high pressure and set the timer for 8 minutes.) *4* Remove from the heat. Release the pressure with a quick-release method. *5* Unlock and remove the cover. Taste and adjust for salt and pepper. Add the lemon juice and parsley. Serve in soup bowls.

Per serving: *Calories 216 (From Fat 58); Fat 6g (Saturated 1g); Cholesterol 0mg; Sodium 960mg; Carbohydrate 37g (Dietary Fiber 10g); Protein 8g.*

Tip: Try serving this dish over gluten-free couscous or basmati rice.

"Barbecued" Tofu

Prep time: 10 min • **Cook time:** 5 min under pressure • **Yield:** 6 servings

Ingredients	Directions
2 tablespoons olive oil	*1* Heat the olive oil in a pressure cooker over medium-high heat. Add the garlic, onion, green and red pepper, and celery. Season with salt and curry powder. Cook 2 minutes. Add the tofu and cook 5 minutes, stirring frequently. (*For Electric:* Select the Brown setting.)
4 cloves garlic, peeled and minced	
1 medium onion, chopped	
1 green bell pepper, cored, seeded, and diced	*2* Add the barbecue sauce. Cover and bring to high pressure over high heat. Lower the heat to stabilize the pressure. Cook for 5 minutes. (*For Electric:* Select high pressure and set the timer for 5 minutes.)
1 red bell pepper, cored, seeded, and diced	
1 stalk celery, diced	
Pinch salt	*3* Remove from the heat. Release the pressure with a quick-release method.
Pinch curry powder	
Two 14-ounce packages extra-firm tofu, cut into 1-inch cubes	*4* Unlock and remove the cover.
One 12-ounce bottle barbecue sauce	

Per serving: Calories 167 (From Fat 88); Fat 10g (Saturated 1g); Cholesterol 0mg; Sodium 502mg; Carbohydrate 13g (Dietary Fiber 2g); Protein 9g.

Tip: Try serving this dish with brown rice.

Part IV
The Part of Tens

The 5th Wave   By Rich Tennant

"Your cigar? Don't worry — if it fell into the pressure cooker it'll be fork tender and delicious."

In this part . . .

Here I've assembled some helpful top-ten lists, which include stumbling blocks you may encounter (and solutions for them) as well as tips for perfect pressure cooking.

Chapter 14

Ten Problems and How to Handle Them

. . . .

In This Chapter

▶ Keeping your cool when things go wrong

▶ Knowing how to fix common problems

. . . .

*B*ecause pressure cookers are easy to use as appliances go and have relatively few moving parts, they hardly ever break or malfunction. Nevertheless, things can go wrong, whether due to user or operational error. So I've compiled a list of ten problems that can occur, along with reasons and advice on how to keep those problems from happening again.

If you experience a problem that I don't touch upon, please consult the printed materials provided by the manufacturer of your pressure cooker. If you still can't find the solution to the problem, contact the company's customer service department.

The Cover Won't Close

Problem: You can't close the cover.

Reasons:

1. The cover isn't sitting squarely on top of the pressure cooker.

2. The rubber gasket isn't positioned properly under the cover.

Solutions:

1. The locking mechanism on most pressure cookers is similar to that of a jar. If positioned at an angle, it won't close. Make sure the cover is sitting squarely on top of the pressure cooker before trying to close it.

2. Before trying to close the pressure cooker, make sure that the gasket is positioned properly and is laying flat.

When the cover is closed, you'll hear a click after it locks in place.

Never force the cover closed, or you may never be able to open it again.

The Cooker's Pressure Won't Rise

Problem: The pressure indicator doesn't rise, or the jiggler valve doesn't turn with vim and vigor.

Reasons:

1. The burner isn't hot enough (for stovetop cookers only).
2. The recipe doesn't call for enough liquid to create steam.
3. The rubber gasket isn't positioned properly under the cover.
4. The pressure regulator valve is dirty or obstructed.
5. The pressure cooker was damaged, and the safety valve has activated or is blocked, inhibiting pressure from building up.

Solutions:

1. Raise the burner heat to high (make this a habit!) when bringing your stovetop pressure cooker up to pressure.
2. Always use at least 1 cup of cooking liquid; some manufacturers suggest using at least 2 cups. Check your owner's manual to determine the correct amount of liquid needed for your particular pressure cooker.
3. Make sure the rubber gasket is positioned properly under the cover.
4. Clean the pressure regulator valve according to the manufacturer's instructions in the owner's manual.
5. The safety valves kick in if the pressure cooker is damaged. Contact the manufacturer for after-sales service and repairs.

Your Cooker Is Leaking Steam

Problem: Condensation or steam leaks from under the cover of the pressure cooker.

Reasons:

1. The cover isn't properly closed.
2. The gasket isn't properly positioned or is damaged.
3. The pressure cooker is overfilled.

Solutions:

1. Release any pressure using a quick-release method (I walk you through these in Chapter 4). Open and reclose the cover as discussed in the earlier "The Cover Won't Close" section.

   For electric pressure cookers, press Stop and then release the pressure.

2. Release any pressure using a quick-release method. Open the pressure cooker. Remove the gasket and check it for tears or cracks. If the gasket is damaged, replace it. If it's okay, check the owner's manual to see whether the gasket has to be positioned in a specific fashion or location (some gaskets have small cutouts or openings that must be lined up in order for the pressure cooker to work properly).

3. Never fill the pressure cooker more than half full with liquid, or more than two-thirds full with food. If above the limit, remove the excess amount and continue cooking under pressure.

Small drops of condensation are normal on the lids of some pressure cookers.

The Safety Valves Went Off

Problem: The safety valves activate.

Reasons:

1. The stovetop pressure cooker reached the level of pressure chosen, and the burner heat wasn't lowered.

2. The vent pipe or pressure-regulator valve has food buildup in it.

Solutions:

1. Never exceed the amount of pressure chosen; lower the burner heat once the desired level of pressure is reached.

   Because the electric pressure cooker automatically adjusts and maintains the cooking temperature needed for the amount of pressure chosen, the user need not worry about this.

2. If using a jiggler-valve or developed-weight-model pressure cooker, remove the weight and look through the vent pipe for a possible clog (or check the manufacturer's instructions). When using an electric pressure cooker or a stovetop pressure cooker with a spring-valve pressure regulator, follow the manufacturer's instructions and remove the valve to check whether there's an obstruction under the valve. Regardless of model, use a toothpick to remove any foreign particles; then flush the opening with clean water.

The Pressure Indicator Doesn't Rise

Problem: The pressure indicator (on certain stovetop models only) doesn't rise as pressure builds.

Reason: The pressure indicator is dirty and therefore stuck.

Solution: Remove the pressure cooker from the stove. Release any pressure using a quick-release method (see Chapter 4 for the scoop on quick-release methods). Remove the cover. Refer to your owner's manual for instructions on how to clean the pressure indicator. Replace the cover. Place the pressure cooker on the stove and resume cooking.

The Cover Won't Open

Problem: You can't open or remove the cover.

Reasons:

1. There is still some pressure in the pressure cooker.
2. A vacuum has formed.
3. The cover wasn't positioned properly when closed.

Solutions:

1. Always release all the pressure before attempting to open the lid.
2. If the lid still won't open after releasing all the pressure, a vacuum may have formed. Bring the contents of the pot up to pressure again over high heat (or use the high pressure setting if you're using an electric pressure cooker) and then try releasing the pressure.
3. Never force the cover into the locked position. If you still can't get the cover off, contact the manufacturer.

Your Food Is Underwhelming

Problem: The food is undercooked.

Reasons:

1. The pressure cooker didn't reach or maintain pressure and thus didn't operate properly.
2. The food wasn't cooked long enough.

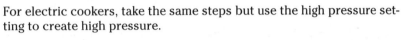

Solutions:

1. When using a stovetop pressure cooker, always bring the unit up to pressure, over high heat. The pressure-indicator valve or the weighted valve must be in the upright position or the jiggler valve must be turning with vim and vigor before you lower the burner to a simmer. After lowering the heat, make sure the pressure cooker maintains pressure. If it doesn't, raise the burner heat a bit until it does.

2. For stovetop cookers, reposition the cover, cook on high pressure for an additional 1 to 3 minutes (the harder or tougher the food is, the longer it needs to cook), release the pressure, and check the food.

   For electric cookers, take the same steps but use the high pressure setting to create high pressure.

Your Food Is Overcooked

Problem: The food is overcooked.

Reason: The food was cooked too long under pressure.

Solution: Make a note and reduce the cooking time when preparing the food next time.

For cooking time accuracy when using a stovetop pressure cooker, always use a kitchen timer. Set the timer for the cooking time needed when the pressure cooker reaches pressure. If using an electric pressure cooker, set the timer for less time. It's always better to undercook than overcook.

Your Food and Pot Are a Charred Mess

Problem: Food burns or sticks to the bottom of the pot.

Reasons:

1. There wasn't enough cooking liquid.

2. The burner heat was too high, causing food to stick to the bottom of the pot or the liquid to evaporate (for stovetop models only).

Solutions:

1. Check the recipe for the correct amount of cooking liquid.

2. When using a stovetop pressure cooker, be sure to reduce the burner heat to low when pressure is reached. On an electric cooktop, use two

burners — one on high heat for reaching pressure and the other on low for maintaining it. Move the pressure cooker from the high burner to the low one after the cooker reaches high pressure.

If you burn food on the bottom of the stovetop pressure-cooker pot, remove as much of the food as possible without scraping the bottom and try cleaning with a nonabrasive cleaner such as Bon Ami. If using an electric pressure cooker, also remove as much of the burnt-on food as you can using a plastic or wooden kitchen utensil, so as not to damage the nonstick finish. Add hot water and allow food to soak to soften before removing any remaining residue with a nonabrasive cleaning pad and liquid dishwashing detergent.

Your Stovetop Pressure Cooker Is Less Than Shiny

Problem: The metal finish on your stovetop cooker is dull.

Reasons:

1. Certain high-acidity foods, such as tomatoes, interact with an aluminum pot and discolor the metal finish.

2. Hard water and foods such as dried beans can leave a cloudy cover on the bottom of the pressure cooker.

3. Heat that's too high in a dry pot or one with little food and liquid can cause scorching when browning.

4. The outside of the pot was cleaned with abrasive cleaners or scouring pads.

Solutions:

1. This condition is normal. To minimize the effect, remove high-acidic foods from the pressure cooker immediately after cooking.

2. Soak the inside bottom of the pressure-cooker pot with a solution made of two parts water and one part white vinegar. Let sit for 10 minutes before pouring the solution out and rinsing the pot.

3. When browning foods, always make sure there is liquid or oil in the pressure-cooker pot as it heats up over medium-high. If there are scorch or burn marks in the pressure-cooker pot, try removing them with a non-abrasive cleaning powder such as Bon Ami.

4. To keep the exterior finish of the pressure cooker shiny, I've learned over the years to never use common abrasive cleaners or scouring pads. Attempt to remove stains or burn marks with a nonabrasive cleaning powder such as Bon Ami.

Chapter 15

Ten Tips for Great Pressure Cooking

*B*ecause pressure cookers cook differently than conventional covered pots do, you have to rethink some old cooking methods and master a couple of new tricks when using a pressure cooker, especially if you want delicious results every time. But don't be overwhelmed or perplexed. In this chapter, I share with you some things that you should be aware of before, during, and after cooking under pressure.

Keeping It Safe

Pressure cooking today is a far cry from the methods used even 15 years ago. Pressure cookers are safer to use than ever before, especially if you follow my five-point inspection checklist (discussed in greater detail in Chapter 5) each and every time you use your pressure cooker:

1. **Following the instructions in the manufacturer's use and care guide, keep the pressure cooker clean.**

   Always wash your pressure cooker well after use or if you haven't used it for an extended period.

2. **Remove and inspect the rubber sealing gasket or ring before using the pressure cooker.**

3. **Check the safety valves to make sure they're clean and in good working order.**

   Consult your owner's manual for the exact procedures.

4. **Fill the pressure cooker properly (no more than half full of liquid and ⅔ full of food).**

    Don't overfill it, and be sure to use enough liquid (at least a cup).

5. **Look, listen, and smell as the pressure cooker cooks.**

    If you see excess steam or condensation coming out of the valves or from under the cover, if you hear steam escaping from the safety valves, or if you smell the food burning, remove the pressure cooker from the stove and immediately release the pressure by using a quick-release method as described in Chapter 4.

    For electric pressure cookers, press Stop and then release the pressure.

Determining What a Pressure Cooker Can Hold

Even though I developed and tested the recipes in this book in 6-quart pressure cookers, you never fill a 6-quart pot with more than 4 quarts of food. Steam weighs nothing, but it requires space as it builds up. Therefore, regardless of your pressure cooker's size, heed these guidelines:

✔ Never fill it more than ⅔ full with food.

✔ Never fill it more than halfway with liquid.

See Chapter 4 for a more in-depth discussion of filling a pressure cooker.

Using Enough Liquid

A pressure cooker cooks under pressure by bringing cooking liquid to a boil in a sealed pot that traps the building steam, causing the temperature inside the closed pressure cooker to rise to 250 degrees. To get this process to work, you must cook with at least 1 cup of cooking liquid; check the manufacturer's owner's manual because some pressure cookers may need up to 2 cups of liquid.

Intensifying Flavors by Searing and Browning First

Today, many people have less-than-fond memories of the food their mothers or grandmothers made in pressure cookers. For whatever reason, a couple of generations ago, overcooked, mushy food was pretty much the norm. Pressure cookers helped the home cook make that happen even quicker! Food was thrown in the pressure-cooker pot with an abundance of liquid and cooked about twice as long as needed. The end result: gray, unrecognizable foods. Nowadays, we like to eat our veggies brightly colored and somewhat crunchy and our meat flavorful and still intact.

To get the maximum flavor out of foods cooked in a pressure cooker, I like to sear and brown them first in a small amount of oil to intensify the flavor and overall appeal. Always do so in the pressure-cooker pot before cooking under pressure. Foods that benefit greatly from this technique include meat and poultry for stews and braised dishes, as well as vegetables like squash, eggplant, onions, tomatoes, and bell peppers. When cooking in a stovetop pressure cooker, brown over medium-high heat.

If using an electric pressure cooker, select the Brown setting.

Cooking under Pressure at High Altitudes

Because foods generally cook slower at higher altitudes, quick-cooking under pressure is a dream come true for most mountain dwellers. Water and cooking liquids come to a boil slower at higher altitudes; therefore, high-pressure cooking times need to be longer. A good general rule is to increase the cooking time by 5 percent for every 1,000 feet you are above the first 2,000 feet above sea level. Table 15-1 provides information for you to use as a guide.

Table 15-1	High-Altitude Cooking Time Adjustments
Altitude in Feet	*Increase in Cooking Times*
3,000	5%
4,000	10%
5,000	15%
6,000	20%
7,000	25%
8,000	30%

The recipes in this book were developed and tested at sea level. If you live at an altitude of 3,000 feet or higher, remember to adjust the given recipe cook times according to Table 15-1.

Building the Right Amount of Pressure

After the pressure-cooker lid is positioned and locked, you're ready to get down to the business of cooking under pressure. In order to build pressure, you must have a combination of heat and liquid. You can't have one without the other.

If your stovetop pressure cooker is a jiggler-valve or weighted-valve type, the weight has to be on the vent pipe. If you have a spring-regulator-valve pressure cooker with a pressure-level indicator, it has to be set on the level of pressure you want. Set the pressure cooker over high heat. When you begin to exceed pressure, lower the burner heat to a simmer — or play "burner hopscotch" (see Chapter 5). Now set the timer for the length of time you need to cook, and voilá! You're pressure-cooking!

Using an electric pressure cooker is even easier. Simply position and lock the lid in place. Turn the pressure regulator knob to the pressure setting. Choose the desired pressure level by pressing either the high or low pressure button on the control panel. Now, set the desired time by pressing the high or low button once for each additional minute or by continuously holding the button down. Press Start and off you go to delicious food cooked in a fraction of the time!

Releasing Pressure without Burning Yourself

Choose the appropriate steam-release method for the type of food you're cooking. Use a quick-release method if steam needs to be released immediately. Use the natural-release method only when preparing foods such as pot roast or stock that benefits from the extended time in the pressure cooker as the pressure drops on its own. Refer to Chapter 4 for the how-to on both methods.

Steam is hot, especially when coming out of a pressure cooker. It usually comes out of the pressure indicator or regulator valve. Check your pressure-cooker owner's manual to see where these are located and make sure you always release the steam away from you, never toward you.

If your stovetop pressure cooker has a steam-release setting or switch, liquid may sometimes spray out the pressure regulator valve along with the steam. To avoid having to clean tomato sauce or bean cooking liquid off your wall or stove, switch the pressure-regulator valve back to high pressure. Release the pressure in the sink using the cold-water-release method. (Just be sure to never use this method with an electric pressure cooker!)

Avoiding the "Too Hard" Scenario

Remember that hard food is better than mushy food; you can always cook it longer with or without pressure! You can do a few things, however, to get whatever you're cooking done right the first time:

- ✔ Cut food into uniformly sized shapes.

- ✔ Because steam needs to circulate around the food, never pack food into the pressure cooker.

- ✔ Never overfill the pressure-cooker pot.

- ✔ Employ what I like to call *stop-and-go cooking.* First cook foods that need more time to cook; then release pressure and add the faster-cooking foods. (See Chapter 5 for more information on stop-and-go cooking.)

- ✔ Never add salt to soaked, dried beans when cooking. The skin will never soften and may even toughen.

- ✔ Cook for the recommended length of time.

See Chapter 14 for more information about avoiding underdone foods.

Avoiding the "Too Soft" Scenario

Nothing is worse than mushy, tasteless, overcooked food. You can avoid overcooking your favorites in your pressure cooker by following a few simple rules:

- ✔ Never cook food in more cooking liquid than the recipe specifies.

- ✔ Never cook naturally soft or tender foods in a pressure cooker. Why bother? They'll only come out softer and mushier! Some things I've learned to avoid (the hard way!) are fish fillets, most shellfish (except live lobster), and snap peas.

- ✔ Cook for the recommended length of time.

- ✔ Don't hesitate to release the pressure after cooking. Even if you remove the pressure cooker from the stove, the food continues cooking as long as there's heat and pressure in the pot.

See Chapter 14 for more information about avoiding overdone foods.

Keeping It Clean

Pot looking dull? Valves a bit sluggish? Gasket frayed around the edges? You'll never get up to pressure if you don't take proper care of your pressure cooker.

Always hand-wash your stovetop pressure cooker after each use with mild dishwashing soap and a nonabrasive sponge or cloth. Remove all caked-on food particles. Towel-dry well before storing. Replace the rubber gasket the minute it begins to look worn or damaged. See Chapter 5 for more details on cleaning your pressure cooker.

 If you have an electric pressure cooker, always be sure to first unplug it and let it cool to room temperature before cleaning. Remove the cooking pot and wash it with warm, soapy water or wash it in the dishwasher. Wipe the outer housing of the electric pressure cooker with a clean, damp kitchen cloth. Don't submerge the housing in water. Be sure to also remove the rubber gasket from the lid and to wash and towel-dry it before replacing it.

Part V
Appendixes

The 5th Wave   By Rich Tennant

ADAPTATION OF THE PRESSURE COOKER:
THE PRESSURE LOCOMOTIVE
TRAVELED FROM CHEYENNE, WYOMING TO LARAMIE
ON 600 lbs. OF COAL AND 900 HEADS OF BROCCOLI

©RICHTENNANT

In this part . . .

These two appendixes are home to important information you'll want to keep handy, specifically, recommended pressure-cooking times and metric conversions.

Appendix A

Recommended Cooking Times Under Pressure

• •

When you cook food under pressure, steam from all that heat builds up in the locked pot, creating pressure that quickly cooks the food for a specific length of time so that it comes out fork-tender and delicious. Perhaps you want to start adapting your own recipes to cook under pressure. Or maybe you're the curious sort and wonder how long it takes certain types of foods to cook in a pressure cooker compared to an oven or stovetop. Either way, this appendix has the information you need. It's filled with tables of recommended cooking times for five major food groups: beans and legumes, fruits, grains, meats, and vegetables.

The recommended cooking times found in the following tables begin when the pressure cooker reaches high pressure. All cooking times are, at best, approximations and should be used as general guidelines.

Start with the shortest cooking time, every time; you can always continue cooking under pressure for an additional couple minutes until the food achieves the texture you desire. You may also find that your particular brand or model of pressure cooker cooks faster or even a bit slower. Therefore, feel free to note any cooking time differences in the right-hand column of the tables.

Beans and Legumes

With the exception of lentils and split peas, the cooking times given in Table A-1 are for cooking *presoaked* beans.

Table A-1	Recommended Pressure-Cooker Cooking Times for Dried Beans and Legumes	
Food	**Cooking Time (in Minutes)**	**Your Notes**
Azuki beans	9–13	
Black beans	13–15	
Black-eyed peas	9–11	
Chickpeas (garbanzos)	20–25	
Cranberry beans	15–20	
Gandules (pigeon peas)	15–17	
Great Northern beans	12–15	
Kidney beans, red or white	12–15	
Lentils, green, brown, or red	8–10	
Navy or pea beans	10–12	
Peas, split green or yellow	8–10	
Pinto beans	8–10	

Fruits

You can cook dried and fresh fruit in a pressure cooker. Table A-2 tells you approximately how long different types and forms of fruits need to cook under pressure before they're ready for eating.

Table A-2	Recommended Pressure-Cooker Cooking Times for Fruits	
Food	**Cooking Time (in Minutes)**	**Your Notes**
Apples, chunks or eighths	4–5	
Apples, slices, dried	2–3	
Apricots, dried	2–3	
Apricots, whole or halved	3–4	
Peaches, dried	3–4	
Peaches, halved	4–5	
Pears, dried	3–4	

Food	Cooking Time (in Minutes)	Your Notes
Pears, halved	4–5	
Plums, whole or halved	2–3	
Prunes	2–3	
Raisins	2–3	

Grains

As you follow the guidelines in Table A-3 for preparing different types of grains in your pressure cooker, consider adding 1 tablespoon of oil to cut back on the foaming of the grain as it cooks.

Table A-3	Recommended Pressure-Cooker Cooking Times for Grains	
Food	Cooking Time (in Minutes)	Your Notes
Barley, pearl	15–20	
Barley, whole (unhulled)	50–55	
Bulgur wheat, whole-grain	10–12	
Oats, quick-cooking	6	
Oats, steel-cut	11	
Quinoa	7	
Rice, Arborio	7–8	
Rice, basmati	5–7	
Rice, brown	15–20	
Rice, long-grain	5–7	
Rice, wild	22–25	
Wheat berries	12–15	

Meats of All Kinds

Not all cuts of meat cook in the same amount of time. Table A-4 offers recommended cooking times for various cuts of beef, chicken, lamb, pork, turkey, and veal prepared in the pressure cooker.

Table A-4	Recommended Pressure-Cooker Cooking Times for Meat and Poultry	
Food	*Cooking Time (in Minutes)*	*Your Notes*
Beef, 1- to 2-inch cubes	15–20	
Beef, corned	50–60	
Beef, roast or brisket	50–60	
Beef shank, 1½ inches thick	25–35	
Chicken, boneless breast or thighs, 1-inch pieces	8–10	
Chicken, pieces	10–12	
Chicken, whole, 3–4 pounds	15–20	
Cornish hen, whole	8–10	
Lamb, 1- to 2-inch cubes	15–20	
Lamb, boneless roast	45–55	
Meatballs, browned	8–10	
Pork, 1- to 2-inch cubes	8–10	
Pork, ham shank	20–25	
Pork, loin roast	40–50	
Pork, smoked butt	30–40	
Pork, tenderloin	15–18	
Turkey, whole breast, bone-in	20–30	
Turkey, whole breast, boneless	30–40	
Veal, roast or brisket	50–60	
Veal, shank, 1½ inches thick	25–35	

Vegetables

If you think vegetables take too long to prepare, you haven't tried making them in a pressure cooker. Table A-5 shows you just how quickly you can whip up a wide variety of vegetables.

Table A-5	Recommended Pressure-Cooker Cooking Times for Vegetables	
Food	*Cooking Time (in Minutes)*	*Your Notes*
Artichokes, hearts	2–3	
Artichokes, whole	8–10	
Asparagus	1–2	
Beans, fresh green or wax, whole or pieces	2–3	
Beans, lima, shelled	2–3	
Beets, ¼-inch slices	3–4	
Beets, whole, peeled	12–14	
Broccoli, florets or spears	2–3	
Brussels sprouts, whole	3–4	
Cabbage, red or green, quartered	3–4	
Carrots, ¼-inch slices	1–2	
Carrots, whole baby	2–3	
Cauliflower, florets	2–3	
Collard greens	4–5	
Corn on the cob	3–4	
Escarole	1–2	
Okra	2–3	
Parsnips, 1-inch pieces	2–3	
Peas, shelled	1–1½	
Potatoes, pieces or sliced	5–7	
Potatoes, whole, medium	10–12	
Potatoes, whole, small or new	5–7	
Pumpkin, peeled, 1-inch chunks	2–3	
Rutabaga, 1-inch chunks	3–4	
Spinach, fresh	2–3	
Squash, summer, sliced	1–2	
Squash, winter, 1-inch chunks	4–6	
Sweet potato, 1½-inch chunks	4–5	
Turnips, sliced	2–3	

Appendix B

Metric Conversion Guide

● ●

*N**ote:* The recipes in this book weren't developed or tested using metric measurements. There may be some variation in quality when converting to metric units.

Volume

U.S. Units	Canadian Metric	Australian Metric
¼ teaspoon	1 milliliter	1 milliliter
½ teaspoon	2 milliliters	2 milliliters
1 teaspoon	5 milliliters	5 milliliters
1 tablespoon	15 milliliters	20 milliliters
¼ cup	50 milliliters	60 milliliters
⅓ cup	75 milliliters	80 milliliters
½ cup	125 milliliters	125 milliliters
⅔ cup	150 milliliters	170 milliliters
¾ cup	175 milliliters	190 milliliters
1 cup	250 milliliters	250 milliliters
1 quart	1 liter	1 liter
1½ quarts	1.5 liters	1.5 liters
2 quarts	2 liters	2 liters
2½ quarts	2.5 liters	2.5 liters
3 quarts	3 liters	3 liters
4 quarts (1 gallon)	4 liters	4 liters

Weight

U.S. Units	Canadian Metric	Australian Metric
1 ounce	30 grams	30 grams
2 ounces	55 grams	60 grams
3 ounces	85 grams	90 grams
4 ounces (¼ pound)	115 grams	125 grams
8 ounces (½ pound)	225 grams	225 grams
16 ounces (1 pound)	455 grams	500 grams (½ kilogram)

Length

Inches	Centimeters
0.5	1.5
1	2.5
2	5.0
3	7.5
4	10.0
5	12.5

Temperature (Degrees)

Fahrenheit	Celsius
32	0
212	100
250	120
275	140
300	150
325	160
350	180
375	190
400	200
425	220
450	230
475	240
500	260

Index

• Q •

• R •

• W •

Warning! icon, 5
washing. *See* cleaning
weight, metric conversion guide for, 254
wine for cooking, 121
winter vegetables, 177

• Y •

yam soup with snipped chives, 100, 105

• Z •

zucchini
  Minestra with Creamy Polenta, 224–225
  Minestrone Soup, 85
  Pressure-Cooker Minestrone Soup, 81, 86
  Ratatouille, 189